# THE EVOLUTION OF GOD

CHANGING CONCEPTS OF GOD FROM JEHOVAH,
THE FATHER AND ALLAH TO YOUR NEIGHBOR'S IDEAS TODAY

*by*

Paul Seydel

**DORRANCE PUBLISHING CO., INC.**
**PITTSBURGH, PENNSYLVANIA 15222**

*All Rights Reserved*
Copyright © 2001 by Paul Seydel
No part of this book may be reproduced or transmitted
in any form or by any means, electronic or mechanical,
including photocopying, recording, or by any information
storage and retrieval system without permission in
writing from the publisher.

ISBN # 0-8059-5218-7
Printed in the United States of America

*First Printing*

For information or to order additional books, please write:
Dorrance Publishing Co., Inc.
643 Smithfield Street
Pittsburgh, Pennsylvania 15222
U.S.A.
1-800-788-7654
Or visit our web site and on-line catalog at *www.dorrancepublishing.com*.

Dedicated to:
Stephen Jay Gould
Dean of Evolutionists

And to:
Mike Lewis and Scott Seydel
Without whose interest and push this MS
would never have seen the light of day.

# Contents

Preface . . . . . . . . . . . . . . . . . . . . . . . . . . . . . . . . . . . . . . . . . . . . .vii

Chapter 1: Natural Selection . . . . . . . . . . . . . . . . . . . . . . . . . . . . . .1

Chapter 2: Origins of Religion . . . . . . . . . . . . . . . . . . . . . . . . . . . .6

Chapter 3: The Pagan Gods . . . . . . . . . . . . . . . . . . . . . . . . . . . . .23

Chapter 4: The God of the Patriarchs . . . . . . . . . . . . . . . . . . . . . .35

Chapter 5: The God of the Prophets . . . . . . . . . . . . . . . . . . . . . .60

Chapter 6: The Father God . . . . . . . . . . . . . . . . . . . . . . . . . . . . .83

Chapter 7: Allah . . . . . . . . . . . . . . . . . . . . . . . . . . . . . . . . . . . .111

Chapter 8: The God of Mormon . . . . . . . . . . . . . . . . . . . . . . . .139

Chapter 9: The Healing God . . . . . . . . . . . . . . . . . . . . . . . . . . .167

Chapter 10: The Universal God . . . . . . . . . . . . . . . . . . . . . . . .192

Epilogue . . . . . . . . . . . . . . . . . . . . . . . . . . . . . . . . . . . . . . . . .217

References . . . . . . . . . . . . . . . . . . . . . . . . . . . . . . . . . . . . . . .220

# Preface

I make no excuse for the following work other than that it was in my thoughts, demanding exit. The subject I seek to address is primarily the religions that followed from and were built upon the Pentateuch in relation to the people and cultures to which they spread. I will focus particularly on the character of the God around which each religion is constructed. Nothing new is presented herewith, although I believe that I have taken a fresh approach to the subject. I hope it will be of interest for this reason.

Although each of the religions I am addressing is essentially monotheistic and derives from the same source, my study has revealed that the different manifestations of God that arose to be worshiped at various historical epochs present sufficient differences in character to actually be identified as separate "Gods." These Gods are presented as found in their autobiographies: the revealed scriptures. Most of these scriptures, a detailed bibliography of which is included in the back of the book, speak for themselves. No attempt is made to present varieties or variations of Gods that have no distinguishing scriptures—such as those of Jehovah's Witnesses, the Unitarian Church, Baptist, Lutheran—but are rather based on varying interpretations of the same scriptures. Nor is there any attempt to take into consideration the wide-ranging and often conflicting theories of modern Biblical scholars. This decision to support the present discussion almost exclusively with excerpts taken from original sources, usually described as "the inspired word of God," was made so readers encountering some of this material for the first time can draw their own conclusions.

In an effort to provide a foundation for our discussion of the Judeo-Christian tradition and its offspring, I have also provided some relevant information on Paganism. My primary resource/reference in this area is Bullfinch's Mythology.

I hereby thank the many friends and acquaintances that have helped with their comments and suggestions, but will not mention names, as I do not desire to discredit them. I was often corrected, but did not always accept the corrections.

You will see that the Gods of which we speak are not the Gods of the theologians. But it is important to remember that the theologians are not our source of knowledge. The only source of knowledge we have of God is self-disclosure. We find that we must take the word of the individual who tells us of God's disclosure, as we have no means of confirming it.

We will seek to compare the attributes and characteristics of the various Gods we will define with the characteristics of the people from whom they sprung, both with the intention of showing how God was created in the image of the people concerned, at least an idealized image, and with the purpose of demonstrating how the God was adapted to the environment in which He prospered.

Certainly there is no expectation that the reader will agree with all or even most of my interpretations. Where there are a hundred people, there will be at least ninety-nine interpretations of religious themes. I would highly recommend that the interested reader turn to the original references, especially for a better understanding. He may still disagree—but understanding is more important than agreement. Still, minor disagreements will not invalidate the main theme: the evolution of the Gods and their adaptability, each to His own environment. I will be content if this book can furnish a basis for thought and discussion.

# Chapter 1: Natural Selection

> So God created man in His own image, in the image of God He created him; male and female He created them. (Genesis 1:27)

The first chapter of the book of Genesis states that God created man in His own image. This first chapter plus a few verses of the second chapter give the first story of the Creation, with a day each for the various labors of God, including the creation of light, the separation of waters and earth, the production of living creatures, and on the sixth day—what we like to consider the crowning glory of Creation—the appearance of humankind.

It is interesting to note that the second story of the Creation, as related in the second chapter of Genesis, inverts some of the chronology of the first story. Instead of building up the background and setting the stage one element at a time in preparation for the creation of humankind, as it developed in the first story, humans were produced from the dust of a barren earth, "when no plant of the field was yet in the earth." Afterwards, the Lord planted the garden of Eden and set in it the man He had formed. Likewise, the creatures of the earth which in the first story were created on the fifth day and part of the sixth day, before humans, in the second story were formed after humans, so that we should not be alone.

We propose to carry the reversions one step further and relate the story of the Creation of God in the image of Man.

Of course, as the Biblical story of Creation is basically allegory, so our exploration will not deal with the authentic creation of God, nor even of the question of whether God actually exists. Still less are we at issue with the question of whether or not our mortal minds can conceive of anything as wonderful as a supreme being capable of the creation and management of the infinite universe as we understand it today.

Our exploration intends, rather, to deal with God as He has been formed or created in the minds of humans, or if you prefer, how humans have perceived God in His various states of evolution. For not only have humans evolved; God has also evolved along with us. We will take this opportunity to note that we will not be confusing things by repeating "man's conception of God" each time we mention God. It is understood that, while many people are certain that they know who or what God is, no one has arrived at a conception of God that is acceptable to even large fractions of the human race, let alone the majority, so I will eliminate the circumlocutions by simply referring to "God" from here on out.

The metaphor we will use in illustrating the changes that occur between various incarnations of Gods in various times and for various peoples is the evolution of God. Evolution, that is, in the Darwinian sense of the term. So let's consider just what that means.

Webster says that evolution is, "in modern use, the fact or doctrine of the descent of all living things from a few simple forms of life, or from a single form." We have a tendency to consider evolution as a development from the simple to the complex, a gradual teleological rise up the ladder of progress one rung at a time, from the virus to the protozoa, through the mollusks, the fish, the reptiles, the mammals, the primates, and so on to man as the culmination of the process.

This is certainly true, but is only part of the picture. Not just man alone, but all living things were produced in the process of evolution. Blue jays, elephants, salmon, streptococci bacteria, amanita mushrooms, oysters, gardenias, cacti, and rattlesnakes, as well as humans, are products of evolution, and not all are in the line of production leading toward humankind.

Let's look for a moment at the scale of evolution. Of the five billion years that the earth has existed, living organisms have been in existence for about one billion years. Of these, *Homo sapiens* have been in existence for a few hundred thousand years. Humans have kept written records for only six to ten thousand years.

To get a better sense of what this means, imagine that the earth began just one year ago. After ten months of cataclysmic geological adjustments and settling down, life, on this scale, began about two months ago. Primitive humans appeared only an hour ago. Historical humankind arrived on the scene only a minute ago, and Christianity has been around for less than half a minute.

It is certainly not impossible that that whole year was designed for just the past few seconds. But when we learn from scientists that the sun will be around without any great change for another few billion years—another full year on our imaginary scale—it is hardly reasonable to assume that things are going to come to an end any time soon, unless, of course, we bomb all the life off the face of the earth. If humans can continue to develop as they have in the past few minutes, just think what might be possible in the next day or two on our year-scale; another few million years on the world scale. We may well have beings as far advanced beyond humans as we are beyond our ancestors, the chimpanzees. Evolution is not simply the development of a protozoa into the man of today; evolution has also developed laterally, branching out into a multiplicity of species, and has the potential to continue developing in new directions. Since it will be as nearly impossible for us to imagine what race or species will be paramount on the earth a few million years hence, as it would have been for a Tyrannosaurus Rex to imagine Roosevelt, Stalin, or Churchill, we won't even dare try. We will concentrate our first study on the origin of species, since it is this aspect of evolution that we intend to portray as metaphorically relevant to our thesis on the evolution of God.

There are essentially two theories proposed to account for the origin of any existing species of plant or animal: the Lamarckian and the mutation theory.

Lamarck proposed that development from one form of life to another was based on the influences surrounding the original forms, influences such as climate, food availability, and predators. From this view, fur coats could have been developed and improved to protect the animal from the cold; black skins or white to adapt to hot or cold climates; a giraffe's long neck enables it to reach the tender new leaves high on the tree; the color change of the chameleon or the mimicry of the moths and the stick insect allows them to escape the vigilant eye of predators.

This view came under scrutiny when biologists objected that, if this theory alone were the basis for the origin of new species, we should find all sorts of intermediate stages in existence, whereas we actually find a great many leaps where no intermediates can be shown to have existed. So, while Lamarck may account for modifications which will produce new species by gradual changes over eons of time, modern biologists prefer to explain the origin of many species by mutation.

Physical effects, such as chance distortion of our DNA molecules, or displacement and rearrangements caused by cosmic rays or other sources of radiation striking these basic molecules which contain the code that determines what the organism will develop into, can produce major changes and can thus account for the appearance of new characteristics.

Obviously, not every change that can be made is desirable. Some will modify the organism to the extent that it will be incapable of survival; others will not be able to compete and will die out. But every now and then a change will occur that will enable the organism to survive better than its neighbors, and it will pass its characteristics on to its offspring. For example, the evolutionary appearance of eyes for sight, wings for flight, and the reasoning powers of humankind enabled certain organisms to do things that previous organisms could not do. Hence, the new organism or animal has a better chance of surviving and proliferating. Thus, it will have more offspring than those without the new beneficial characteristics and others of its kind, without these advantages, will tend to die out.

This proliferation of advantageous characteristics is called "natural selection."

We intend to show that God has also evolved to His present form or forms through a similar process. In this way, a God who is better suited to His surroundings will tend to survive, while those gods that are not well adapted to their surroundings will tend to disappear, or die out. Before we move on to discuss fully the relevance of this process to the evolution of God, however, let's develop a little further our understanding of species and of "natural selection."

Biologists, beginning with Carl Linnaeus, have been able to take any individual organism and classify it as belonging to a "species." Variations exist within these species, but the certain essential characteristics are almost always such that any individual can be classified as belonging to a certain species.

Humankind, as a species, is called *Homo sapiens* by the classifiers, and all people belong to this species, which has been divided into races, depending upon the conditions of the various places where the species spread. It is generally considered that a characteristic of a species is its ability to produce fecund offspring, even among wide variations of its subdivisions or races, while interbreeding with other species generally produces no offspring at all, or produces sterile offspring, as in the case of mules.

Even this is not a strict rule, as we have several widely variant species of dogs, which are able to interbreed. Possibly, domestication has produced varieties which became highly differentiated by careful breeding. Still, we can imagine that any differentiation due either to Lamarkian influences or to mutation could produce a variation sufficiently close to the original that it should be able to interbreed, and thus have the possibility of passing on its own qualities. The ability of various species of dog within the genus Canis to interbreed should demonstrate this.

Each species has its own niche, where it fits its surroundings. For instance, three species of the giant land tortoises that live in the Galapagos Islands are characterized by differences in the shells, which have greater or lesser arches in the shell above the neck, so that the head can be lifted higher with the greater arch. This enables the tortoise with the higher arch to graze higher on the vegetation that he uses for food. Each species lives in a different area and is adapted to the surrounding food source. They breed true to form, the offspring having arches similar to those of the parents.

The changes that came over a certain antelope-type animal which produced the long-necked giraffe, enable this new animal to utilize a food source that was not available to other lower cattle and antelopes, and thus to fill a different niche. Life thus being easier for him with less competition, he developed and multiplied, while some of his cousins are today only fossils in the rocks of antiquity.

Pleasure and pain as a basis for evolutionary development, if for the right reasons, increase the chance for survival. Obvious examples are the pleasure derived from sexual intercourse, which will tend to produce more offspring; and the pain derived from contact with fire, which will cause the animal to avoid the fire in the future. We shall see that, in the same way, the reactions of God to what pleases and what displeases Him will contribute to the survival of any particular species of God. The pagan gods died out due their lack of adaptability to a changing environment; their reactions were not compatible with the developing philosophies and ideals of humankind.

We find that a common characteristic of species, and even varieties in natural habitats, is to associate primarily with its own kind. This tends to maintain the differentiating characteristics of species, even in the rare cases where cross-breeding can produce fertile offspring. For example, experiments were made a few years ago in which the experimenters captured individuals of a certain species of seagull, painted its feathers to resemble another species and released the birds. It was observed that its own kind would have nothing more to do with the masquerading birds and chased them off as if they were undesirable interlopers.

We find a similar set of conditions with the evolution of God. Small, gradual variations and development exist, similar to the Lamarckian developments, as the "climate" or other surrounding influences change—if there is no sudden change in His environment—God will continue true to form or change only gradually. A God who developed in one set of conditions, among people of a certain characteristic and temperament, can generally not survive under widely varying conditions, at least not without making some drastic variation in His own characteristics, in order to adapt to the new environment. A well-known example of this is the God of the Haitians, who, although He was introduced into the black slave milieu as the purely Christian God, found it expedient to adapt to the new surroundings by incorporating a heavy dose of African religion, resulting in voodooism, in order to survive.

Mutational changes also occur. We might consider the change of the Old Testament God into that of the New Testament a sudden change, especially in that God became an international God rather than just a national God. True, along the way there were some tentative movements in the direction of influence outside the Hebrew nation, but they lasted only a short while and were highly localized. The Old Testament God still survives and fills the "niche" of a limited group of people, the Orthodox Jews.

In the subsequent chapters, we will consider the evolution of God: how He developed from the primitive forms of animism to become the Gods existent today. As in the evolution of the species, where there have been many paths leading to a variety of species all of which are adapted to their surrounding environment, so also God exists in various forms which are adapted to the groups of people among whom He dwells.

We will seek to compare the attributes and characteristics of the various Gods we discuss with those of the people from whom they sprang. The intention is to show how God was created in the image—at least an idealized image—of the people concerned and was adapted to the environment in which He prospered.

Many people would like to think that humankind is the ultimate achievement of evolution. In the case of the evolution of God, we cannot yet point to any particular God species and say, "This is the true conception of God that we have been waiting for."

It is, of course, understood that many people will take issue with that statement and present their own Gods as the ultimate goal. That will simply have to remain the basic disagreement between us. And we would like to add that, when we look around at what evolution has produced materially, we can anticipate that a species better adapted to live peacefully among their fellow-beings than humankind will come along.

# Chapter 2: Origins of Religion

> It is natural for the mind to believe, and for the will to love, so that for the want of true objects, they must attach themselves to false. (Pascal, *Pensées*, 81)

> He who only knows one religion can no more understand that religion than he who knows only one language can understand that language. (Tylor, *Primitive Culture*)

"So God created man in His own image...." says Genesis 1:27. But just what does this mean? Certainly not that man is an exact copy of God in all respects. God, being one and eternal, as the Old Testament holds Him to be, He obviously has no need of genitals, either male or female. Since God probably does not subsist on ordinary food, one can infer that He has no need for teeth or digestive apparatus. As God is omniscient, either He does not use eyes, or if He does, they must be aimed, as those of Argus, in all directions.

So we must assume that, even though Michelangelo was inspired to paint God as a venerable patriarch with an imposing muscular frame and flowing white beard, this depiction is, in essence, allegorical. God must have some other form, or no real form at all, as we understand form.

Hence, if people are in the image of God, then it must be our inner quality that is God-like, and not our visual appearance. Here we may have a better argument, for we find that there is often a close correspondence between the personalities of a given god or group of gods and the people who worship them. As we glance over a vista of gods who have existed within their given contexts of race and era, we are presented with gods with widely variant characteristics that are often typical of the people who worship the incumbent god, or typical of their ideals, we are gradually forced to the conclusion that it must be God who is made in the image of man. Thus, in the words of Feuerbach, "The personality of God is nothing else than the projected personality of man." (*The Essence of Christianity*)

Naturally, for God to be worthy of the concept of God, He must be superior to mortals. This superiority may be manifested in various ways, such as immortality, omnipotence, wisdom, and so on. It is also manifested in other ways, as humans advance from more primitive existences to populate emergent civilizations as beings who begin to consider ideals. We will find as our story progresses, that as humankind becomes more and more idealistic, God evolves into a being characterized less and less by jealousy and vengeance, and more and more by love and charity.

The story will concentrate on the God of the Pentateuch, as He evolved through religions based on the Bible, either wholly or in part. For now, let's go back and see how the whole thing started.

When the earliest written records were being made, a parallel study of ancient architecture and art reveals that religions were already fairly well developed. As we do, however, have no written record of earlier religions, our ideas of the beginnings of religions must be based on conjecture. It is generally considered that humans probably derived their concept of the existence of something beyond visible physical life from their dreams. The dream experiences certainly had a different quality that was not characteristic of waking life, but neither the early human's education or experience substantially demonstrated that the dreams were not, in their own way, as real as his waking life. That friends or family members insisted that one's body remained in place in the corner of the cave while dreams were occurring could best be explained by assuming a spirit that could detach itself from the body and circulate on its own.

The step from conceiving of a spirit or soul to developing animism as a primitive religion is no more than logical. It may have taken a hundred years; it may have taken ten thousand years; no matter, primitive humans had plenty of time. From learning from their fellows and finding that they, too, had souls that were capable of independent wandering while the body slept served to reinforce this idea and to lay the foundation for what we recognize as religion.

Primitive peoples experienced the motion of the sun as it rose in the east, sailing unhurriedly but invincibly across the blue vault to return each night to its home to rest, just as man himself rested at night. There was a force from this golden orb, a power in its heat that man could feel deeply. Above were also clouds, sailing majestically across the sky, changing shape and form, appearing and disappearing, and swelling and darkening to produce the rain and sometimes flaring dangerously with lightning and growling with thunder. The rivers, which streamed from unknown sources and flowed on to unknown other worlds, sometimes overflowed their banks and flooded the land, carrying destruction with them. And there were the trees, which grew just as did animals. In the winter, they shed their garment of green leaves, and slept the season through, to wake again with new foliage in the spring.

Obviously, all these entities must be alive, like humans. And since they are alive, they must also have spirits or souls of their own.

There was the wind. The wind itself must be alive, else how could it come and go as it does, how could it change direction, how could it one moment caress gently, and the next shriek and scream so that the waters built up into frightened waves desperately trying to escape from its force; dust was thrown into the air, and leaves and branches were torn bodily from the sturdy trees.

Of the phenomena knowable to man, only the immutable stone and the eternal mountains showed no motion and therefore no evidence of life. But why leave them out of the general scheme of things? Many primitive peoples also awarded spirits to the rock or to the mountains, to the lakes, the seas, and the earth itself.

This, then, was animism, the consideration that all objects possessed a soul, the Latin *anima*, a living, breathing thing. Though these spirits had not yet evolved into gods, we already see the effect of man's creating them in his own image. He has decided that he has a spirit, therefore all other beings must have a spirit. This applied to what we today consider inanimate objects as well as living beings, for primitive humans had no way of determining what was alive or what was not. Motion was not a criterion; all things that moved were probably alive, but then plants and trees were obviously alive, and yet did not move except to grow or in response to the motion of what was around them (i.e., wind).

The next step in projecting their image onto the spirits was in endowing them with a human capacity for benevolence and malevolence. The clouds which could bring the beneficent rain and help the needed fruit and vegetables grow could also produce the terrifying lightning which could smash trees or kill.

Sometimes the hunting was good; sometimes it was scarce. People could become the victim of vipers or of bears or their homes could be carried away by floods. Children and adults could be tortured or killed by disease. All this required explanation.

At this point, animism begins to evolve from being merely explaining life, to being a religion: something that not only explains the functioning of life, but admits that this functioning can influence humankind, and that there is at least a remote possibility that humans can influence or otherwise interact with the influences.

While a strong man has no problem obtaining what he wants from a weaker man simply by asking and threatening, the weak man finds that he can often obtain what he wants from the strong man by being subservient, by doing him favors, by offering gifts. Children have no difficulty learning how to manipulate their elders, even though their elders are perfectly capable of imposing their wishes on children.

Hence, although spirits may have powers that are irresistible in relation to man, this does not mean that they cannot be influenced. Several avenues of approach were developed. The spirits were propitiated with sacrificial offerings. A sacrificial offering to the sun would be made on some high place: as near to the sun as one was able to get. Sacrificial offerings to the river were made on a bend of the river; to the rain spirit, it was set up in some place where the rain was desired. The ancient Phoenicians sacrificed to the spirit of the cedars before harvesting the trees. A prominent stone could serve as sacrificial altar. The fact that the sacrificial food did not always disappear was no problem; it was the spirit of the food that was to be accepted by the spirit for whom it was intended.

Talking to the spirit to be propitiated or appeased was another approach—whether just general persuasive talk or calling the spirits to the sacrifice and explaining what was expected in return. From this we have the beginning of prayer: the effort to communicate with a hypothetical being whom the maker of the prayer believes exists and believes can hear the prayers, but from whom the prayer does not expect direct acknowledgment. He could only hope that subsequent happenings will produce favorable evidence that the prayer has been heard and acted upon. Primitive humans did all they knew how to do and hoped for the best.

Another means of influencing the spirits was found in the efforts of primitive peoples to frighten off evil spirits, sometimes on the birth of children, sometimes on the inauguration of a new building, often when a person was sick and obviously under the influence of malevolent spirits. Terrifying masks were worn; loud noises were resorted to: cymbals, clappers, yelling and screaming; threatening dances all conspired to inspire fear in the malignant spirit and cause it to scramble to escape.

The primitive use of amulets or talismans, good luck charms, has carried down to the modern age. We are pleased to find a four-leaf clover, and many people tack up horseshoes (be sure to keep the points up, or the luck will spill out!) or carry a rabbit's foot. The primitive talismans or charms were thought to keep away evil spirits, and were often made out of the teeth of large animals, or unusual stones which might be agate, jasper, jade, or other precious stones.

When these practices first appeared, man lived in family gatherings, or in clans of several families. The fact that people those days lived by hunting and gathering meant that there was no advantage to living in large groups. As a matter of fact, it was a disadvantage. A blackberry patch, a group of fig trees, a herd of wild deer suitable for food, could support only a limited number of men, women, and children. If there were too many people, the food would be quickly consumed or the animals would be frightened away by excessive predation. At most, a group of men would need to act as a team in attacking the large animals like the buffalo or the hairy mammoth, or in helping to construct shelters.

Religious activities were therefore either the preoccupation of the individual or were left to the head of the family clan. It was the leader's responsibility to organize the hunt, to locate and supervise preparation of shelters, to allocate the chores, to decide when to move on and where to move. It was therefore only natural that the person filling this role should also assume religious responsibilities.

Hence, we have at this stage a miniature theocratic dictatorship. What was the human picture of the religion at this time? We have already seen how humans' conception of the nature of spirits derived from their self-concept. They had yet to arrive at a point in cultural development when there was sufficient time to consider the origin of things. Humans had therefore not yet developed any myths or legends of creation, hence they had no need to consider supernatural beings as creators.

He endowed all things with souls, because he had come to the conclusion based on his dream life that he had a soul. His life was generally unorganized, families getting together only when expedient, to hunt large game or to build shelters, and then only for brief periods. So his supernatural world was unorganized, his spirits individualistic, each operating in its own sphere, taking no notice of the others. They, like men, could be either benevolent or malignant; often simply neutral, going their own way without regard to humankind, as the individual man went his own way without regard to others for most of his waking hours.

The spirits could be propitiated or appeased, just as the strong man could be influenced by clever manipulation on the part of the weaker person. But man was not surprised when the spirit did not respond to his overtures—neither did the strong person always respond favorably to the appeals of the weaker. And although the pater familias was the acknowledged boss of the family or clan, his need to exercise that power was comparatively rare, so that individualism was the order of the day. Concern for others was not an essential part of the daily life. So the spirits were imagined with the same characteristics.

Not until humans learned agriculture and to domesticate animals and develop a herding industry, was there any reason for them to gather into larger communities. With agriculture, people learned to control nature to the extent that they were no longer dependent on chance harvests. They could concentrate the food production instead of just taking it as they found it, so as not only to remain in one area and enjoy the food supply, but to also take care of larger groups of people. Herding had a similar effect. Domesticated cattle and sheep were not so likely to wander off without warning as were wild beasts. Furthermore, the larger gatherings of people were of advantage, in that they could protect each other against the ravages of beast and wolves, who quickly learned better than to approach a group of men armed with clubs and stones. Cooperation made animal husbandry easier, and continuous supervision of herds more practical.

At the same time, it was found that the individual responsibility originally carried by the head of each family became subordinate to governorship by the leader of the community. Whether this leader was chosen by popular acclaim, by heredity, or whether the succession was determined when an aging, weakened leader was deposed by a new leader who removed him with threats or physical force, the general organization and community were the same. In the beginning, the organization was loosely knit, subject to the direction of the leader only as a judge to settle disputes, or as a leader on fact to determine when community projects should be done, who should do them. He might have functioned as a battle leader in case of attack and invasion by an enemy group, or as a leader of the warriors in a foray into neighboring territory.

With the coming of these larger communities, the shape of religion began to change. There was no need for each family head to make individual offerings, when they could be done by one person for the whole tribe. At this point, either the leader himself took over the duties of what we begin to recognize as a priest, or someone was selected from the tribe to be solely responsible.

The function of priests in these primitive societies, whether they be also the governing leaders of the tribe or not, was to take over the relation of the tribe as a whole and the individual responsibilities of the tribe members in dealing with the spirits. He did the praying, the sacrificial offerings, the noise-making, and mask-wearing that were the tasks of the shaman, or witch doctor, in the efforts to drive off the evil spirits. He might and generally did require cooperative effort of the tribe members in ritual prayer, song, and dance, since on the one hand the spirits are likely to be more impressed when wooed by larger numbers of people than by individuals, and on the other hand the tribal members would take their religion more seriously when they themselves were part of the process. This participation, incidentally, served to enhance the importance of the priest's position in the tribe.

Somewhere along the line, these "spirits" became "gods." Just where is both unimportant and impossible to determine, not only because it is lost in the dim mists of antiquity, but also because there is no great real difference between the primitive spirits and the primitive gods. We find, for example, the common reference in American Indian folklore, the "Great Spirit." There is no real way to translate from another language into English the word *spirit* or the word *god* as either one or the other, unless that language itself has two words that make some differentiation which could lead us to choose one or the other. In most cases, especially in the primitive tongues, the word used for the governing supernatural beings could just as well be translated as either spirit or god without changing the sense of the reference. It is quite likely that we find the term "Great Spirit" used in reference to the Amerindian god because the Christian missionaries who first began to communicate with these Indians did not want to call anything God except their own Christian deity. Semantically, "The Great Spirit" and "Almighty God" are one and the same to any person approaching the concept as an unprejudiced outsider.

Life among primitive peoples changed with accretion into larger groups. The relations among any group of persons may be described by "anarchy" or "organization." A pure black or white, however, never exists; there is always some shade of gray. Small groups can approach anarchy, with no stated rules between themselves governing their behavior, but larger groups must have some rules, which leads to government and governmental authority. In the most primitive life, the authority was the father, and the rules governing life were fairly loose, formed over periods of many generations of experimentation to find the most effective systems of living together.

In small groups, the rules are unspoken, but nevertheless exist. It is generally accepted that one does not kill his neighbor without extreme provocation. One does not take one's neighbor's property—unless the accepted rules are based on communism, in which case no one may retain property for exclusive use. One does not grab food from the mouths of the elderly or from children. And so on. Pure anarchy can exist only in theory.

Likewise, pure government does not exist. Even under the tightest dictatorial control, persons are free in many ways. They make their own friends, control their own sex life, decide what to eat (if there is a choice); they have free time they can spend as they will—at least within certain limits.

As Thomas Jefferson expressed in the Declaration of Independence, the power of government derives from the consent of the governed. It is likely that he was not the first to express this basic truth.

Still, there are many ways in which this consent can be obtained. In the case of democracy, it is a result of the consensus of the governed that life is much more agreeable if the people can arrive at a mutually accepted set of rules, and the realization that it is necessary to have an authority and some sort of organization to ensure that everyone follows the rules. No set of rules will please each and every person, but it is generally conceded that it is better to accept a few rules one doesn't like, in exchange for acceptance by others of rules one does believe desirable.

Consent, however, while necessary to a government, does not need to be strictly voluntary. The schoolboy member of a gang of kids consents to the leadership of the bully, because otherwise he would be beaten. The citizens of a tyrannical dictatorship likewise consent to be governed because the consequences of withholding individual consent can be highly unpleasant. Yet it is possible for a revolution to occur when a large enough number of subjects withhold consent, so that the government loses its power and falls.

In ancient times, the government of small groups of citizenry was often conducted by an authority who had set himself up by force. As long as government was anything approaching reasonable, he continued to maintain his position until someone stronger decided to replace him. If he was bad enough, his subjects could gang up on him, and select a replacement for the recently deceased, but continuance generally depended on individual strength.

As the groups grew larger, it was found effective to organize a small nucleus of loyal friends who kept the chief in power, in return usually for special treatment. In this way, brains began to be more important than muscles.

Somewhere along the line, some political genius discovered that there was a way of effectively receiving the consent-to-be governed other than by physical threats. The chiefs found that their subjects had more fear of an invisible spirit than they had of human form that they could see, watch, and touch. It was possible to threaten a human agency; it was impractical to threaten a spirit or a god. Furthermore, the invisible spirit might be present at any time, while a human chief was not always around.

Hence, while one might conceivably avoid trouble with the chief by acting secretly, one could not maintain a secret from the invisible, omnipresent spirit. There was also the advantage that, if the chief presented himself as a representative of the invisible spirit or god, and managed to persuade his subjects of the validity of his representation, he was automatically under the god's protection and need not fear that he would be removed from his position of authority as a result of aging or enfeeblement.

This was a great turning point in the story of religion.

Up until the development of larger communal units than the family or the clan, religion had been more of a personal concern. Tradition and interclass communications had developed the concept of animism's spirits to the status of more-or-less widespread understanding of the spirit world. Agreement that spirits existed that could influence people as well as operate the bodies they occupied—the sun, the clouds, and the animals—was fairly common. The details, the names of the spirits, and their relative malignancy or capabilities varied widely, but the general principles were commonly accepted.

Among these principles was that of the individuality of the spirits and the individuality of each person's or family's relation with them. The spirits were capricious; no general laws were laid down. No standard of conduct was available to serve as a guide for primitive people.

With the turning point, the priest, or priest-chief—the contact person representing the tribe in its relations with the gods, who arranged the offerings and made the sacrifices, who did most of the official praying or verbal attempts to communicate with the gods—went a step further. The gods began to answer this person. It would be too much to expect a shaman to resist the temptation to improve his position, to increase his authority, by claiming a two-way communication with the gods. Nothing could be lost—there was no way of proving that the gods did not speak to him—and everything was to be gained.

The gain in authority was tremendous. The priest need only say that the gods had told him that certain things should be done and certain other things should be avoided, and the fear of the supernatural world made people obey. Even those few individuals who were not easily frightened were kept in line by their neighbors, who were anxious that the wrath of the gods not descend on the tribe because of the misbehavior of one member. It needed only the shaman's assertion that the gods had told him that the drought was ruining their harvest because of the misbehavior of one person, and they became an instant pariah.

It was not even necessary that the priest have a specific example in mind to thrust before the public. Reference to a hidden sin could immediately cause all and sundry to reform and obey in the fear that the prevalent air of suspicion might result in catching someone sinning and lead to ostracism, punishment, or banishment, in an effort to appease the gods and persuade them to let the life-giving rain return. Thus, religion and government mutually reinforced each other.

Meanwhile, as the human mind and the ideas it contained developed, the human philosophical approach also developed. The spirits gradually assumed more and more of the characteristics of gods. Their abodes were no longer in natural objects, but somewhere in the sky or below the earth. Death itself, which had once seemed a natural and accepted end to things, began to be questioned. If there was a spirit which could leave the body in dreams, why should it not be able to continue its existence after the demise of the body? As life became more complex—more than just a search for food—people began to feel a need for something beyond their limited visible horizon. They yearned toward a conviction that there was more to their existence than merely the monotonous daily routine of feeding themselves and their families; they felt frustrated that the world might continue its course towards eternity without them, that they were as insignificant as they seemed in the scheme of things.

This meshed readily with the evolution of the spirits into gods, and fell right in with the further development of the gods by the priests. The authority of the gods increases greatly when they can control not only the bodies, but also the souls of people. If they could promise eternal bliss to those who did their bidding or eternal damnation to those who crossed them, how much more effectively could that keep potentially errant people in line than could the threat of a simple run of bad luck engendered by malignant spirits.

Whatever reflected the policy of the governing chiefs became the commands of the gods. The gods of the Vikings or the Japanese promised heavens complete with feasts, fighting, and sometimes beautifully seductive women to those who died fighting for their nations. The high priests, with the help of legends and myths developed over many years, and with their claim to have privileged communication with the deities to back up their authority, maintained control over the citizenry in a way they never could have approached if they relied only on respect for human authority. Even where the people recognized the imperfections or outright vices of the priests, they would continue to obey the "divine" laws which they were brought up to believe.

Beliefs in religious systems—called "superstitions" by persons who disbelieved or who believed in a different system of religion—were used to maintain governmental authority, either via a theocratic government or through a government in which the religious authority paralleled a civic authority. This was not in itself either good or evil; the beliefs were simply tools in the hands of those in authority which could be used for either good or evil. Generally, they were used for what the authorities considered to be the good of the nation.

Just as the armies of our country or of our allies can be considered forces for good, while those of our enemies, though having almost identical characteristics can be considered potential forces for evil, so the religions we are brought up with and which maintain our style of life we consider good, while those of other peoples with other life styles can be considered evil, or at the least questionable and founded on ignorance or superstition.

Aside from the impetus behind using religion as a legalistic basis for enforcing ordinances and moral systems, progress in development of religious thought and beliefs came with the development of people's ability to think, to reason, to philosophize. Slowly across the years, the original ideas became ever less acceptable to the thinking person. The first superstitions, the beliefs in beneficent and malignant spirits that inhabited the rocks, rivers, and trees became less admissible. Still, people's yearning to believe in something less evanescent than the short, brutal lives they saw around them made them open to persuasion that something else really did exist.

Since the original spirits reflected both the good and evil characteristics that people themselves possessed, it was only natural that gods should appear to be, in many ways, similar to humans. The pagan gods were often full of human lust for the good things of life; drinking, feasting, and chasing members of the opposite sex—plus an ability for a miraculous control of persons and events, miraculous interventions in the weather, the wars, and the adventures of human life. These capabilities made the gods useful to the clergy and to the authorities.

Although these gods were an advancement over the spirits, they were all too human to be accepted by some individuals. Among other ideas that emerged, the consideration of the wonders of the universe by the ancient philosophers led to an urge to explain the origin of such marvelous organization, the infinite variety, and the harmony in nature that was everywhere one looked. As long as the gods existed, it was just one step further to consider them powerful enough to have created all these wonders. There was only one rational problem. Suppose we admit that it is reasonable to consider a universe so wonderful, so complex, and so well planned and operated that it must have had a Creator. If we must believe in an origin, a creation of the universe, then it is logical to ask who created the Creator?

Evidently, the average person is incapable of simply accepting as an insoluble mystery the theory of creation. We must have some sort of hypothesis in order to relax mentally, whether we can prove it or not. So we come to the hypothesis of the Eternal Creator God, and left the question of His origin in limbo.

This hypothesis cannot really be proved or disproved; it can only be accepted or denied. Thus, we cling to this explanation until something better comes along. Something better could come along, yet we are no more capable of predicting the philosophical ideas that will arise ten thousand to fifty thousand years in the future than were the primitive peoples capable of seeing beyond their sylvan spirits and river demons to the pagan gods of the Greeks and on to the Christian God of Love.

The Creator God quite obviously must be something far beyond the anthropomorphic gods of the pagans. With such fantastic powers, He cannot possibly be one of a group of human-like gods—He must stand alone. And, if He is powerful enough to create a universe, then where can He be limited? He must be also omniscient, omnipotent omnipresent.

Yet humans, even with the dawn of the idea of such a god, could not resist the temptation to shape this god in their own image. Or perhaps it was not a question of temptation but simply a question of the limitations of their imaginary vision. The Creator God who became the founder of the religions of the Western world, Jehovah, was a jealous God, a God of vengeance, a God who would send blights on those who did not worship Him. Jehovah was bloodthirsty to the extent that He commanded His people, the Israelites, to slaughter the inhabitants of the lands that His wanted them to have—even including all women and children.

This method of claiming land was the order of the day when people were still controlled by animal instincts to an even greater extent than they are today. Might was right, at least when your tribe confronted another tribe that possessed something you wanted. Vengeance and envy were considered perfectly normal human characteristics, and deceit was simply a tool for obtaining one's desires. Practicality demanded that one rein in one's tendencies when dealing with one's family members, neighbors, and fellow citizens. Such considerations became increasingly diluted the farther one was removed in one's relations from the other people in view; still, there were numerous instances of fratricide and parricide where the goal thereby attained was of sufficient importance to the doer of the deed. Small wonder that the God of these people was pictured as jealous, vengeful, and ever ready to help His people destroy their enemies.

The improvement of people's attitude toward their fellows-beings came slowly, but it did progress. Two thousand years ago, it had progressed to the point that the teachings of the carpenter of Nazareth were understandable and acceptable to many people of His day. Jesus as a preacher and prophet expressed the essence of the advancing morality, crystallizing its expression and systematizing its precepts. That Jesus was not accepted by everyone is not surprising; the laws and commands, the philosophy of the old Jehovah were too thoroughly ingrained in the minds of the people—all aside from the fact that the priests had a profound influence and great incentive to maintain their own positions of authority. The fact that Jesus was accepted at all, and by so many in such a short period is due to the previous development of moral attitudes and a thirst for the expression of something more adapted to these evolving attitudes.

Even centuries before Christ, Buddha had developed an advanced moral position in the East. Buddha went even further, separating the moral viewpoint from the direct control of a deity, and being so vague in his approach to deity in general that Buddhism has been called an "atheistic religion." However, Buddha and his followers were so far removed geographically and practically from the Western world, that their influence was virtually negligible, and Western religion developed essentially on its own.

Still, the teachings of Jesus and His disciples did not free people from some of the less desirable aspects of religious thought. Christ's promise of Paradise to those who believed in Him may well have made life's problems more acceptable to the poor and underprivileged, but His insistence on belief has been the source of both religious wars, such as the Crusades, and the outrageous terrors of the Spanish Inquisition.

Meanwhile we find that those among Christ's brethren who could not accept His divinity still progressed morally along the same path. Conservative and Reform Judaism are leaning away from the harsh unyielding Jehovah of their ancestors toward a more beneficent Creator. For charity and consideration of their fellow men, the Jews, as a group, are in the forefront of moral development.

Contemporaneously, it is difficult for those on the sidelines to understand what has happened in Ireland. There two sects of the followers of Jesus are at each other's throats, committing all sorts of atrocities, nurturing gnawing hatreds, all based on the fact that one group claims to follow Jesus through the leadership of the Pope, while the other finds the Pope unnecessary, or even an obstruction to proper worship.

Of course, the fundamental dissension is not the result of this minor difference in religious beliefs. The difference is not the reason for the violence, but is a tool used by the authorities on both sides to keep the factions apart and keep those in power in a position to continue in their power, while those on the outside are trying to get in. For nowhere is faith actually the cause of war, fortune, or dissension, but it can be a highly effective tool in the hands of those in authority to require submission, obedience, sacrifice, and heroism in order that the authorities may attain their personal goals.

Whence comes this power that religion has over our lives? We have been told by psychologists and anthropologists that people have a vital need to believe in something beyond just what they see in their physical environment. These beliefs do not always require a concrete belief in God, as witness the religions of Buddha and Confucius, which are, for all practical purposes, agnostic religions, and yet appeal to a multitude of people. Humanism in the Western world is somewhat their equivalent, in believing in the basic morality of humankind and not requiring, as Descartes once expressed it, the "hypothesis of God." Communism, in theory if not in application, is atheistic but highly moral as it was originally propounded by Karl Marx. We find highly placed members of Christian churches who are themselves atheistic or agnostic—witness the "God is Dead" movement, which is not as new as it might appear to the general public, having had its initial great impulse in the philosophy of Nietzsche in the past century.

Yes, the average person needs to believe in something. But a great many other influences also strengthen the position of religion. To some it is a crutch, to others it is a reaction to materialism; some look to religion for health, and others to satisfy their desire for brotherhood and mutual love; some find in religion a tool for power, and others, satisfaction of an innate desire to serve their fellow people. Many also adhere to their religion simply because of a youthful training that set their personalities on rigid tracks that subconsciously, they are unable to escape.

Religion can be a buttress in at least two ways. The poor person, the underdog, the economic slave, the person chained to a harassing family, the one in an unhappy position because of mental incapacity to compete or because of a personality weakness, the person left behind in the stream of life because of mental or physical handicaps—all these can benefit by the idea that a merciful God exists who will take care of them. Perhaps they only need the assurance that if they sincerely believe and avoid sinning to the best of their ability, and are honestly repentant when they do succumb to temptation, God will take care of them, and they will have their reward in Paradise. It may also be that they need to feel that the individuals who are responsible, in their minds, for their wretchedness will be punished. In either case, they have a real need for the consolation that religion can afford them. Thus, through the support of religion they are able to suffer "the slings and arrows of outrageous fortune" with something approaching equanimity.

Karl Marx said that "religion is the opiate of the people." Marx proposed to make a better world by removing the opiate and replacing it with a system that would be of benefit to all. Unfortunately, all attempts to install such a system on anything more than a very small scale have stumbled upon human nature: those at the top seem mainly interested in their own welfare, and those beneath them do not have not enough influence to overcome the extremes that cause the system to fail in its theoretical aims.

Hence, it may be preferable for those in need to preserve their religious beliefs until someone comes along who can replace them with a reliably effective proposal.

Religion can also be a buttress to those who are not permanently deprived. Even those who are otherwise well-off have problems, days when luck abandons them, when friends turn unfaithful, when loved ones pass on. It can mean much to them to be able to abandon themselves to "the will of God," and to the hope that they will be reunited with those they loved in the future.

So too, those faced with difficult decisions, have often found themselves aided by a few moments of silent prayer or meditation, in which they call on a power beyond them to help choose their direction. Whether such a power actually responds is irrelevant; as long as they maintain their belief, they are reinforced and strengthened by it.

The gross materialistic world of today calls in some, especially the young, for an intensified interest in religion as its antidote. The Jesus movement, the Hare Krishnas, the Moonies are all examples of people embracing philosophies that will lead away from the specter of materialism. As they begin to mature and perceive the world surrounding them—the frantic rush for the dollar, the kaleidoscopic color ads in magazines and on TV—they revolt in disgust and look for something that must have more meaning. Some find it in poetry and literature, some in art, some in nature, some in the simple and eternal beauty of love. Some of these find life meaningful in religion, especially in religions that promote interpersonal relationships, losing oneself in teamwork rather than the mad individual scramble to amass useless artifacts.

Perhaps the catalog of miracles in the Bible is the foundation for those who turn to religion for reasons of health. We are taught by our preachers that God answers prayer, that when someone is ill or his friends are sick, recovery can be hastened by prayer. This belief is reinforced by the existence of faith healing. Miracles of faith-healing do occur, though not to all supplicants at shrines such as Lourdes or by laying on of hands. The unbeliever will claim that the cure is of a psychosomatic disease; that the faith in the shrine or in the healer produces certain changes in the flow of fluids in the bodily organism which result in the healing.

Faith in cures can be faith in formulas such as that of Émile Coué, who found that many people were cured by repeating many times a day, "Every day, in every way, I'm getting better and better." Physicians have known that a person who is convinced that he will get well and who strongly desires his recovery will be out of bed much sooner than one who abandons hope. Basing this type of faith on religion certainly cannot diminish one's health, and may well help to strengthen it. Certainly, belief in the efficacy of such faith strengthens the position of religion.

Religiously, this faith in supernatural curing is carried still further by the Christian Scientists, who call sickness an "error," and whose religion is based on a credo that health is the natural aspect of a humanity which has the capacity to maintain perfect health solely by the proper understanding of the Divine Mind and its functions. We will consider this at length further on in our exploration.

We find a deep-felt need for religion among those unfortunates who have a craving for appreciation and love, which is not satisfied in their daily lives. A nagging spouse, a tyrannical boss, selfish neighbors, a demanding, unappreciative family—or just simply being ignored by those around him—can be morbidly depressing to a person. It requires a strong character to rise above such situations and find ways to get enough out of life to declare independence from this type of feeling.

For the average person, such a declaration of independence does not come so easily. He or she can find much comfort in the fellowship of a small-town or country church, especially where the preacher teaches love and brotherhood. They look forward to the smiles and friendly handshakes of the Sunday congregations or the Wednesday night prayer meetings, when enough warmth can be stored in the heart to last through the tribulations of the next few days.

Life in a religious commune may be the answer for those with the strongest needs. But this can sometimes lead to disaster, such as the tragedy of the mass suicides of the followers of preacher Jones in California. Men and women, blacks and whites, who came to Jones and found a loving acceptance, a pat on the back, and a friendly hug, felt that they had found their Paradise on earth. What Jones's religion meant to these people cannot be appreciated by those who do not know the feeling of starving for love. What Jones gave these people meant so much to them that they chose to follow him out of this life rather than abandon him for a return to their sordid lives. We can see in this scenario how the need for love and acceptance and the concepts of religion can reinforce each other.

In quite a different way, there can be mutual reinforcement between the individual and religion, when a person pursues the priesthood in response to an inner need for power. In all walks of life we find an urge for power over one's fellows: the clerk works hard with the hope of being some day made an office manager, and it is a rare soldier that does not accept a promotion. Nor are all persons who accede to power automatically capable of handling the job. Too often in industry, a chemist or a salesman is promoted to a management position as a reward for doing his work well, only to have the boss discover that he has lost a top-notch chemist or salesman and gained a poor manager. Desire alone does not guarantee capability, but the desire for the status concomitant with a position of power or authority is present in many if not most individuals.

Graduation from a theological seminary almost guarantees that the graduate can become a priest, a minister, or a rabbi, and have carved out his/her own little niche in the midst of a flock of parishioners. Certainly not all who receive the call to the ministry have this in the forefront of their minds or even in their subconscious, but even those who start out without such thoughts do enjoy basking in the admiration of their followers. As with any teacher, it would be difficult to deny that it is soothing to the ego to have people look to one for guidance and insight.

Like the political atmosphere of a university, the church hierarchy may not be without intrigue. There are professors and priests who are satisfied with their positions, and want no part of the politics in which those who wish to advance must engage. But advancement is based also on having produced an above-average performance, so that an ambitious person contributes more to his religion as it in turn provides him with the opportunity for the power and the influence he seeks.

Nor must such power always be on the grand scale to be enjoyed. We recall some years ago meeting a missionary in a tiny settlement in the depths of the Amazon jungle. He had taken a vow of poverty, and certainly by the standards of the friends he had left behind in his Canadian hometown, he had little of the world's material goods. But by the standards of the natives around him, he was very well off. His house had the only galvanized roof, the others being of thatch; had the only stove, the others being pits in the ground; had the only flush toilet, served by a tank on the roof into which water was pumped by one of his two teenage helpers who worked for him and for the glory of the church in return for a few scraps of food. He enjoyed his position of authority and to recompense, he performed to the advantage of the church, spreading the word as best he could among the Indians who knew only a few words of Spanish, and were hard put to understand the transubstantiation or the significance of the Virgin birth but who allowed themselves to be baptized and introduced to ritual marriage ceremonies.

The desire to be of service to one's fellows can also find its opportunity in religious organizations. In some cases we are not sure whether a person joined a religious organization because they found it helped them utilize their altruism, or did they develop the desire to be altruistic after being exposed to the teachings of the religion.

Until recent times, religious organizations were the only mechanisms which furnished ready access to service opportunities. Monasteries and nunneries were training grounds for those who wanted to help the sick, contribute to education, and care for the poor. Today not only at home, but also in the underdeveloped countries of the world, medical and educational missionaries spread over the globe under the aegis of some church or other with the financial support of that church's congregation. There are no more inspiring stories in our libraries than those of Albert Schweitzer and his fellow medical missionaries, trying to alleviate the sufferings of some part of the world's destitute, and often suffering martyrdom from attacks by unappreciative natives or unthinking hordes of strange bacteria.

Religious organizations like the Salvation Army help bring bed and bread to the urban hungry and destitute, and a comforting feeling that somebody cares, even if it seems that most of the world does not.

Certain organizations, such as the Masonic lodges and the Elks clubs, are very active in performing charity work, especially hospital service. While these are not religious organizations, they are thoroughly infused with religious philosophies, and religion is an integral part of their thought.

In the modern world, there are also avenues of service that do not require passing through religious gates. Not all social service workers are religiously inclined; not all Red Cross and Grey Lady workers go weekly to church. Many people go into Boy Scout or Girl Scout work without any thought of religion as an incentive. Atheists work hand-in-hand with priests in Community Fund enterprises, and Peace Corps and Vista do not require religious affiliation. Governmental politicians and employees work on the all pervading welfare programs.

The service clubs, such as Rotary, Kiwanis, Pilot, and many others can almost be considered a contemporary religion in their approaches, though they are service-oriented rather than God-oriented. Though they usually open their meetings with a prayer, this is all that one hears of religion in their operations. The members seek opportunities to be of service to the community and its youth, and pride themselves on never turning down a request for aid from a fellow member who is trying to organize a team for a service project.

From the foregoing, we find that religion, as we know it today, is built on a foundation of three sturdy columns.

The first is the human's discovery of the soul, the "anima." The development of this discovery, made through dream experiences, led to assignment of souls to other natural phenomena, such as animals and plants; objects which seemed to have life and movement such as the wind, rivers, the sun and moon; and eventually, to rocks and mountains.

The second column of the foundation was the discovery by persons in position of authority, that they could utilize this belief in spirits to enhance their authority. Not only could they keep their subjects in line with greater facility by threats of retaliation from these unseen spirits or gods whenever they misbehaved; but priests or theocratic heads of the tribe were also able to deliver the impression that they were in direct contact with the spirits. This set him apart from the common person and conferred on him an aura which would have been impossible to have otherwise attained.

The third column of the foundation is composed of people's psychic needs, which are several in nature. One is the need to feel more important than what is substantiated by the evidence of the senses alone—which generated a belief in immortality of the soul on the one hand, on the other hand a belief in a special relationship to God which He denied to other animals. In its ultimate form, this exists as a belief that the whole of the universe was constructed to serve as a foil for humankind, and that the human being was the prime object of Creation. We find this underlined by the egotistic statement that humankind is created in the image of God.

The other components of the third column, the psychic needs, are several in nature: the moral support given by religious teachings which make of religion a crutch or a bulwark, the human need for fellowship, the need for self-importance which can be observed in non-spiritual context, such as the pleasure of being able to guide and influence one's fellow-beings which the missionary or the parish priest experiences, and the sensation of power of abbots, bishops, high priests, and others in advanced administrative positions. Additionally, there are the needs arising from altruism: a sincere desire to help one's neighbor, to be of service, and otherwise to do one's part in building a better world.

These are three very solid foundations, indeed. Over the ages, they have maintained a religious structure in society which persists in spite of the humanism of such events as the French Revolution and the atheism of the so-called Communist governments. As time passes, the force of human intellect is always seeking something better and more acceptable to a logical and reasoning mind. In each era, it strives to build the edifice of religion into a monument that will satisfy both people's aesthetic senses and their demand for a construct that will have the strength to withstand the furious buffeting of the winds of contrary intellectual opinion.

The product of this effort we find in the evolution of the gods, from the animistic spirits through the pagan gods to the monotheistic gods of people's later historical development. These efforts have produced the biblical Gods, the Urdu pantheon, the now-defunct Egyptian gods, the nearly extinct Zoroastrian dual deities, as well as the religions such as Buddhism and Confucianism, in which God Himself is relegated to a secondary role.

The new Gods or religious systems are never universally accepted, and indeed, are generally only gradually accepted and only by a fraction of humankind. The older Gods, from which the new ones have evolved, may survive either as a result of intellectual disagreement, or because of intellectual inertia on the part of their followers—or they may gradually lose their following and become unimportant or even extinct as a species. We will follow this evolutionary process in the subsequent chapters.

# Chapter 3: The Pagan Gods

So saying, Minerva goddess azure-eyed,
Rose to Olympus, the reputed seat
Eternal of the gods, which never storms
Disturb, rains drench, or snow invades, but calm
The expanse and cloudless shines with purest day.
There the inhabitants divine rejoice
Forever. (Homer, *Odyssey*, translation by Cowper)

Many students of religion who look on the Biblical story of creation as allegory consider that the six "days" of creation represent extended eras—thousands or possibly millions of years were taken by God for each stage in the production of the cosmos, of earth, of lands and seas, of plants, of animals, and finally of humankind. When one considers that, to God in His infinite duration, a million or a billion years might be the equivalent of what we consider one day, the assumption becomes logical.

In like manner, the creation of God in the mind of humans was a process that lasted over many millennia, and is still going on. And in a manner similar to the creation of the universe as we know it, the creation of God occurred in stages.

We have considered the origin of animism, in which people had already begun the process of creating supernatural beings in their own image. They were still far removed from being gods, these mind-created spirits, but they were quite obviously based on people's experience with their minds, their memories, and their dreams. If people were conscious of something stirring within them that seemed to be a spirit or soul, by whatever name they may have called it, it was only natural for them to project the same sort of spirit onto animals, or onto anything that moved or grew. Wolves and bears, trees, the rivers and the breeze, volcanoes, and the sun were all supplied with spirits which could be looked upon with anxiety, fear, or hope for help, and with an impression of the advisability of appeasing or currying favor through prayer and sacrificial gifts.

Within the anarchy of animism, these spirits did not yet constitute gods. All this supposed phenomena existed simply as a transference, somewhat enlarged and elaborated, of humankind's own experience of other objects within its ken.

It was only with the dawn of philosophy that the gods began to appear. The organization of the life of humans passed beyond the stage of continual individual concern about finding the next meal, and avoiding becoming a meal themselves. Larger groups afforded the opportunity of expressing and exchanging ideas. Having at least a small bit of leisure for this exchange, humans' innate curiosity surfaced. They began to look beyond the end of their noses, to wonder where all this came from and what kept it all on the right track. How did the sun know to rise each dawning; what magic turned the egg into a chicken?

The original animistic spirits possessed human attributes: sight, the ability to reason, take action and react, aggressiveness and docility, love and hate, good and evil. Then came the attributes of the gods, possessing those characteristics people desired for themselves: an idealized being of infinite wisdom, eternal life, unlimited strength, omniscience, perfected virtues. Nor did all these desirable qualities arrive at once, but rather gradually. The pagan gods themselves had many of the limitations: the imperfections and the vices of the mortals whom they neither created nor supervised.

For one raised with the knowledge of the Father God of Christianity preaching love, it might be difficult to jettison the inculcated idea that God made humans in His image and entertain the idea that the process was actually in reverse. Even the consideration of such a thought might be considered blasphemy by the orthodox.

Logic and history can help. Logically, an infinite God will have no need of the bodily organs and members required by humans for their encounter with the world around them. Also, it is not very respectful on our part to consider that man's prejudices, envies and ambitions, and other miscellaneous failings are part of an image of God. If humankind is in the image of God, we can only hope that humans, as a mirror, are producing a very distorted image.

From the vantage of history, it is quite simple to trace the image of God formed by humankind, based on itself, through the various evolutionary stages we have just mentioned, to the later stages where we realize that if the God we have created is to resemble what one should rightfully expect from a reasonable, infinite, omniscient, omnipotent, perfectly virtuous God capable of creation, He must be brought beyond the stages of evolution known to our ancestors into today's world of science, reason, and the beginnings of altruism.

In this chapter we will explore briefly the intermediate stage of the evolution of God, in which He evolved from a simple spirit to a God recognizable as such, with godly and creative powers. Comparing the stages of evolution of God to those of humankind, we might say that the tribal limited gods that appeared after the primitive animism, were in a stage intermediate between spirits and genuine gods, as was *Homo erectus* a stage between the animal primates and the evolution of *Homo sapiens*. Similarly, the hunter-caveman *Homo sapiens*, the first recognizable as a genuine modern man, could be thought of as being on an evolutionary level equivalent to the first real gods, the pagan gods of Rome, Greece, Scandinavia, and others.

In this and successive chapters, we will follow the evolution of God down to the Gods that still remain viable and thriving today.

Paganism is a rather indefinite term generally applied by those who consider their own beliefs those of a true religion to those whom they consider victims of superstition. It includes belief in Gods who have passed the primitive stage of animism, but which have not yet developed into the principal religions recognized today, religions under the aegis of Gods that are capable of creation and who have something of the characteristics of omniscience and omnipotence. Certain religions with multiple gods, such as those of ancient Egypt and the Hindus, have some of the characteristics of paganism.

Paganism generally includes the religions developed in Greece, in Scandinavia, and in Arabia before Mohammed; that copied from Greece by the Romans; as well as the religions of Polynesia. It is essentially a progressive evolutionary step beyond animism which we can best characterize by pointing out that the personifications of natural phenomena represented by the spirits, turn into persons in the form of gods who control these phenomena. In the process, the disappearance of personifications allows consolidation of functions, so that one god can handle several duties, thus materially decreasing the numbers and variety of supernatural beings.

That this did not happen all at once we see from the fact that the families of the gods of the pagans were quite numerous. Hermes, as an example, was the god of science and commerce, of wrestling and other gymnastic exercises, the patron of both travelers and thieves, and being the messenger of the gods would preside today over the communications industry. Yet even with consolidations such as this, not only were there literally hundreds of gods and demigods crowding the heavens, the earth, the sea, the rivers, and the underworld. Dryads, nymphs, and satyrs roamed the woods. Nymphs splashed in the fountains; tritons and nereids sported in the ocean depths. Lares and penates guarded the home and hearthside; agriculture and related occupations had a long list of gods including Tellus, Demeter (Ceres), Cybele, Sylvanus, Pan, Faunus, Bona Dea, Vertumnus, Pomona, Dionysus (Bacchus) among others. Pluto and his lieutenants supervised the underworld. Apollo drove the chariot of the sun. Athena (Minerva) was the goddess of wisdom, Aphrodite (Venus) the goddess of beauty. The nine Muses were patrons of the performing and literary arts, and the three Graces presided over the dance, social relations, and the elegant arts. The Parcae (the Fates) spun the web of destiny, while the Furies made certain that the wicked were punished. No action, occupation, quality, vice or virtue was without its divine steward.

One of the normal characteristics of paganism is idolatry. The presence of an idol was not a necessary requisite in a temple or at an altar, but in common with Christianity, especially Roman Catholicism, the idol or the symbol was generally there.

To an outsider, it is difficult to understand why the Catholics, with their preponderance of paintings and statues of Jesus, the Madonna, and the saints, should look disdainfully upon the idolatry of the pagans, as if it were completely and qualitatively different. Many Christians have the idea that pagans worshiped the idol itself, but pagans were only doing what Christians do when they pray in front of a statue or painting of Jesus: using the image to help themselves visualize and communicate with the idea behind the image.

Mohammed, at least, was consistent. In denouncing the idolatry of the Arabian pagans, he refused his followers the use of anything even vaguely resembling idols in the worship of Allah, with the exception of the Black Stone in the Kaaba at Mecca, which is an object of pilgrimage and veneration by Muslims the world over, and to some extent serves the function of an idol.

The theologian will argue that the difference lies in the assumption that there was nothing behind the pagan idol, whereas Jesus did exist and so did the saints. And the philosopher will reply that in all likelihood, neither the pagan gods nor the Catholic God is an exact reproduction of what the Supreme Being actually is like, if He exists at all. Hence, both the pagan and Christian worshipper are on the same ground., simply worshipping the best possible idea currently available to him concerning what God really is, with the understanding that God is God, by whatever name He may be called. In our exploration of paganism, we will study principally the Greek and Roman gods; those most closely related to the western world and its development. It is noteworthy that, in the progress of religion, one step did not follow another in logical sequence along the spread of the calendar. Although the pagan gods of Greece and Rome continued to be worshiped for several centuries after the birth of Jesus, just centuries before Christ, Pythagoras and Plato along with many others, postulated a single, all-powerful Creator God similar in nature to the Biblical God. While for some, this God was essentially a monotheistic God, for others, He was simply a higher-level God, creator of the minor gods as well as of man and earth.

The pagan gods familiar to the common man were without any shadow of doubt created by man after his own image. The evolution from spirit to god, from personification to person, was a mutational change, a step-wise progression that by-passed gradual developmental processes. It was a change brought about in response to humans beginning to think and to wonder. The spirits of animism were not suited to the new environment of intellect, and could no longer survive, except in fewer and fewer isolated regions around the globe where humans were confined to a primitive stage of thought. While not yet completely extinct, the spirits of animism are certainly a threatened species.

The pagan beliefs, which today we call myths, were by no means uniform. As today we have many sects of varying Christian belief, there were then many variations of the myths about the origin of the world and the stories of the gods. Still, all these variations had common features. In all, the characteristics of the gods were those of men, but on a grand scale, man's vices, as well as his virtues, were those of the gods. The powers and capabilities of the gods were those of mortals, but carried to an idealized extreme and infused with magic, which although beyond ordinary human powers, was believed to be within the powers of adepts.

The gods that were generally worshiped were not creators. The creators of the world were believed to have been antecedents of the usually venerated gods such as Zeus (Jupiter) and his relatives. Possibly these antecedents were added later to mythology for the purpose of explaining creation. There were several conflicting accounts of creation from Chaos, an agglomerate of earth, sea, and heaven without form, but containing the seeds of all living things. The earth goddess Gaea and Erebus (Darkness), among others, were credited with having a part in the separation and placing of earth, sea, and sky. The first beings, offspring of Earth and Heaven, were a race of god-like giants, the Titans. Two of the Titans, Cronos (Saturn) and Rhea, produced a large family which included the most important of the gods and goddesses. Zeus, the chief of the gods, and his wife Hera (Juno) were among these, as well as Poseidon (Neptune) and Hades (Pluto).

Saturn's children, once grown, rebelled against their father. When the other Titans came to his aid, there ensued a fierce battle in which the gods were victors, and we hear little more of the Titans, except for Atlas, who was condemned to carry the weight of heaven on his shoulders; and Prometheus, the creator and friend of man.

Following the separation of the earth, the sea and the sky, some anonymous god took on the labor of shaping the mountains, the valleys, the rivers, the islands, the forests, and the plains. For all his effort, he was given no credit, and his name escapes history.

Prometheus himself did not end well. He molded a handful of mud into human form—in the image of the gods, it was said—giving him an upright stance so that unlike the rest of the animals, he could look up at heaven and the starry skies. As a final touch, Prometheus lighted his torch from the chariot of the sun and took the lighted torch as a present of fire to man, thus giving him supremacy over the beasts of the fields and woods.

In the Adam story of creation, we read that after Adam had partaken of the apple, God lamented that Adam, with his knowledge of good and evil, had thereby become more god-like, and that, at all costs, He must prevent Adam from eating the fruit of the tree of life and becoming immortal—as God said, "becoming one of us." To avoid this eventuality, Adam and Eve were ousted from the garden of Eden. With the gift by Prometheus of fire to man, a similar reaction occurs to Zeus. As in the case of Adam, the deed, once done, cannot be recalled. To punish Prometheus, and to prevent him from acting further to make his creation, man, more god-like, Zeus chained Prometheus to a rock, and sent a vulture to feed eternally on his liver, which grew back as fast as it was consumed.

The first woman was Pandora, who was sent in the beginning to Prometheus' brother, Epimetheus. While in Epimetheus' home, Pandora's feminine curiosity got the better of her, and she peeked into the famous box, which she had been cautioned by Epimetheus not to touch. Before she could replace the lid, the plagues, evils, and vices escaped and left the world no longer the perfect ideal home for humankind.

Evidently neither the story of Eve nor the story of Pandora was authored by women, as in both we find women receiving credit for the origin of all the evils that have beset the human race.

In the Biblical and many other religions, man was a creation of the highest or the only god, and was therefore a subject of the utmost interest to God. By contrast, the pagan gods, who were not the creators of man, had little direct interest in the fate of man, either as an individual or as a race. We have a condition similar to the feelings of parents: their own children are of prime importance, and everything possible must be done to see that they prosper.

Children of other parents are of interest to them only in passing, or when these children approach them and beg assistance—which may or may not be given. Gods and mortals have this sentiment in common.

The neglect was not complete. Mortals could be approached when they were in a position to serve the wishes of the gods, or when the gods found themselves sexually attracted to mortals, which especially in the case of the rake, Zeus, was a not infrequent happenstance.

As a result, in paganism we find a lack of several features which are prominent in later religions. Although the gods appear to mortals from time to time, there is nothing which we can relate to the "revelations" of most of today's major religions. These were essentially for the purpose of explaining to man the nature of God and of God's will. Zeus would not understand the first commandment of jealous Jehovah. He does not demand belief from man, and it is a matter of the utmost indifference to him whether man recognized him or not. Appearance of the gods that did ensue were from some ulterior motive, as often as not for amorous pursuits.

Hence there were no appearances or communications from the gods with the purpose of enlightening mortals regarding their nature or their desires. Nor were they expected. We are here moving from animism to the gods, and there have been no experiences with revelations as we understand them, other than some claims of priests to personal communications.

Another missing feature present in many other religions is the legalistic dictates of the gods. For instance, Jehovah dictated a long and complete code of laws to Moses, in addition to the Ten Commandments. Allah, although He dictated no specific code as such, was legalistic in the extreme, and it was the responsibility of each Moslem to determine the full will of Allah and to follow it without deviation. The God of Mormon not only dictated His moral likes and dislikes, but went so far as to dictate the organization of the church and the names of the officials.

None of this do we find in the orbit of the pagan gods, who are too taken with their own personal concerns to worry about mortal action or inaction—again the non-parent relation.

Nor are they moralistic. It could hardly be expected from a group of gods whose own morals left something to be desired. There is no urging on their part for mortals to be obedient, to indulge in charity, or to tithe. Humans' contribution to the temple upkeep and to the sacrifices did not come from any requirements passed down by the gods, but by their own initiative arising from attempts to placate the gods or to importune the gods for one favor or another.

The one outstanding exception to the rule of indifference to mortal morals came when humankind degenerated so thoroughly that even Zeus became disgusted, and resolved to wipe it out and to replace it with a better race.

Zeus and his brother Poseidon, working together, produced from the clouds and from the seas the waters for a deluge that covered the world. No ark was built, but the waters did not quite reach the peak of Mount Parnassus, and Deucalion and his wife Pyrrha found refuge there. The had led exemplary lives, and Zeus spared them for the start of a new and hopefully better race.

Like wise there is no evidence of a select group, a "chosen people." The gods are simply not interested.

This does not imply that the gods did not have their individual favorites. There were plenty of these, generally based on personal attraction to the individual, such as the stories of the amours. There was also the attachment of Aphrodite to Paris, in gratitude to him for having chosen her the fairest of the trio of claimants which included also Athena and Hera. The result of this was the presentation of the fair Helen to Paris by the intervention of Venus. The subsequent elopement to Troy had as its consequence the war between the Greeks and the Trojans. During this war, the gods showed favoritism, but the gods themselves were divided, and with the occasional help of the gods on one side or the other, the war see-sawed into a drawn-out conflict that lasted over ten years before it was ended by the ruse of the so-called Trojan Horse (actually a Greek horse).

One by-product of this disinterested attitude of the gods was a lack of sin. Sin is, by definition, a transgression of the laws of the deity. If the deity made no laws, there can be no sin. Man's transgressions are then either violations of his own laws, or acts that, while legal, are immoral and detrimental to the good of one's neighbor or the community.

Such transgressions were noted and properly punished. Virgil relates the story of the descent of Aeneas into the nether world ruled by Hades, accompanied by the Sibyl as a guide. His object was to search for his father Anchises.

In the process he was regaled with a full sightseeing tour of Hades' realm, and saw the varieties of tortures of the damned; the dreary sad regions of the suicides; the unending labor of Sisyphus, who could never reach the top of the hill with his huge rock before it rolled down again; the tortuous thirst of Tantalus who could never quite reach the cool water or the juicy fruits that eluded his grasp each time he reached for them. Punishment was meted out by the infernal judge, Rhadamanthus, and the three sister goddesses, the Furies, of horrid mien with serpent-wreathed heads, whose duty it was to see that criminals who escaped justice in the mortal world were punished in after-life.

We note here that the underworld, or Hades, of the ancients showed much more imagination than the Hell of Christianity or Islam, which were little more than lakes of fire. In the pagan Hades, the punishment fits the crime, and there is as varied a catalog of punishments as of crimes. For an expanded picture of this, the best reference is Dante's "Inferno," in which the pagan Hades has become Christianized, and Dante has been given a guided tour of the region by the shade of the poet Virgil. Probably, at one time, many Christians accepted this presentation of a many-circled Hell with its fantastically imagined tortures, but the church itself remained with its simpler Biblical affirmations.

The heroes, priests, and poets as well as others who had done service to humankind, were found by Aeneas in Elysium, the pagan Paradise, where his father resided. There the shades of the dead rejoiced in glowing groves, chatting, singing, dancing; engaged in games of skill or strength or listening to the enchanting music of Orpheus and others.

None of this is of concern to Zeus, Hera, Hephaestus, Aphrodite or the other gods resident on Mount Olympus. Each God had his own function, own bailiwick. Punishment and reward are handled by gods who specialize in these areas alone.

We observe here a further characteristic of the intermediate state between animism and monotheism. Within the pagan pantheon, no one god can do everything, or even come close to it. Still, each god may preside over what was once the field of several animistic spirits. We have already mentioned the variety of duties assigned to Hermes (Mercury). Demeter, goddess of agriculture, embodied a whole catalog of spirits which once lived with each type of fruit, with corn, with wheat, and other plants. Apollo was not only the sun-god, he was also the god of prophecy, archery, and music.

It is interesting to compare the Elysian Fields of the Greek pagans with the Valhalla of the Scandinavians. While Jesus, Allah, the God of Mormon, and others required strict belief as a ticket of admission to Paradise, the pagan gods were more unconcerned. In the first place, the pagan gods took it for granted that everyone knew they existed; in the second place, belief profited them nothing, and they remained completely indifferent to mortal credence.

Although we take the story from the Roman poet Virgil, it is essentially a Greek story. In the Elysian Fields, we find the souls of the dead in what was to the Greeks an ideal existence—participating in earnest discussion or in sporting games of skill and strength, enjoying the dance, song, and the music of the lyre. The war heroes are relaxed, weapons aside, spears stuck in the ground, chariots unused, the war horses unharnessed and peacefully grazing.

Farther north, among a race of warriors from the harsh Northlands, the picture is completely different. The dead are divided into two groups, as with the Greek afterlife, but not with regard to morals. The chosen are the war heroes who died in battle, and are brought to the halls of Valhalla by the Valkyrie. All others, those who die of sickness or old age, are sent to the domain of Hela, the goddess of Death, called Hel, or Niflheim, a rather neutral, vaguely unattractive abode reminiscent of the Old Testament Sheol.

All the best is given to the warriors, and the best for them is a heaven where they can fight all day. Toward evening, the wounds heal themselves, they retire to a feast of mead and roast boar, and rest for another round the next day.

Thus we find that not only are the gods created in the image of humans, but Paradise is also created in the image of human desires. This compatibility finds the gods to have such characteristics that they adapt well to their environment and survive as a species. It was only when humans themselves changed their intellectual ideas, that the pagan gods were no longer adapted to the environment, and faded out of history.

Zeus often appeared to mortals, predominantly to the fairer sex. He was constantly slipping away from his wife, Hera, and indulging in adultery with both goddesses and mortals. Several of his well-known amours were Leda, Io, and Callisto. For those who view of the "virgin birth" of Jesus, in which a mortal is impregnated by a divine being, as something original, we call attention to Hercules, to Dionysus,, and to the twins, Castor, and Pollux, all offspring of mortal virgins by the activity of the god Zeus, in consort with Alcmene, Semele, and Leda.

Nor is dalliance with mortals limited to male gods. Venus, the goddess of love, got around a bit herself. Her more celebrated amours were those with the mortals Adonis and Tannhauser.

As for other characteristics of the pagan gods, we find that although they have been given greater capabilities than those possessed by mortals, they are not, like later gods, either omnipotent or omniscient. While they were able to watch the affairs of the world from a position in their palaces on Mount Olympus, much could be done without their knowledge, both in the lands of mortals and among themselves. They were continually doing things secretly without the others' knowledge.

Sometimes however, an effort to remain clandestine backfired. When Zeus created a cloud to conceal his courting of Io, Hera noted the shadow and brushed away the cloud for a look, discovering her husband on the river bank with a lovely heifer. Because of Zeus's efforts at concealment, Hera correctly guessed the transformed shape was that of a luscious wench.

The tale of Midas was based on a god's lack of omniscience. Dionysus had been searching for his old schoolmaster, Silenus, who had wandered away under the influence of' alcoholic indulgence. He was found by King Midas who took care of him for a few days, then brought him back healthy to his pupil. Grateful, Dionysus granted Midas a wish, which was the famous desire that everything he touched should turn to gold. The wish was granted, and Midas was ecstatic till dinner time. When his food and drink turned to gold, he nearly dies of hunger and thirst before he found Dionysus again and persuaded him to withdraw the mixed blessing.

And the goddess Demeter searched over half the known earth before she learned from the fountain Arethusa that her daughter Persephone (Proserpine) had been abducted by Hades and taken below to become queen of the underworld.

As for omnipotence, the gods often had to call on each other for help. Hera had the maiden Io, in the form of a heifer under the watchful eyes of the hundred-eyed Argus, who always slept with only a few eyes at a time. Zeus has to call on Hermes and his magic wand to bring on a somnolence with all one hundred eyes, at which he cut off Argus' head and rescued Io. Hephaestus (Vulcan), the smith of the gods, was often called on for impregnable armor or invincible weapons.

Raising individuals from death or protecting them from dying, which Jesus handled with calm aplomb, was not within the capabilities of the pagan gods, as we found in the death of Hyacinthus while Apollo was looking on, and in the death of Adonis, the favorite of Venus. Adonis, in a careless demonstration of courage during a hunt, was gored by the tusks of a wild boar. He expired painfully from loss of blood before Venus was able to return to help. The best that she could do was to turn the flowing blood into a memorial flower, the beautiful anemone.

The lack of omnipotence was partially compensated by the gods' abilities with magic. No one spoke of miracles on the part of the pagan gods, but some of their repertoire included machinations that certainly had aspects of miracles.

Aeolus, for instance, presented Odysseus (Ulysses) with a leather bag which contained the unfavorable and tempestuous winds, so that he could proceed on his voyage with the ships sails bellying out, full of favorable winds. Unfortunately, a curious crew member opened the bag for a look, the contrary winds broke out, and all hell broke loose.

The gods were continually changing mortals into other than human form for one odd reason or another.

Zeus turned his love Io into a heifer to hide her from Hera; he turned himself into a bull to carry off the beautiful Europa and into a swan for the courtship of Leda. Hera turned one of his amours, Callisto, into a bear, to make her less attractive. The river god, Peneus, turned his daughter Daphne into a laurel tree to enable her to escape ravishment by Apollo. Venus, irked by the ingratitude of Atalanta and Hippomenes, changed them into lions in her fit of pique. Minerva changed Arachne into a spider for having the presumption to challenge her to a duel of weaving artistry. The list goes on ad infinitum.

As for Christ's miraculous feeding of the multitude with the loaves and the fishes, we have equivalents of the bottomless market basket in the liver of Prometheus which grows back as fast as it is devoured by the vulture. We have the tale of Valhalla, where the deceased heroes feast on the flesh of the boar Schrimnir. The beast was roasted every morning in preparation for the nightly banquets, then became whole again at night, ready for another barbecue the next day. The most well-known story may be of Ope and the famous Horn of Plenty.

Other than the powers of magic, the powers of the pagan gods are generally those of the mortals raised to a much higher degree. Human qualities carried to perfection are represented by Athena for wisdom, Ares (Mars) for courage, Aphrodite for beauty, Hephaestus for skill, Hermes for adroitness, and Dionysus for geniality. One of the best examples of this is presented by the demigod, Orpheus, son of Apollo and Calliope, whose music had charms far beyond those "to soothe the savage breast." Not only were people and gods enchanted by the music of his lyre, but wild beasts came to listen, and suspended their carnivorous activities in their ecstasy. Even the oaks and willows crowded around, and the granite rocks softened to hear him play. When he penetrated the confines of the nether world, seeking to persuade Hades to free his wife Eurydice, the very ghosts shed tears. Tantalus, in spite of his thirst, stopped for a moment his efforts for water, Ixion's wheel stood still, the vulture ceased to tear at the giant's liver, the daughters of Danae rested from their task of drawing water in a sieve, and Sisyphus sat on his rock to listen. Then, for the first time, it is said, "the cheeks of the Furies were wet with tears—Pluto himself gave way...." (Bulfinch, *Mythology*)

Speaking of music brings us to a tale of two other human characteristics: mischief and an aversion to appearing ridiculous. Athena had invented the flute; Cupid, watching her play one day laughed at the odd contortions of her face while playing. Athena was so annoyed that she threw the instrument away and never played again.

The gods were inventive in other directions. From dipping into the past to development musical instruments, one, Hephaestus, moved into the future and produced the first robots. For Zeus, he produced a series of chairs and tables that moved themselves wherever they were commanded. For himself, he fabricated of gold several lovely serving maidens that took care of his household needs.

The pagan deities had human tastes, loving a good feast, a bit of sport and games, some adventures now and then, as well as the amorous pursuits we have already mentioned. Full of life, the adjective sedate could be applied to none of them. They raced, the ladies had weaving competitions, and they often gathered at the palace of Zeus for gay banquets. At one of these, we find the human fault of pride something also characteristic of the gods and goddesses. We quote from Bulfinch's *Mythology*:

> ...all the gods were invited with the exception of Eris, or Discord. Enraged at her exclusion, the goddess threw a golden apple among the guests, with the inscription 'for the fairest'. Hera, Venus and Minerva each claimed the apple. Zeus, not willing to decide so delicate a matter, sent the goddesses to Mount Ida, where Paris was tending his flocks, and to him committed the decision. Hera promised him power and riches, Minerva glory and renown in war, and Venus the fairest of women for his wife.... Paris decided in favor of Venus—thus making the two other goddesses his enemies....

Paris did obtain the gorgeous Helen, but the enmity he had earned made some of the gods allies of the Greeks, and he eventually lost his life in the Trojan war.

Which demonstrated another human failing among the gods: vengeance. Another example of the exercise of vengeance we find during the preparations by the Greeks for the Trojan siege. Agamemnon carelessly killed a stag which was sacred to Artemis (Diana) In revenge, she sent a plague to the Greek army, and calmed the winds so that the ships could not leave port. Many a mortal suffered because of the vengeful reactions of the gods to some often unintentional or unavoidable slight.

Such vengeance was often caused by jealousy. This was quite frequent on the part of Hera, jealous of the dalliances of Zeus. Poor Callisto, once an object of Zeus's affection, was turned into a bear by Hera. Her revenge on the unfortunate Io, who had been turned into a heifer by Zeus in an attempt to escape Hera's detection, was to send an extremely annoying gadfly to pester the heifer, who ran all over the world in a futile attempt to escape the buzzing beast. Vengeance was taken by the goddess Latona on a group of peasants who maliciously sought to prevent her from slaking her thirst in the cool waters of a limpid stream. She became so annoyed at their comments and their jeers, that she changed them all to slimy green frogs. They are still there in the water, croaking hoarsely at all who approach.

In short, the whole history of the pagan deities, the whole catalog of myths, is one story after another demonstrating the human-like characteristics of the gods. They have their jealousies and deceits, their intrigues, their indulgence to favorites, their response to praise and petitions. They are capricious, willful, envious, licentious. They are anything but altruistic. There is no planning for the future; the life of the gods was lived day by day, taken as it came.

Perhaps if they had planned for the future, they might still be with us today. But they did not survive. They were better adapted to their environment than were the spirits of animism, but the environment continued to change, and the pagan Gods, unchanging, were left behind. More and more, man felt the need for a genuine creator, a need for a less confusing pantheon and a more satisfying monotheistic deity, one with even more power than the gods of Olympus, an omnipotence worthy of a god. And why should god have to sit on the ramparts of Olympus to be able to watch what is going on? It was only befitting that god should be omniscient; that nothing should escape him.

As a creator rather than one created, He could earn the respect of man. Humans could, themselves, feel more important, being the subject of creation, the crown of the efforts of an Almighty God, a God who thought enough of His creation to control properly this work of His. If His control did not extend to the details and to day-to-day operation of the universe, it was at least consolidated on Judgment Day, when corrections were made for everything that had escaped the divine volition.

The complexity of the pagan system did not allow for adjustment or adaptation to the new environment. Already weakening in the Mediterranean area, when Christianity was introduced as a state religion by the emperor Constantine, the death throes of the pagan deities began, twilight descended, and they never fully recovered. The principles of evolution were demonstrated once more, and the survival of the fittest left the field to Christianity, while the pagan gods went into hiding, gradually starved to death, and became extinct. Today's world has no pagan priest, no pagan worshipper; their altars and temples are only occasional ruins. The tombs of the pagan gods are the libraries and the museums of the world.

# Chapter 4: The God of the Patriarchs

> You shall have no other gods before me....I the Lord your God am a jealous God, visiting the iniquity of the fathers upon the children to the third and fourth generation of those who hate me but showing steadfast love to thousands of those who love me and keep my commandments. (Exodus 20:3, 5, 6)

When we consider God as He is conveyed in the Christian Bible, we find three essentially different concepts of God. We propose to call these different conceptions the God of the Patriarchs, the God of the Prophets, and the Father God. The God of the Prophets and the Father God we will address in the two subsequent chapters; we will address the God of the Patriarchs in the chapter that follows.

There seems to be no recorded connection between the ancient pre-history of the religion of the Hebrews and the beginning of the Old Testament. Orthodox Judaic teaching states that the world began with Chapter One of Genesis, and history originated with Adam in Chapter Two. Jewish history does not articulate a stage of development from animistic beginnings through polytheism to Jehovah.

Evidence indicates and many historians, both clerical and secular, support the idea that the stories of the Creation, the Flood, and the first man were derived from Babylonian legends. The Jews were exposed to these legends during the Exile, after Nebuchadnezzar invaded Jerusalem and carried them off to Babylonian captivity in 597 and again in 586 B.C. Certainly, there are many parallels. And it is generally accepted that very little if any of the present Old Testament was in written form before the Exile. It is likely that what had been written was either lost or highly modified in the subsequent writings. In the days when neither king nor commoner could make sense of the scribbles on parchment or clay, there were few scribes and little demand for written records. Oral recitation sufficed to pass on the traditions of the tribes.

The first five books of the Bible, the Pentateuch, are called the "Books of Moses," because ancient tradition holds that they were written by Moses. Yet nowhere in the Pentateuch is there any reference to an author, and sections of these books leave it very doubtful that they were written by the great prophet himself—especially the description of his death at the end of Deuteronomy. Certainly, this could have been added by a subsequent editor, but it is more likely that the books were ascribed to Moses to lend them greater authority.

In this book, we are particularly concerned with presenting God as is documented by authoritative sources—a God made in the image of the people that conceived Him and in the image of their contemporaries. Since a contemporary group is never homogeneous, there will always be variations amongst the Gods worshiped by particular groups, but it is always possible to derive a description of a particular God that will make it decisively clear to which God we are referring. From this, we hope to demonstrate that each God evolved and survived because He was better adapted to his particular environment.

What was the environment of the God of the Patriarchs? The ancient Jews were tribal and nomadic. Families or clans made their living from some tillage of the soil, but their main occupation was animal husbandry. City life, even in the small cities that existed in those times, was not a large part of their experience. The early parts of the Bible refer repeatedly to tent life. We find that the attempt to build a city around the tower of Babel was frustrated by God, who confused their language and scattered them abroad over the face of the earth. (Genesis 11:9) Herding required appreciable areas for maintaining the forage, and just a few people for supervision of the herd. Since there were no large Hebrew communities in these antediluvian times, only family ties and family loyalties were important. Alliances outside of the family amongst these nomadic or semi-nomadic peoples were never permanent, and were uncertain at best. Interfamily arguments could burgeon into blood feuds, in which the deep dependence on blood ties became ever more strongly reinforced. Genealogies were hence important to these people; they wanted to know who they could count on, and in the anarchic world in which they lived, the nearest thing to this surety was familial relationship. Few written records were kept, but the oral traditions and the genealogies were thoroughly drilled into each succeeding generation.

This was the situation up until the time when Joseph and his family migrated into Egypt. From there is a hiatus of four hundred years in the Biblical record. The Pentateuch takes up Jewish history again in the times of Moses and his brother Aaron. Due to Joseph's administrative genius, he and his family were heartily welcomed by Pharaoh and the people of Egypt. Evidently, some changes occurred with the succeeding generations, and the Israelites were eventually forced into slavery. Thus set apart from the Egyptians, they were able to maintain the integrity of their own religion to a large extent. From the time between Joseph's family's coming to Egypt and the Exodus, however, as seen by the angel killing the first-born of the Egyptians (Passover), living conditions must have been favorable—when Moses took the census after leaving Egypt, he counted 603,550 able Israelite men over twenty.

> So the whole number of the people of Israel ... from twenty years old and upward, every man able to go forth to war ... was six hundred and three thousand five hundred and fifty. (Numbers 1:45, 46)

This implies a total population of around two million, including women, old men, and children, plus the Levites, who were not counted at that time, as God appointed them members of the priesthood and exempted them from military duty (Numbers 1:48–50). This represents quite an increase in population for four hundred years.

It is significant to note that, at this point, the family unit was central to Hebrew society. The census was taken by families; each descendant of one of Joseph's brothers divided into a tribe of his own. The strength of family solidarity evidently had not been weakened by a four-century sojourn in Egypt. The whole people were known from this time as Israelites because of their descent from Jacob, whom the angel renamed Israel.

> Your name shall no more be called Jacob, but Israel, for you have striven with God and with men, and have prevailed. (Genesis 32:28)

Despite the Lord's demonstration of prodigious power by the miracles of the plagues He sent to Egypt, the crossing of the dry land in the midst of the Red Sea, the daily supply of manna and the fresh water from the rock, the Israelites were skeptical about their God. They were still homeless in the wilderness, and when Moses left them for some days to receive his instructions from God on Mount Sinai, they decided to better themselves by sacrificing to an idol—the famous golden calf. I have chosen this an excellent juncture in which to begin our study of the characteristics of the God of the Patriarchs. Upon learning that the Israelites had built and begun to worship the golden calf, God said:

> "I have seen this people, and behold, it is a stiff-necked people: now therefore let me alone, that my wrath may burn hot against them and I may consume them...." (Exodus 32:9, 10)

Repeatedly, we find Him quick to anger: a God of wrath.

We also discover the following two other characteristics in Him: a self-doubt and jealousy. He time and again states what He intends to do, then allows Himself to be talked out of it by a mere mortal. In this case, Moses pleads with Him:

> Why should the Egyptians say, "With evil intent did He bring them forth, to slay them in the mountains"....turn from thy fierce wrath....Remember Abraham, Isaac, and Israel, to whom thou didst swear, "I will multiply your descendants as the stars of heaven, and all this land that I have promised I will give to your descendants,"...and the Lord repented of the evil which He thought to do. (Exodus 32:12–14)

Despite the omniscience, power, and wisdom attributed to God, He is still, like a human being, sufficiently uncertain of Himself that He could be convinced by Moses that His stated intents were evil, and repent of them.

One might also think that an omnipotent, almighty God would simply laugh at people who set up empty idols, or at least pity them in their profound ignorance, yet the God of the Patriarchs feels, quite prominently, the essentially human emotion of jealousy. So much is it a part of God that it provided as the most significant the reason behind the first two of the Ten Commandments:

> You shall have no other gods before me, you shall not make yourself a graven image....you shall not bow down to them or serve them: for I the Lord your God am a jealous God, visiting iniquity of the fathers upon the children to the third and fourth generation....(Exodus 20:3–5)

Of course, one thing we should remember is that, in the days of the Patriarchs and their close descendants, Jehovah was not actually without competition from other deities. The henotheism characteristic of much of the ancient world, although it called for a single or at least central god, considered that the province of that god was limited to a particular tribe, nation, or people. In essence, henotheism is localized monotheism. Other people had their own gods, which were dominant in their own local territories. The early Israelites accepted that, among others, the Egyptian Ra, the Babylonian Marduk, the Assyrian Asshiur, Chemosh of the Moabites, and the Ammonites, were real gods, valid for their people and in their location. Their own God was Jehovah, who had presented Himself to Abraham to inform him that He had chosen Abraham and his descendants to be His people.

Seen in this light, His jealousy is more understandable; the God of the Patriarchs is concerned that some of his Chosen People could turn to other gods. This presumption was at least partially accepted even as late as the days of Jonah, who fled when called by the Lord to preach against the wicked at Nineveh:

> But Jonah rose to flee to Tarshish from the presence of the Lord. (Jonah 1:3)

Jonah hoped to avoid a dangerous task by fleeing from the Lord's jurisdiction, but God caught him at sea before Jonah could arrive at his destination which would presumably be under the jurisdiction of some other god. That such ideas persisted for so many centuries despite the fact that, even at the time of Moses, it had been stated that there were no other gods, demonstrates how basic and fundamental a part henotheism played in the religion of the Hebrews.

Because this is one of the principal circumstances that differentiates the environment of the God of the Patriarchs from that of the other Gods we will discuss in this book, and because this factor often goes unacknowledged, we will delve further into the subject. The first really definite statement of monotheism is:

> To you, it was shown that you might know that the Lord is God; there is no other besides him....the Lord is in heaven above and on the earth beneath; there is no other. (Deuteronomy 4:35, 39)

And yet, if God is unique, why does He settle on a single small group, the Israelites, as:

> ....a people for his own possession, out of all the peoples that are on the face of the earth.... (Deuteronomy 7:6)

While we find that that later on, after the death of Moses, Joshua refers to "the Lord of all the earth" (Joshua 3:13), we also find that many other references occur both before and after this which consider Jehovah as a tribal, henotheistic God. Jethro—high priest of Midian and Moses' father-in-law—impressed by what Jehovah has done for the Israelites, expressed this in a way that acknowledges other gods:

> Now I know that the Lord is greater than all gods, because He delivered the people from under the hand of the Egyptians. (Exodus 18:11)

They are also acknowledged in the following passage:

> God went to redeem [Israel]... driving out before his people a nation and its gods. (2 Samuel 7:25)

God himself tells Moses:

> ...on all the gods of Egypt, I will execute judgments. (Exodus 12:12)

The above passages illustrate the common contemporary henotheistic belief in localized gods. Even Solomon, to whom God had given wisdom and understanding, evidently recognized the existence of other gods. Instead of building the temple to the only God, he built one to the "greater" God:

> The house I am to build will be great, for our God is greater
> than all gods. (2 Chronicles 2:5)

Another variety of evidence is found in the story of Naaman, one of the captains of the king of Syria, who was a leper. An Israelite maidservant, taken as captive, told him of the miraculous powers of the prophet Elisha. Naaman journeyed to Israel, where Elisha proposed a treatment, including washing seven times in the Jordan river. The treatment worked, and Naaman thereby became a zealous convert, asking Elisha:

> ...let there be given to your servant two mules' burden of earth;
> for henceforth your servant will not sacrifice to any god but the
> Lord. (2 Kings: 5:17)

Sacrifice to Jehovah on Syrian soil would have no value, as Jehovah would have no power there, but if Naaman could stand on a bit of Israelite soil to perform the sacrifice, a proper relationship could be attained.

The crowning Biblical testimony to henotheism is:

> When the king of Moab saw that the battle was going against
> him...he took his eldest son...and offered him for a burnt offering upon the wall. And there came a great wrath upon Israel;
> and they withdrew from him and returned to their own land.
> (2 Kings 3:26, 27)

Not only does the author of 2 Kings admit to the power of another god, many years after Deuteronomy had proclaimed monotheism, he even demonstrates that the power was great enough to overcome the people of Jehovah.

The existence of the henotheistic—a single, tribal god—is a logical intermediate step along the road from animism to pure monotheism. It is certainly reasonable to consider that the God who created the universe must either be alone, or so powerful that none of the other supernatural beings are in His class. The Hebrew Scriptures begin with God the Creator, and Adam, the first man, knew God, as did his progeny and his descendents. If one accepts the Bible as literally true, the Hebrews did not go through the stages of animism and polytheism as did the rest of the world: There were no primitive Hebrews.

We will try to follow the early scriptures of the Hebrew Bible/Old Testament as closely as possible in determining the characteristics of the God of the Patriarchs, but at some points, it is necessary for us to make a slight detour. The internal evidence in these scriptures of the existence of henotheism leads us to believe that the Hebrews also progressed through their own quite normal primitive stages of religious belief, but that at the time of reduction to writing, it was either omitted or missing from their history. Probably because they were by then convinced that the old ideas were no longer valid.

We must remember that these tribal gods existed in the days before written records were common, and when most of history was oral tradition. We have mentioned that most, if not all, of the Old Testament as it stands today was probably put into written form during and after the Babylonian Exile. We find nothing that can tell us for certain whether the Creation of Genesis is an adaptation of Babylonian tradition, or if the Hebrews had already developed their own creation theory. In any event, the story of the monotheistic Creator God evidently overlaid more ancient traditions without careful expurgation of all conflicting concepts. As a result, evidence of the old tribal god shows through.

In the days when the spirits of animism evolved into gods, humans lived an isolated life. Their families or clans, or the small tribes, ranged through a limited area, keeping apart from other groups. Since they had no precise concept of the physical boundaries in their world, they could not conceive of its extent. Having no understanding of the extent of the universe, there was no basis for consideration of a universal God.

Though they knew other tribes existed, they knew little or nothing about the integrity of the tribe. Divine jealousy must have had its function in maintaining the coherence of a group, and integration with others was not approved:

> You shall make no covenant with them or their gods. They shall not dwell in your land, lest they make you sin against me. (Exodus 23:32, 33)

> If . . . among you . . . a man or woman . . . has served other gods and worshiped them, or the sun or the moon or any of the host of heaven . . . you shall stone that man or woman to death.... (Deuteronomy 17:2–5)

Intermarriage is repeatedly condemned, because of the danger of the spouse's influence in diminishing the attachment to Jehovah.

> For if...you marry their women and they yours....they shall be a snare and a trap for you...till you perish from off this good land.... (Joshua 23:12, 13)

In his desire to maintain His power over humans, the God of the Patriarchs is also jealous of humankind, as we saw in the garden of Eden:

> The Lord God said, "Behold, the man is become like one of us, knowing good and evil."....He drove out the man...and placed the cherubim and a flaming sword...to guard the way to the tree of life. (Genesis 3:22, 24)

And during the attempted construction of the tower of Babel:

> ...this is only the beginning of what they will do....let us go down and there confuse their language. (Genesis 11:6, 7)

Not only must tribal integrity be maintained, the maintenance of authority is important to proper tribal functioning.

Considering then the rather limited range of the tribal gods in those days, and the fact that each of the other nations already had a god of its own, the fact that Israel was chosen by Jehovah could have a completely different significance than what is generally considered. Possibly at the time Jehovah approached Abraham He was an unemployed deity; having found all positions filled in other nations, He selected Abraham to found a nation of which He could be the undisputed Lord.

So far, we have considered as characteristic of the God of the Patriarchs His liability to monumental wrath when crossed, His jealousy, some limitations on His omniscience, His wavering in His intentions when convinced by mortal pleas, and His position as a strictly tribal God, which is what one might expect of a God made in the image of a people fiercely restricted in their tribal loyalties.

We will proceed to consider some of the other qualities which distinguish the God of the Patriarchs, among which are omnipotence, justice, loyalty, an interest in legalities, masculinity, an avenging nature, bloodthirstiness, pride, an occasional tendency to intrigue, and superstition. He is also a God who is by nature severe, but can also be forbearing and forgiving, personal yet eternal.

Many volumes have been written on miracles, and much dispute has arisen over whether the miracles actually happened or whether they are part of legend.

Basically, whether an individual can accept miracles as a fact or designates them as legend depends on his concept of God. All of the Biblical Gods—the God of the Patriarchs, the God of the Prophets, and the Father God—performed miracles, either directly or through representatives. It seems reasonable to suppose that a Supreme Being who had the consummate power to create a universe out of chaos, to produce the wonderful complexity that we see in the laws of nature and in the organic structure of animals and men, should have the power to temporarily suspend those laws. Or, as some have suggested, to use those laws in ways beyond the limited knowledge and capabilities of humankind. If one can believe in a Creator God—a God who is personal in nature and instructs us in knowledge of Him and His will through revelations—there should be no difficulty in allowing Him a few miracles from time to time to advance His cause, either through changing the course of events, or by giving "signs" which can help convince the skeptical. Since all of Judeo-Christianity is based on revealed religion, the revelation demonstrates the personal interest of God and furnishes the incentive for miracles which should be within the power of a Creator.

Miracles can range from the trivial, such as Christ's changing water into wine for the wedding guests (John 2:1–11) and the finding of a lost ax-head:

> But as one was felling a log, his ax-head fell into the water; and he cried out, "Alas, my master! It was borrowed." Then Elisha said, "Where did it fall?"....he cut off a stick, and threw it in there, and made the iron float. (2 Kings 6:5, 6)

to miracles that change the course of history, such as the plagues in Egypt described in Exodus, the manna that kept the Israelites alive in the wilderness, and the halting of the sun in its course for the benefit of Joshua and his armies:

> Behold, I will rain bread from heaven for you; and the people shall go out and gather a day's portion every day....on the sixth day, it will be twice as much.... (Exodus 16:4, 5)

The stalling of the sun was something else again as it required the laws of inertia to be temporarily suspended; a full-scale miracle by any measurement:

> "Sun, stand thou still at Gibeon, and thou Moon in the valley of Aijalon." And the sun stood still and the moon stayed, until the nation took vengeance on their enemies. (Joshua 10:12, 13)

Other miracles may have been wrought as signs to convince the skeptical. There was the contest between Elijah and the four hundred and fifty prophets of Baal, who called without avail upon Baal to light an altar fire. The Lord lit Elijah's fire for him even after it had been thoroughly soaked with water:

> Then the fire of the Lord fell and consumed the burnt offering and the wood, and the stones.. and licked up the water.... (1 Kings 18:38)

Such miracles could even be disastrous to innocent bystanders. When king Ahab sent a captain and fifty men to bring Elijah into his presence:

> ...fire came down from heaven and consumed him and his fifty. (2 Kings 1:10)

Or when the prophet Elisha was annoyed by small children jeering at his bald head, in his annoyance:

> ...he cursed them in the name of the Lord. And two she-bears came out of the wood and tore forty-two of the boys. (2 Kings 2:24)

This must certainly have been more effective than a simple admonition.

All in all, whether any person chooses to accept these miracles or not, we must accept them in considering the God of the Patriarchs, for they are part and parcel of Him; of the God that man made in those days in his image. For, among other things, people in those days, having no knowledge of modern science, believed in magic and the ability of the power of spirits, of sorcerers, or court magicians and others.

Whatever His other characteristics, there can be no doubt of the loyalty of the God of the patriarchs. From the time of the making of the covenant with Abraham (born Abram) on, with the exception of three centuries in Egypt, God kept a close eye on His chosen people.

> I am God Almighty, walk before me and be blameless....you shall be the father of a multitude of nations....I will give to you and your descendants after you...all the land of Canaan....this is my covenant, which you shall keep....Every male among you shall be circumcised. (Genesis 17:1–10)

A strict and severe God, He punished His people when they transgressed, but He was always ready to come to their aid when they needed help. God had even planned to help His people far in advance, telling Abraham:

> ...your descendants...will be slaves there [in Egypt]....will be oppressed for four hundred years, but I will bring judgment on the nation they serve, and afterward they shall come out with great possessions. (Genesis 15:13, 14)

The individual cases of the munificence of God towards those who found favor in His sight are too numerous to list. The prospering of Abraham, the saving of Lot and his family from the destruction of Sodom, the position obtained by Joseph in Egypt with God's help, the military might of Joshua, the power given Samson, the authority given David, and the wisdom and prosperity of Solomon are but a small part of it.

The Israelites as a nation were given a good start, as Joseph's family was well received in Egypt:

> The Lord was with Joseph, and he became a successful man....the Lord caused all he did to prosper. (Genesis 39:2, 3)

When their lot deteriorated into slavery, God sent the plagues to persuade Pharaoh to let them go, and Himself served as a guide and help through the years in the wilderness:

> And the Lord went before them....the pillar of cloud by day and the pillar of fire by night did not depart from the people. (Exodus 13:21)

Even after He had punished and scattered the Israelites, He remained loyal, and we have the source for Zionism:

> ...return to the Lord your God...and obey his voice....then the Lord your God will restore your fortunes...and gather you again from all the people where the Lord your God has scattered you. (Deuteronomy 30:2, 3)

This loyalty was characteristic of both God and His tribes. Jehovah's loyalty also included a certain amount of forbearance. The whole book of Judges is one continual history of backsliding on the part of the Israelites, followed by God's punishment:

> And the people of Israel again did what was evil in the sight of the Lord...and the Lord sold them into the hand of Jabin, king of Canaan.... (Judges 4:1, 2)

Yet, whenever misery overwhelmed the Israelites, they had only to straighten out their lives, return to their beliefs in Jehovah and plead for help, and God was ready to welcome them into His protection again. Thus, when they cried to the Lord for help, the prophetess Deborah, with the help of Barak, raised an army and freed the Israelites:

> So perish all thine enemies, O Lord!....and the land had rest for forty years. (Judges 5:31)

In spite of the evil done by Manasseh, even including human sacrifice, and in spite of dire threats against him by God, God's forebearance was such that Manasseh continued to reign for a total of fifty-five years.

The relations of people who live in a harsh land with their neighbors often turn to violence in attempts to obtain an adequate portion of what the land has to offer. A sample of this behavior is provided in 1 Samuel. Despite the fact that Ahimelech insisted that David was really faithful to Saul, Saul caused a mighty massacre:

> Then [Saul] said to Doeg, "You turn and fall upon the priests."...and he killed on that day eighty-five...and Nob the city of the priests, he put to the sword; both men and women, children and sucklings, oxen, asses and sheep he put to the sword. (1 Samuel 22:18, 19)

Likewise, we find that the God of the Patriarchs is also sometimes violent, even to the point of seeming bloodthirsty. There is really no other adequate adjective to describe some of the acts and commands of the God of the Patriarchs. Also, it must be remembered that what will shock the modern man was something perfectly normal in those times. Whereas, we react today with horror at the fate of the victims of the Holocaust, large-scale massacres were commonplace in the Old Testament, and accepted as one of the facts of life.

> In the cities of these peoples that . . . God gives you . . . you shall save alive nothing that breathes, but you shall utterly destroy them, the Hittities and the Amorites, the Canaanites and Perizzites, the Hivites and the Jebusites.... (Deuteronomy 20:16, 17)

The excuse given is that survivors might teach the Israelites the "abominable practices which they have done in the service of their gods." To avoid this obscenity and rather than converting the other peoples, the God of the Patriarchs comes up with His own solution.

Let us recall the status in Egypt, after God had visited the Egyptians with a series of plagues, from the annoying one of flies to the disastrous death of all the cattle. Eleven there were in all, and each time it was to make a greater impression upon Pharoah, who had promised Moses each time that he would let the people go if the plague were lifted. But the Lord hardened his heart and caused him to change his mind. Now one might be inclined to ask why, if the Lord was capable of hardening Pharoah's heart, would it not be easier and kinder to soften his heart, and let him keep his promise. But we cannot expect that the God of the Patriarchs will always act as we moderns think we would have done in His place. To make one last final impression on Pharoah of His terrible powers:

> At midnight the Lord smote all the first-born in the land of Egypt, from the first-born of Pharaoh...to the first-born of the captive who was in the dungeon, and all the first-born of the cattle. (Exodus 12:29)

The Nile must have run red with the blood shed from that massacre, executed solely to impress Pharoah so that "the Egyptians shall know that I am the Lord." (Exodus 7:5)

Time and again we find in the Old Testament that the common individual has no significance for God. God concerns Himself with the kings, the priests, and the nations. Innocent by-standers—men, women, babes-in-arms—must simply suffer God's demonstration. How many innocent children must have died in the destruction of Sodom and Gomorrah, in the Flood, in the battles to seize the land of Canaan! The first-born victims of Egypt who suffered because of God's determination to let the Egyptians know He was the Lord were only a small fraction of the legions sacrificed to the pride and jealousy of the God of the Patriarchs. When David arranged for Uriah to be killed in battle so that he might possess himself of Bathsheba, God was mightily displeased, but He needed David as king. The sin was paid for in blood through the death of an innocent child:

> Nathan said, "...the child that is born to you shall die"....and the Lord struck the child....on the seventh day the child died. (2 Samuel 12:14–18)

How else but bloodthirsty can we consider a God who tells Saul:

> Now go and smite Amalek, and utterly destroy all that they have; do not spare them, but kill both man and woman, infant and suckling, ox and sheep, camel and ass (1 Samuel 15:3)

When Saul spared king Agag, and saved some of the cattle for a sacrifice to the Lord, God, angered, had Samuel chastise Saul and tell him:

> The Lord has torn the kingdom of Israel from you this day....the Glory of Israel will not lie or repent; for He is not a man, that He should repent. (1 Samuel 15:28, 29)

This brings us around to another aspect of the God of the Patriarchs' character. His commands must be obeyed to the letter, no matter how unreasonable they may seem to us.

Related are the qualities of vengefulness and vindictiveness. While some of the slaughter directed by God was in revenge for the "abominations" of other tribes, God repeatedly let it be known that He would take revenge for disobedience, meting out much stronger punishments in retaliation than modern man would consider reasonable. Right in the beginning, God tells Cain:

> ...If anyone slays Cain, vengeance shall be taken on him sevenfold. (Genesis 4:15)

In the Song of Moses, God says:

> I will take vengeance on my adversaries....I will make my arrows drunk with blood, and my sword shall devour flesh... (Deuteronomy 32:41,42)

It was not enough just to eliminate the enemy; God often gloried in His revenge.

When Onan's father Judah instructed him to marry his dead brother's wife and produce offspring for his brother as was the custom, Onan spilled his semen on the ground to avoid producing offspring. God responded vindictively:

> And what he did was displeasing in the sight of the Lord, and He slew him also. (Genesis 38:10)

Instead of being grateful for the manna they were given in the wilderness, the Israelites wanted more, asking Moses for meat. Their greed angered God, and He responded:

> ...the Lord will give you meat, and you shall eat...until it comes out at your nostrils and becomes loathsome to you.... (Numbers 11:18–20)

> And there went forth a wind from the Lord, and it brought quails from the sea...about two cubits deep on the face of the earth. And the people...gathered the quails....While the meat was yet between their teeth...the anger of the Lord was kindled...and the Lord smote the people with a very great plague. (Numbers 11:31–33)

The vindictiveness of God was not always demonstrated through harsh measures. Sometimes it was shown by simply ignoring the people and letting them stew in their own juices. The Israelites, after years of judges, wanted a king, as other nations had. This irritated God, who pointed out kings' habits of taking the best of everything, putting the sons in his armies and the daughters in his kitchens, and taxing the produce and the herds mightily. When the people insisted, God said:

> ...they have rejected me from being king over them. (1 Samuel 8:7)

> And in that day you will cry out because of your king...but the Lord will not answer you. (1 Samuel 8:18)

And God was right. After the death of Solomon, who behaved just as God had predicted, amassing wealth and subjugating the people, they plead with his son Rehoboam to "lighten the hard service of your father and his heavy yoke upon us," but to no avail (1 Kings:12:1–15).

The harsh, intolerant God of the Patriarchs would be expected to punish without hesitation. As a matter of fact, the God of the Patriarchs had neither heaven nor hell, meting out His retribution on this earth. Sheol, mentioned from time to time in the Old Testament, is mistakenly equated with hell by some fundamentalists, but was not actually conceived of as a place of punishment. Like Niflheim of the Nordic pagan religion, there was neither torture nor joy. It was an extremely nebulous conception, not held by everyone; a place where the deceased souls wandered in semi-oblivion.

Robert Ingersoll made an interesting observation:

> In the Old Testament, there is no promise of another world. I have sometimes thought that while the Jews were slaves in

Egypt, the doctrine of immortality became hateful.. they carried so many burdens to commemorate the dead; they saw a nation waste its wealth to adorn its graves, and leave the living naked to embalm the dead, that they concluded the doctrine [of the afterlife] was a curse and never should be taught. (Ingersoll, *Interviews*, p. 156)

Rewards and punishments are to be of this earth, some immediate, some a bit delayed, but all temporal. Adam was punished for disobedience, Cain for fratricide, Ham for disrespect, the flood and the destruction of Sodom and Gomorrah for general wickedness. Hannah's song (1 Samuel 2:1–10) tells how God makes the poor and the rich, cuts off the wicked, and takes care of the feeble, the poor, the hungry, and the barren. As long as the Israelites walk in His commandments, they prosper and their enemies are defeated. God Himself tells the Israelites:

> If you observe my commandments, I will give you your rains....the land shall yield its increase....I will give you peace....will remove evil beasts....the sword shall not go through your land....but...if you spurn my statutes...I will appoint over you sudden terror, consumption, and fever that waste the eyes....trees...shall not yield their fruit....I will bring more plagues....loose wild beasts....cast your dead bodies....lay your cities to waste.... (Leviticus 26:3–31)

Nothing here is mentioned of either heaven or hell. All punishment and reward is immanent: understandable by the simple mind. God Himself, immanent and personal, acts swiftly and irrevocably:

> If a man lies with his uncle's wife...they shall die childless. (Leviticus 20:20)

The God of the Prophets was a firm believer in capital punishment, even for what we today consider less heinous offenses:

> If a man is found lying with the wife of another man, both of them shall die.... (Deuteronomy 22:22)

> If...the tokens of virginity were not found in [the bride]...the men of her city shall stone her to death. (Deuteronomy 22:21)

> And if anyone [other than the Levites] comes near [the tabernacle], he shall be put to death. (Numbers 1:51)

With God speaking thus, we can well believe that Moses could say:

> Your eye shall not pity; it shall be life for life, eye for eye, tooth for tooth.... (Deuteronomy 19:21)

God did have other means of punishment, some on a grand scale. Repeatedly, the backsliding Israelites were defeated by their enemies:

> ...the king of Assyria captured Samaria, and he carried the Israelites away...because the people of Israel had sinned against the Lord.... (2 Kings 17:6, 7)

Another example of God's punishment is when the Israelites were condemned to forty years in the wilderness because of their faithlessness after the Exodus (Numbers 14:26–35). On a smaller scale, when Moses' sister Miriam spoke against him for having married a Cushite woman, despite the fact that she was chiding him for something that God had repeatedly forbidden:

> And the anger of the Lord was kindled against [her]... and...behold, Miriam was leprous, white as snow.... (Numbers 12:9, 10)

We can do no better than refer to Chapter 28 of Deuteronomy for a picture of the consequences of obedience and disobedience. The language is inspired, and apocalyptic:

> And as the Lord took delight in doing you good and multiplying you, so the Lord will take delight in bringing ruin upon you and destroying you.... (Deuteronomy 28:63)

The subordinate position of women in ancient Hebrew society began in the garden of Eden:

> ...your desire shall be for your husband, and he shall rule over you. (Genesis 3:16)

It is not surprising that the patriarchal God of this patriarchal society values men above women:

> ...your valuation of a male from twenty years old...shall be fifty shekels....if the person is a female, your valuation shall be thirty shekels. (Leviticus 27:3, 4)

> When a man vows...he shall not break his word....when a woman vows...if her father expresses disapproval...no vow of hers...shall stand.... (Numbers 30:2–5)

Responsibility was the province of men; women remained in the background. The one really outstanding exception was the judge and prophetess Deborah in the book of Judges. Esther and Judith also played prominent roles in Biblical history, but as wives and seductresses. Men were the priests and obtained the inheritances, although a woman could inherit in the absence of brothers:

> If a man dies, and has no son, then you shall cause his inheritance to pass to his daughter. (Numbers 27:8)

Still, it was required of the heiresses that they marry within their own Israelite tribe:

> But if they are married to the sons of the other tribes of the people of Israel, then their inheritance will be taken...and added to the inheritance of the tribe to which they belong.... (Numbers 36:3)

A man could divorce his wife at will, but the wife had no such privilege. On the other hand, it was recognized that the subordinated position of women necessitated protecting them:

> If a man seduces a virgin...he shall give the marriage present for her, and make her his wife. (Exodus 22:16)

> If [a man]...dies and has no son...her husband's brother shall go in to her, and take her as his wife. (Deuteronomy 25:5)

The God of the Patriarchs was legalistic, setting forth carefully and in great detail instructions and regulations for the daily life of His people. Before Moses, we have no record of the content of His regulations, although they already existed in Abraham's time:

> Abraham obeyed my voice and kept my charge, my commandments, my statutes, and my laws. (Genesis 26:5)

Till a much later date, most of God's laws must have been a part of the oral tradition, despite the statement that they were written on tablets of stone on Mount Sinai. When Hilkiah, the high priest, found the lost book of law (Deuteronomy?) centuries later in the temple, there was much concern and anxiety because they found laws therein that had evidently not been obeyed; which led to the great reform under king Josiah (2 Kings 22 and 23).

The laws of Israel were for many centuries the laws that Moses brought down from Sinai. With the Ten Commandments as a base, they expanded to cover all circumstances imaginable at that time, from the rules whose violations were punishable by death to the dietary laws and the manifold architectural particulars for the construction of the tabernacle. We will not attempt to go into these laws in detail, but enough will be mentioned to illustrate the extent of their effect upon Israelite life. Besides the injunctions against making and worshipping idols, and the death sentence for murder, adultery, sodomy, and other less serious offenses, there were many laws which required the criminal to make good the damage suffered by the victim, and laws which required sacrifices for expiation:

> ...he shall restore what he took by robbery, or what he got by oppression, or the deposit that was committed to him...or anything about which he had sworn falsely; he shall restore it in full, and shall add a fifth of it, and give it to him to whom it belongs.... (Leviticus 6:4, 5)

Many laws are also given without specifying how their infringement should be punished:

> ...you shall not strip your vineyard bare....you shall leave them for the poor and for the sojourner....you shall not steal, nor deal falsely....you shall not swear by my name falsely....the wages of a hired servant shall not remain with you all night....you shall do no injustice in judgment....you shall not go...as a slanderer....you shall love your neighbor as yourself....you shall not let your cattle breed with a different kind...nor...a garment of cloth made of two kinds of stuff. If a man lies carnally with a woman who is a slave...they shall not be put to death because she was not free; but he shall bring a guilt offering....you shall not round off the hair on your temples or mar the edges of your beard. You shall not...tattoo any marks upon you....do not profane your daughter by making her a harlot....do not turn to mediums and wizards....you shall do [a stranger] no wrong....you shall have just balances, just weights.... (Leviticus 19:10–36)

Among other references, Leviticus 1,7, and 17 and Numbers 28 and 29 provide detailed instructions regarding how to perform sacrifices. Offerings may be made to atone for guilt or sin; there are peace, thanks-giving, votive, and free will offerings, and they may be of meat, of cereal, and of unleavened bread.

As to land, Leviticus 25:23 states that "land shall not be sold in perpetuity," and the chapter continues with the rules of redemption. Last, but for the orthodox not least, are the dietary laws and those referring to ritual cleanliness. Although God told Noah, "Every moving thing that lives shall be food for you...." (Genesis 9:3), He changed His mind when dictating to Moses, setting up strict limits.

> Whatever...is cloven-footed and chews the cud...you may eat....the camel...the rock badger...the hare, because it chews the cud but does not part the hoof, is unclean....the swine because it...is cloven-footed but does not chew the cud, is unclean....Everything in the waters that has fins and scales...you may eat. But anything...that has not fins and scales...is an abomination to you.... (Leviticus 11:3–12)

Not only is touching unclean animals defiling, also anything on which any of them falls, whether an article of wood, a garment, a sack, or a vessel, becomes unclean (Leviticus 11:32). Defilement requires that the defiled person wash his clothes, and he remains unclean till evening. Limitations are even imposed on the eating of clean animals:

> The Lord said to Moses, "...You shall eat no fat of ox, or sheep or goat....you shall eat no blood whatever, whether of fowl or animal...." (Leviticus 7:22, 26)

> You shall not boil a kid in its mother's milk. (Deuteronomy 14:21)

Even today, the orthodox do not eat meat and dairy products at the same table.

Cleanliness applies not only to certain animals, but also to the touching of the dead. And women are also considered unclean at certain times:

> If a woman bears a male child then she shall be unclean seven days....if...a female child, then she shall be unclean two weeks.... (Leviticus 12:2, 5)

> When a woman has a discharge of blood which is her regular discharge...she shall be in her impurity for seven days.... (Leviticus 15:19)

At the end of these times of uncleanliness, cleansing is obtained through ritual sacrifice.

Strict observance of the laws contributes to unification of a people: a sense of having something in common that other nations do not have. Like military drill, the strict laws function as disciplinary training. Furthermore, much inherent good can be recognized in laws which eliminate child sacrifice, demand respect for parents, charity toward widows, orphans, and the poor. Laws against incest eliminate one possible source of unhealthy offspring; laws regarding the isolation of lepers, and avoidance of or washing after touching the dead help to avoid the spread of disease. The dietary laws are partly ritual, for solidarity, and partly may do much to promote health, enjoining them to avoid foods that spoil easily, and are thus beneficial healthwise. Hence, what had been considered by the experience of the tribal elders to be advisable, was made part of the image of God.

In passing, we may also note that the God of the Patriarchs, like human kings, made laws for others, not for Himself. He did not hesitate to abrogate His Ten Commandments, or to prompt people to do so when it suited His convenience. God slew without hesitation those who displeased Him and allowed His people not only to covet the property of the Canaanites in the land of milk and honey, but told to steal it, murdering in the process.

The God of the Patriarchs is sufficiently akin to human beings that He is not above being deceitful. When Samuel was instructed by God to find a successor to Saul among Jesse's sons, God suggests a bit of deceit:

> And Samuel said, "...If Saul hears it, he will kill me." And the Lord said, "Take a heifer with you and say, 'I have come to sacrifice to the Lord.'" (1 Samuel 16:2)

God tacitly approved of Abraham's deceit in presenting his wife Sarai as his sister to Pharaoh, for He allowed Pharaoh to make Abraham rich with gifts. After the unfortunate king had innocently taken Sarai into his house, God afflicted Pharaoh with vile plagues, and Sarai and Abraham were sent on their way much richer than when they had arrived (Genesis 12:10–20).

When Jacob disguised himself as his elder brother Esau, and came to his blind father Isaac for the elder brother's blessing, Isaac was deceived and delivered the blessing. Evidently, the blessing itself was irretrievable, and God must have accepted it, even though He must have known of the deceit. Here, Esau was not only deprived of his rightful blessing, but Isaac told him:

> ...I have made him your lord, and all his brothers I have given to him for servants, and with grain and wine.... (Genesis 27:37)

Thus, with the connivance of God, both Abraham and Jacob profited by their deceit. It is certainly advantageous to have God on your side. Another element God shared with humankind of the times was superstition. Not only do we find magic in Pharaoh's court, where the court magicians duplicated the miraculous sign given by God of having Aaron's rod turn into a serpent, and duplicated also the turning of water into blood and the miraculous production of frogs (Exodus 7 and 8), we find that God Himself takes augury, magic, and sorcery sufficiently seriously to forbid it:

> Do not turn to mediums or wizards...to be defiled by them....
> (Leviticus 19:31)

> A man or a woman who is a medium or a wizard shall be put to death; they shall be stoned with stones.... (Leviticus 20:27)

Whether God is concerned by competitive supernatural powers, or if He considers them demonic, and so wishes them destroyed to protect humankind is not quite clear, but these laws caused the cruel burning, torture, and drowning of countless unfortunate "witches" over the ages. If God acknowledges their existence, who are humans to deny it?

One characteristic of the God of the Patriarchs was that, not only did He speak to His prophets, but He also manifested Himself to them in some physical form, beginning with Adam:

> And they heard the sound of the Lord God walking in the garden in the cool of the day.... (Genesis 3:8)

> ...God called to him out of the [burning] bush, "Moses, Moses!"....and Moses hid his face, for he was afraid to look at God. (Exodus 3:4, 6)

Interestingly enough, there are times when God manifests Himself as an angel, recounted as if the angel were equivalent to God, not a separate individual, but a manifestation of God Himself. Thus, the story of the burning bush begins:

> And the angel of the Lord appeared to him in a flame of fire out of the midst of a bush.... (Exodus 3:2)

Immediately afterwards, God called from the bush. Elsewhere in the scriptures, a man, evidently an angel, wrestled with Jacob, and later blessed him, causing Jacob to say:

> ...I have seen God face to face, and yet my life is preserved. (Genesis 32:30)

Note that it is written "the angel of the Lord," not simply "an angel." Evidently a theophany; surely it must be interpreted as a manifestation of God in an apparently human form. These visitations demonstrate a highly personal relationship between God and certain of His people.

Yet in spite of this, we find that God does not always talk directly to the person He wishes to contact, but often imparts His messages through His prophets. For example, God's communications with Saul were generally through Samuel, among many others. As a rule, God did not talk to the Israelite kings after David, other than through prophets.

Although the people are admonished against pride, God Himself is not above demonstrating His own pride. The great detail lavished on the tabernacle, the strict rules for observation of the Passover and other feasts, the complex formulas for sacrifices, and service of the priests to God may simply be requirements to impress the people and help maintain their cohesion, but one also suspects that there is also a measure of pride, vanity, and love of glory.

> And I will harden Pharaoh's heart, and he will pursue them, and I will get glory over Pharaoh and all his host.... (Exodus 14:4)

Is it possible that the insistence on holiness is related to pride?

> ...the sons of Kohath shall come to carry these, but they must not touch the holy things, lest they die. (Numbers 4:15)

One difficulty in dealing with the God of the Patriarchs was that, like humans, He was not always consistent. When Balaam was hired by king Balak of Moab to go curse the people of Israel, God became concerned:

> God came to Balaam at night and said, "If the men have come to call you, rise, go with them; but only what I bid you shall you do." (Numbers 22:20)

and then follows the famous story of Balaam's talking ass. But why did God become angry when He Himself had told Balaam to go, just a few hours before? Since one would assume that the curse would have to be carried out by God, would it not be simpler to let him go and just ignore his cursing? Yet we must remember that Balaam was probably originally supposed to do his cursing in the name of the god of the Moabites, and it was this that made Jehovah nervous.

Again, with David, when God demanded a census:

> ...he incited David against them, saying, "Go, number Israel and Judah." (2 Samuel 24:1)

Which David obediently did, then regretted having done it:

> And David said to the Lord, "I have sinned greatly in what I have done." (2 Samuel 24:10)

Evidently God agreed, for as a result:

> So the Lord sent a pestilence....there died seventy thousand men. (2 Samuel 24:15)

Not only does it seem inconsistent that God agreed with David that he had sinned in carrying out His original command, but it makes still less sense that seventy thousand innocent men should die because of David's sin. The Lord truly moves in mysterious ways!

As God is supposed to be good, it seems inconsistent for evil spirits to be in his employ, but:

> Now the Spirit of the Lord departed from Saul, and an evil spirit from the Lord tormented him. (1 Samuel 16:14)

And does it not seem highly inconsistent that although God has more than once forbidden human sacrifice:

> And Jephthah made a vow to the Lord...."If thou wilt give the Ammonites unto my hand, then whoever comes forth from the doors of my house to meet me shall be the Lord's, and I will offer him up for a burnt offering."....the Lord gave them unto his hand. (Judges 11:30–32)

This story did not have a happy ending, for the first one to run to greet Jephthah was his virgin daughter, his only child, who was accordingly sacrificed.

The God of the Patriarchs is also characteristically omnipotent and omniscient. We will later find that omnipotence is a common attribute of all the Biblical Gods. From time to time, the God of the Patriarchs announces that He will do something, then changes His mind or postpones it, but whenever He actually starts something, it gets done. He successfully managed the whole performance in Egypt, from the signs to the plagues, from the hardening of Pharaoh's heart to the separation of the waters of the Red Sea, and letting them fall back to inundate the host of Pharaoh's army. His control was accurate and efficient; in visiting the plagues on Egypt; only the Egyptians suffered, and all the Israelites were spared: there were no flies in Goshen, nor any hail, Israeli cattle were not affected by the plague that destroyed the Egyptian cattle, there was no darkness for the Israelites, and none of their first-born died (Exodus 7–9).

God or His angels enabled the Israelites to defeat, time and again, forces far superior to themselves, and when the Israelites were in disfavor, He transferred His power to the enemy, and the Israelites did not have a chance of success. He engineered the terrible destruction of Sodom and Gomorrah. He brought on the universal deluge. Yet none of this even approaches the great and wonderful masterwork of the Creation.

The greatness of His omnipotence is shown in that His power is applied not only on a grand scale, but also penetrates into the small scale processes of the world. Angels were sent to announce to Abraham that Sarah, old as she was, would bear a son. Sarah doubted, laughing at the very idea, but God said:

> Is anything too hard for the Lord?....Sarah shall have a son. (Genesis 18:14)

And so Isaac was born.

Whatever God set His mind to, He accomplished, seemingly without effort. Or almost everything. The one exception we find:

> At a lodging place along the way the Lord met Moses and sought to kill him. (Exodus 4:24)

Without success, it turned out. Zipporah, his wife:

> ...took a flint and cut off her son's foreskin, and touched Moses' feet with it.... (Exodus 4:25)

Is the point of the story that the power of circumcision is such that it could prevent even God from killing Moses, or simply that it made Him change His mind? But this exception is such a strange occurrence that we must be allowed to consider either that an error arose in this report or that a basic fact was omitted that would help us to understand it. We cannot even begin to comprehend why God should seek to kill Moses just after He had enlisted him to persuade Pharaoh to let the people go. In the light of everything else that God carried through successfully, we must assume that there is some other explanation. The story will just remain a mystery.

Having established God's omnipotence, we do not intend here to enter into the age-old controversy as to why if God is so powerful, He allows evil to exist in the first place. Our object is not to explain why God does anything, but rather to describe the character of God as it was presented in the scriptures. It is sufficient to observe that, while He can harden hearts and soften them at will, in the main, He has left humans to decide for themselves how, when, and whether to follow His precepts and thereby suffer the consequences or enjoy the rewards.

The omniscience of the God of the Patriarchs probes both into the present and into the future, both near and far. He foresaw the four-hundred-year sojourn and servitude of the Israelites in Egypt, as well as the backsliding of the Israelites after they had been led out of Egypt.

> And the Lord said to Moses, "Behold, you are about to sleep with your fathers; then this people will rise and play the harlot after the strange gods of the land...will forsake me and break my covenant.... (Deuteronomy 31:16)

His clairvoyance was both general and individual:

> And the Lord said to [Rebekah], "Two nations are in your womb, and two peoples born of you, shall be divided....the elder shall serve the younger." (Genesis 25:23)

> He [Ishmael] shall be a wild ass of a man, his hand against every man, and every man's hand against him... (Genesis 16:12)

Throughout the centuries, God observes whether His people are behaving or misbehaving. Even while occupied in conference with Moses on Sinai, He knows what is going on elsewhere:

> And the Lord said to Moses, "Go down, for your people...have corrupted themselves....they have made for themselves a molten calf, and have worshiped it...." (Exodus 32:7, 8)

His omniscience, however, misses occasionally. It is amusing to note here that again God is presented in the image of man. When the people are misbehaving, they are not "my people," but "your people."

After talking to Abraham about his future, He seems uncertain of what is going on in Sodom and Gomorrah, for:

> I will go down to see whether they have done altogether according to the outcry which has come to me....(Genesis 18:21)

God has heard the news, but does not know whether to trust it.

If God's omniscience and clairvoyance were perfect, why did He select Baasha as king over Israel? God asks, indirectly through the prophet Jehu:

> Since I exalted you...and made you leader over my people Israel...you...have made my people Israel to sin, provoking me to anger.... (1 Kings 16:2)

This sounds like another case of the clouded crystal ball. With all the human efforts made to conceive of God as we imagine He should be, we have conceived one that is somehow not quite perfect. We find in Him many of the qualities and characteristics that are common to humankind in the days of the patriarchs. Again we pose the question: in whose image?

# Chapter 5: The God of the Prophets

> They say to the prophets, "Prophesy not to us what is right; speak to us smooth things...." (Isaiah 30:10)

The God of the Patriarchs was the God of the grand ages of Biblical times, when history marched in majestic pageantry across the pages of the Scriptures. We begin with the wonder of the Creation story, pass on through the cataclysmic destruction of Sodom, Gomorrah, and the Flood. He was the God not only of the Patriarchs, Abraham, Isaac, and Jacob; but also of the great Lawgiver, Moses, who led his people out of the Egyptian slavery with so much fanfare. We continue with the invincible military campaigns of Joshua into the times of the Judges, with Israel basically still a tribal entity, and see the beginnings of Israel's development into a nation under its first kings: Saul, David, and Solomon. David, with a few minor faults in his character, was the greatest of these kings, successful as a military campaigner as well as a ruler, loyal to the people and to his predecessor Saul, even when Saul sought to kill him. Solomon is more of an enigma. Despite his renowned wisdom and the fact that he was obviously favored by God, he used his position and his intellectual faculties for self-aggrandizement, amassing wives and concubines, and surrounding himself with all the trappings of wealth and materialism. Not only did he flaunt God's will in marrying multiple and foreign wives; he committed the heinous crime of building temples for the gods of some of his favorites from other lands. While he was strong enough to maintain a heavy yoke of taxation and forced labor during his reign, the people revolted when his son Rehoboam sought to continue the harsh rule.

The God of the Prophets began to develop about the time of the break-up of the nation, when Israel separates from Judah. We can point to no sharp dividing line between the God of the Patriarchs and the God of the Prophets; they have coexisted for some time, for they are both well-adapted to their environments. As in evolution in the animal kingdom, where many species are co-existent, so both species of God can co-exist. On earth we find still living and thriving the anciently developed possum and the crocodile, both of whom have been around for millions of years. There are still environments to which the God of the Patriarchs is well-adapted, particularly amongst the congregations of some fundamentalists churches which, while having adopted the later concept of heaven and hell, still live with the awe-inspiring and terrible Jehovah of the cataclysmic days. The God of the Patriarchs, too, is still alive and thriving, with perhaps some minor modifications, principally amongst the orthodox Jews.

So the God of the Prophets began to make His appearance on the stage of history along with Samuel and the first of the kings, about eight or nine hundred years before the birth of Jesus. The most significant change in Him was the loss of the henotheistic character of Jehovah as a tribal God, and His evolution into the one God, sufficiently almighty that idols and graven images no longer present a threat. Concurrently, faith in timely retribution began to waver, and sacrifices began to lose their predominant position. There will be further discussion on the matter of rite versus right.

Up to the time the Israelites marched out of the wilderness under the leadership of Joshua, they had essentially been an isolated people. Before Egypt, they had been mostly nomadic herdsmen, having minimal contact with their neighbors. No evidence exists that they ever integrated their lives with those of the Egyptians, and their fall into slavery would have curtailed whatever integration may have occurred, keeping them socially isolated. Evidence of Egyptian influence on their ways and their religion is slight, especially in comparison with the evidence of later Babylonian influence. This is likely due to the fact that they were slaves in Egypt, while in Babylon, they lived more in the mainstream. During the Exodus, they were again isolated, wandering as nomads in the wilderness of the Negeb.

Following Joshua as a conquering army, devastating and annihilating all that stood in their path—Canaanites, Hittites, Hivites—the Israelites remained a group unto themselves. More outside contacts came throughout Judges, when the Israelites were sent into bondage to a series of kings, interspersed by periods of prostration and depression when they had nothing turned back to religion and called on God to deliver them. Which God did, always relenting in His love for His chosen people—only to find that as soon as they were again free and become prosperous, they no longer felt the need for His help, and went their merry irreligious way till God again ran out of patience. These contacts, along with the trade and commerce that had already begun, allowed the Israelites a better view of their surrounding world. Their view broadened and for the first time their concept of the world extended beyond just themselves and their immediate neighbors.

The henotheistic concept is slow to disappear; we have already mentioned its continuance in the mind of Jonah, and with Micah, it still clings:

> For all the peoples walk, each in the name of its god, but we will walk in the name of the Lord our God for ever and ever. (Micah 4:5)

This was two centuries after Solomon. The idea was so tenacious that it had not yet completely disappeared in the time of David:

> For I know that the Lord is great., and that our Lord is above all gods. (Psalms 135:5)

It is not until Isaiah that He is firmly established as the God Almighty:

> Says the Lord..."Before me no god was formed, or shall there be any after me. (Isaiah 43:10)

> I am coming to gather all nations and tongues; and they shall come and shall see my glory...and some of them also I will take for priests.... (Isaiah 66:18, 21)

> For God is the king of all the earth, God reigns over all the nations.... (Psalms 47:7, 8)

Indeed, God Himself no longer hesitates to step outside the confines of Israel:

> Now I have given all these lands into the hands of Nebuchadnezzar, the king of Babylon, my servant....All the nations shall serve him...until the time of his own land comes.... (Jeremiah 27:6, 7)

God in His admonitions to His people no longer warns so much against "serving other gods," but rather against worshipping empty idols. Henotheism as a theological philosophy is officially dead with Isaiah; any subsequent appearances are those of a wandering ghost.

A superficial reading of the latter half of the Jewish Bible/Old Testament might give the idea that Jehovah is bloodthirsty as ever. But more careful perusal shows that much of this impression derives from the highly dramatic language of the prophets of Isaiah, or Jeremiah, or Ezekiel. Through them, God threatens all sorts of dire calamity, but His threats are rarely fully carried out. We no longer find the demands for annihilation of women, children, and the weak and helpless that were accepted in the days of Saul. Though great destruction and slaughter does occur, it develops more in line with standard warfare. Not too much mercy can be expected when the vengeful exiles in Babylon can be as shocking as:

> Happy shall he be who takes your little ones and dashes them against the rock! (Psalms 137:9)

Vengeance and wrath are still the order of the day:

> The Lord is a jealous God and avenging, the Lord is avenging and wrathful....his way is in whirlwind and storm.... (Nahum 1:2, 3)

> "I will take vengeance [on Babylon], and I will spare no man." (Isaiah 47:3)

Ezekiel goes on to quote God as saying that, because Tyre was glad when Jerusalem was being laid to waste:

> I will scrape her soil from her and make her a bare rock. (Ezekiel 26:4)

This presents a dramatic picture. Let us look at some other spectacular language of the prophets:

> I trod down the peoples in my anger, I made them drunk in my wrath, and I poured out their lifeblood on the earth. (Isaiah 63:6)

> I will make Jerusalem a heap of ruins, a lair of jackals....I will feed this people with wormwood, and give them poisonous water to drink....the dead bodies of men shall fall like dung on the open field, like sheaves after the reaper, and none shall gather them. (Jeremiah 9:11, 15, 22)

Truly inspired is the terrible poetry of the Dies Irae of Zephaniah, from which:

> He will make Nineveh a desolation, a dry waste like the desert....the vulture and the hedgehog shall lodge in her capitals; the owl shall hoot in the window, the raven croak on the threshold. (Zephaniah 2:13, 14)

Yet fortunately, though Nineveh did fall, the outcome was not as horrific as had been threatened. Nineveh had already been spared once by the God of the Prophets, who sent Jonah to warn them of their wicked ways. Jonah evidently did an excellent job, for the king and the people of Nineveh repented, and donned the customary sackcloth. Jonah was evidently a disciple of the bloodthirsty God of the Patriarchs, for he was annoyed that God had relented and accepted the repentance of Nineveh. God chided him:

> And should I not pity Nineveh, the great city, in which there are more than a hundred and twenty thousand persons who do not know their right hand from their left, and also much cattle? (Jonah 4:11)

The divine mercy the God of the Prophets shows by first giving a warning and then sparing the repentant people is very different from the practice of the God of the Patriarchs.

Still, there remains some elements of cruelty in the new God. From the times of the Judges, we have seen that Israel has been repeatedly chastised by God, who sent foreign kings as His tools to harass and to capture them. Yet God, in His vengeance delights in punishing these foreign kings even after He Himself has delegated them to punish the Israelites (2 Kings 18:12 and 24:3, Isaiah 10:5, 6).

One thing we cannot avoid remarking about God is that He takes Himself very seriously. Christian apologists over the ages have maintained that for a God who takes Himself seriously it is only natural that He be vengeful, quick to anger, showing His wrath whenever He is crossed. Time and again, He expresses a love for His chosen people, and requires that they love Him. His love is, however, a possessive sort of love, demanding gratitude, appreciation, and obedience. God's fury is unleashed most fully when He is scorned, when His chosen people "go whoring after other gods." He obviously does not agree with Shakespeare's comment that "Love is not love which alters when it alteration finds." God not only takes Himself seriously, He also expects everyone else to take Him seriously.

The one aspect of humanity that we never find in the Biblical Gods, nor in any of the Gods derived from the Bible, is a sense of humor. It is practically impossible to imagine God laughing at a joke, or even smiling at some ridiculous situation in philosophical acceptance. When Sarah laughed at the idea of bearing a son in her old age, God did not join her laughter, but took it extremely seriously:

> The Lord said to Abraham, "Why did Sarah laugh....is anything too hard for the Lord?" (Genesis 18:13–15)

Nowhere do we find the slightest hint of humor, which is strange when we consider that God from time to time demonstrates most of the other characteristics we find in humankind. Perhaps people lacked humor in those days when life was hard and such effort was required to scrape a living from the sparse soil so thus could not comprehend a God with a sense of humor.

In a way, it is natural to expect seriousness from one with the unfailing power and omnipotence of God, expressed in the following passage:

> Thou didst set the earth on its foundations....thou makest springs....give drink to every beast....thou didst cause the grass to grow....the high mountains are for the wild goats....thou hast made the moon to mark the seasons.... (Psalms 104:5–15)

God interprets dreams for Daniel (Daniel 2:45), and protects His worshippers in the fiery furnace:

> Then Shadrach, Meschach and Abednego came out of the fire...the hair of their heads was not singed, their mantles were not harmed and no smell of fire had come upon them. (Daniel 3:26–27)

And on the larger scale, God works for the Israelites when they behave, and punishes them when they do not:

> The Lord...turned the heart of the king of Assyria to them, so that He aided them in the work of the house of God. (Ezra 6:22)

> Ah Assyria, the rod of my anger....Against a godless nation (Israel) I send him...to tread them down like the mire of the streets. (Isaiah 10:5, 6)

Jeremiah tells us that it was the Lord, not the king of Babylon, who carried out the destruction of Israel. Yet there is always hope:

> And He will come to Zion as Redeemer, to those in Jacob who turn from transgression.... (Isaiah 59:20)

Overweening pride and the demand for recognition is still an important element of the God of the Prophets. He was not hesitant to demonstrate His power:

> Woe to the rebellious children...who carry out a plan, but not mine...who set out to go down to Egypt, without asking for my counsel.... (Isaiah 30:1, 2)

> It is not for your sake, O house of Israel, that I am about to act, but for the sake of my holy name....then they will know that I am the Lord. (Ezekiel 36:22, 23)

> Arise...O daughter of Zion, for I will make your horn iron and your hoofs bronze; you shall beat in pieces many peoples, and shall devote their gain to the Lord, their wealth to the Lord of the whole earth. (Micah 4:13)

> Edom...may build, but I will tear down...and you shall say, "Great is the Lord, beyond the border of Israel!" (Malachi 1:4, 5)

While He is unfailingly omnipotent, His omniscience is, like that of the God of the Patriarchs, less than complete. Although the Psalmist conceives of God as observing the minutest detail:

> Thou knowest when I sit down and when I rise up....even before a word is on my tongue....thou knowest it altogether....even the darkness is not dark to thee....in thy book were written...the days that were formed for me when as yet there were none of them. (Psalms 139:2, 4, 12, 16)

He evidently misses from time to time, admitting that:

> They made kings, but not through me, they set up princes, but without my knowledge. (Hosea 8:4)

For example, Satan succeeds in persuading Him that He doesn't really know Job, and He allows Satan to test Job by taking away his wealth, his servants, and his children (Job 1). Not only is Job himself afflicted, but God allows Satan to murder the innocent servants and the sons and daughters of Job for the sole purpose of a test that an omniscient God should find unnecessary.

Still, God knows most of what is current; it is when He looks into the future that His vision is less than clear:

> Behold, Damascus will cease to be a city, and will become a heap of ruins. Her cities will be deserted forever...says the Lord.... (Isaiah 17:1, 2)

> For out of the north a nation has come up against [Babylon], which shall make her land a desolation....both man and beast shall flee away....she...shall be an utter desolation.... (Jeremiah 50:3, 13)

Yesterday's newspapers indicate that Damascus is still thriving. While it is true enough that Babylon succumbed to Cyrus the Persian, it was not destroyed, continuing to be a rather important city until it dwindled into being a village some time after the founding of Baghdad in 762 A.D., some fourteen hundred years later.

Nor is God appreciably more successful with His predictions regarding the Israelites:

> I will take the people of Israel....will gather them from all sides, and bring them to their own land....I will save them from all backsliding....they shall dwell in the land....they and their children and their children's children shall dwell there forever...the

> remnant of Israel...will...gather them from the farthest parts of the earth....for I am a father to Israel, and Ephraim is my first-born. (Ezekiel 37: 21, 23, 25)

Judah did return some years later from Babylon, but Israel (Ephraim), which had been scattered by the Assyrians, was never heard from again. God was also completely unsuccessful in His efforts to prevent backsliding, which went on as usual, and resulted in negating the prediction that they should dwell there forever.

The story of Solomon illuminates further the character of the God of the Prophets. God loved Solomon from the time of his birth on, and, at the beginning of his reign, He appeared in a dream and offered to grant him a wish. The still humble youth responded:

> Give thy servant therefore an understanding mind to govern thy people, that I may discern between good and evil. (1 Kings 3:9)

The God of the Prophets was pleased with Solomon and granted his request. Solomon became at first an exemplary king, and later fulfilled God's prediction that the kings would amass wealth unto themselves, and not only tax the people, but also press their sons and daughters into his service. Solomon constructed a magnificent temple for the Lord, and in the eyes of God, this was the ultimate in righteousness. As a result, God continued to look with high favor on Solomon, and he amassed riches and women beyond even the most flamboyant dreams of anyone else in history.

Among Solomon's seven hundred wives and three hundred concubines, there were several foreign princesses. Like some of his compatriots before and after his time, Solomon saw the riches and the power of the great nations surrounding him, and felt undoubtedly that this was derived from the power of their gods. Partly to appease the religious fervor of his foreign wives and partly to cover all eventualities, Solomon:

> ...built a high place for Chemosh the abomination of Moab, and for Moloch the abomination of the Ammonites....And so he did for all his foreign wives, who burned incense and sacrificed to their gods. (1 Kings 11:7, 8)

This naturally incurred the wrath of God. Still, He could not bring Himself to exercise His wrath on His favorite, crediting David with His lenient attitude towards Solomon:

> I will surely tear the kingdom from you. Yet for the sake of David your father, I will not do it in your days, but will tear it out of the hand of your son.... (1 Kings 11:11, 12)

We are thus back to the status of the sins of the fathers being visited on the sons. And He was true to His word. While Solomon retained his kingdom through the rest of his life, his son lost all but the tribe of Judah. The rest of Israel came under the reign of Jereboam, never to reunite with Judah.

One definite difference we find between the God of the Patriarchs and the God of the Prophets is in their respective attitudes toward sacrifice and burnt offerings. Now that the people of Israel were moving beyond their primitive stages and losing some of their superstitions, the complications of city life and commerce left less time for ritual and made more demands on their ethics and morals. The majority of the people, no longer herdsmen and animal keepers, did not have livestock available for ready sacrifice, and their tithing in the form of gold and silver coins was not suitable for burnt offerings.

While God dictated to Moses an extensive catalog of sacrificial praxis, described in the minutest detail and designed for the expiation of sins, guilt, payment for prayers answered, love offerings, and offerings made simply to stay in God's favor, these lost their importance for the God of the Prophets:

> Sacrifice and offering thou dost not desire....burnt offering and sin offering thou hast not required....thy law is within my heart. (Psalms 40:6, 8)

> I have had enough of burnt offerings of rams and the fat of fed beasts; I do not delight in the blood of bulls....who requires of you this trampling of my courts? bring no more vain offerings....make yourselves clean....cease to do evil, learn to do good.... (Isaiah 1:11–17)

> I hate, I despise your feasts....even though you offer me your burnt offerings and cereal offerings I will not accept them....but let justice roll down like waters and righteousness like an ever-flowing stream. (Amos 5:21–24)

It is at this point that right becomes more important than rite. Although God still has His rules and regulations, the God of the Prophets begins to sound more like a God of morals and ethics than a dictatorial legislator, demanding strict obedience without allowing for question. Having already forbid human sacrifice, converting it to ritual sacrifice, where the sacrificed animals are eaten after the roasting, He is now allowing compassion to dominate His creed, insisting upon the defense of orphans and pleading for the widow and the poor. These considerations now take precedence over the demand for sacrifices.

In some ways, God is also becoming more a remote presence. He still speaks directly to His prophets for His communication with the kings. His visual apparitions become mostly limited to His angels and a few signs. Only Amos and Ezekiel are visited visually by the God of the Prophets:

> I saw the Lord standing beside the altar.... (Amos 9:1)

> And above the firmament...there was the likeness of a throne, in appearance like sapphire, and seated above...a likeness as it were of a human form....such was the appearance of the likeness of the glory of the Lord. (Ezekiel 1:26, 28)

This limitation of appearances did not prevent Him from sending various signs or performing miracles. Isaiah tells Hezekiah that God will send him a sign.

> This is the sign to you from the Lord....I will make the shadow cast by the declining sun on the dial of Ahaz turn back ten steps. (Isaiah 38:7, 8)

Ezekiel spends chapters 40 through 47 describing the vision of the temple that God expected him to help build, complete with detailed measurements, directions for sacrifices and operation of the temple, as well as a miraculous river issuing from the temple in the vision.

There was also the sign of the handwriting on the wall:

> [Belshazzar], his lords, wives and [concubines] drank wine, and praised the gods of gold and silver....Immediately the fingers of a man's hand appeared and wrote on the plaster of the wall....and the king saw the hand as it wrote. Then the king's color changed....his knees knocked together. (Daniel 5:4–6)

There were signs in the sky:

> For the space of almost forty days there were seen horsemen running in the air ... and troops and horsemen in array.... (2 Maccabees 5:2, 3)

Another sign appeared in the temple, when Heliodorous was prevented from taking money from the temple by the miraculous appearance of a horse and rider and two young men with whips. (2 Maccabees 3:23ff)

When, as was somewhat unusual, a number of Jews were slain in battle, it was afterwards found that the following miracle of retribution occurred:

Under the coats of every one that was slain they found things consecrated to the idols of the Jamnites.

Whether the following two quotations are miracles or just typical examples of prejudiced media reporting, we will leave for someone else to decide. After vicious battles in which many thousands of the enemy were slain:

> ...all the people returned safe to Joshua. (Joshua 10:21)

> There were burnt offerings because not one of them were slain until they had returned in peace. (1 Maccabees 5:54)

Verily, these were great warriors—or great reporters.

The zeal of certain factions among the Jews resulted, after the end of the history given by the canonical books of the Old Testament, in a brief reign of prosperous Jewish independence under the Maccabees, after which the fall of Judea and the final dispersing of the Jewish people occurred. Both the God of the Patriarchs and the God of the Prophets took credit for winning wars; whenever the Jews lost a battle, this was blamed on the withdrawal of divine assistance as a result of Jewish apostasy. The courage their faith gave Jewish soldiers produced strong and valiant warriors, and often resulted in their ability to overwhelm much larger forces.

> And when you draw near to the battle...do not fear...or be in dread of them; for the Lord your God...goes with you...to give you victory. (Deuteronomy 20:2–4)

> ...none that put their trust in him shall be overcome. (1 Maccabees 2:61)

On occasion, God expressed His resentment when the Israelites sought allied assistance instead of relying wholly on His support.

> Woe to those who go down to Egypt for help and rely on horses...but do not...consult the Lord! (Isaiah 31:1)

Generally, the help was provided under cover, and it seemed to the enemy that it was dauntless Israel who carried the day.

> God helped [Uzziah] against the Philistines, and against the Arab ...and against the Meunites. (2 Chronicles 26:7)

At other times, the action was outright miraculous. When Hezekiah called on God for help against the Assyrians, God waged His battle during the night, while everyone was sleeping peacefully:

> And that night the angel of the Lord went forth, and slew a hundred and eighty-five thousand in the camp of the Assyrians.... (2 Kings 19:35)

When the Seleucid king Antiochus defamed the temple in 167 B.C., the horror of this brought on the Maccabean rebellion. Again, their deep faith in God enabled the Jews, fighting on home ground, to defeat much larger Seleucid forces. This would probably not have been enough, but Seleucid succession politics at home and troubles with the Parthians on another front divided Seleucid efforts and enabled the Maccabeans—first under Judas Maccabeus, then under his brother Jonathan—to eventually win their independence. This independence lasted about eighty years, until the Romans took advantage of a family fracas among the Jews and themselves obtained power.

The Jews lived under Roman hegemony for over a century, till the Zealots, remembering the success of the Maccabees, and with a firm faith in God, rebelled against the Romans between 66 and 70 A.D. They were, however, unable to withstand the might of the Roman Empire, with the result that the rebellion was put down and the Jews finally scattered among the nations, not to regroup till the founding of Israel in the twentieth century.

From the evolutionary point of view, the God of the Prophets showed Himself to be vital and resilient. Well adapted to His Jewish environment, even the scattering of the nation did not threaten His existence. Quite compatible with Jewish philosophy, He accompanied them on their exiles, and they in turn revered their Lord. Undoubtedly, their conviction that they were the chosen of God had much to do with His survival amongst their scattered communities.

Jewish insistence on apartheid did much to maintain the integrity of their religion:

> You yourselves know how unlawful it is for a Jew to associate with or to visit any one of another nation....(Acts 10:28)

Peter, who tells us this, even though he is beginning to preach to Gentiles and becoming more open in his ways, knows the rules. Business and casual contacts are permitted, but socializing and especially eating with others is taboo. The resultant impression that non-Jews may have had—that they were unclean or inferior to the Jewish people—may well have contributed to the persecution of the Jews in predominantly non-Jewish societies.

No small contribution to the God of the Prophets' survival came from scriptural history, where the Jews saw that, time and again, they were victims of the wrath of God. Repeatedly in Judges, and more recently in the Babylonian Exile, they had submitted to the rightful retribution of God, knowing that underneath it all, He loved them, and that sooner or later they would regain His favor, and become once more the heirs and rulers of Jerusalem.

Although God is evolving to have less visual personal contact with His people, His presence and immanence remains. God follows His people closely, and can change His plans to suit the course of events or to answer the pleadings of His people. In this we see clearly that God has given humankind the gift of free will. He reserves the right from time to time to step in and make a few changes, such as the hardening of Pharaoh's heart or helping Jacob along the way of life, but humans are left to meet their destinies as best they can.

The logical result of this attitude is that God is at times flexible, willing to forgive when His people repent and hold off on threatened retribution. God is also willing to listen. As when the Israelites built the golden calf at Sinai:

> ...the Lord God was calling for a judgment by fire....[Amos] said, "O, Lord God, cease, I beseech thee! How can Jacob stand? He is so small!" The Lord repented concerning this; "This also shall not be." (Amos 7:4, 5)

When Hezekiah prays to the Lord for life, saying, "Remember, I beseech thee, how I have ...done what is good," the Lord replies, "I have heard your prayer....I will add fifteen years to your life."

When the armies were having some trouble, the men asked the prophet Jeremiah for help, and he prayed to God:

> Thus says the Lord...,"If you will remain in this land...I will plant you, not pluck you up; for I repent of the evil which I did to you." (Jeremiah 42:9, 10)

From this we get an insight into the force of prayer. Some say that God, all-wise and omnipotent, knows what is best for everyone, and that it is absurd for mere humans to suggest to Him what should be done through prayer. Yet both the God of the Patriarchs and the God of the Prophets did respond on many occasions, essentially as a result of man exercising his free will in a way that pleased God enough to bend Him from His original intent.

There is still the nagging thought that God should have been able to foresee the actions and pleas of man and therefore should not have made the threats in the first place. Yet, if He had not made the threats, man would not have behaved as he did, or would have had no reason to plead as he did. A dilemma. On another subject, the God of the Prophets, following in the ways of His predecessor, is not above a bit of deceit or beyond some inconsistencies:

> Moreover, I gave them statutes that were not good and ordinances by which they could not have life; and I defiled them...making them offer by fire all their first-born, that I might horrify them; I did it that they might know that I am the Lord. (Ezekiel 20:25, 26)

While this is not precisely what one might expect of a benevolent God, we are not expected to understand God.

> Speak to Zerubbabel, governor of Judah, saying, I am about to shake the heavens and the earth, and to overthrow the throne of kingdoms....I will take you...and make you like a signet ring; for I have chosen you.... (Haggai 2:21–23)

This might be interpreted as inciting a revolt against Babylon, but some have considered it even greater, a declaration of Zerubbabel as the Messiah. In any event, there was nothing to it. After the construction of the temple, it all fizzles out, and Zerubbabel is heard from no more.

Note the following inconsistency between the first passage and the one that follows it sequentially in the scriptures:

> I will not again destroy Ephraim; for I am God and not man....
> (Hosea 11:9)

> Ephraim has given bitter provocation....I will fall upon them like a bear robbed of her cubs, I will tear open their breast...as a wild beast would rend them. I will destroy you, O Israel....
> (Hosea 12:14 and 13:8, 9)

Perhaps the following contradiction implies a confusion among the prophets:

> Satan stood up against Israel, and incited David to number Israel. (1 Chronicles 21:1)

On the subject of Satan: he is a rather nebulous figure in the Jewish Bible/Old Testament. Tradition equated him with the serpent who tempted Eve. Unlike Ahriman in Zoroastrianism, who is on equal footing with the benevolent god Ormazd, Satan is assumed to have been one of God's creations who rebelled against Him in the early days.

In the Old Testament, we find him successfully tempting God to test Job; in the Gospels, he unsuccessfully tempts Jesus. Satan does not have the power to force anyone to do anything, but with his wily ways, he can tempt man to sin. Although God has not so stated, evidence indicates that Satan has a function in God's plans. In his efforts to tempt humankind, he exercises the human soul, strengthening it if it is made of the proper stuff. Further, he acts as a filter to Paradise, separating the worthy from the unworthy souls.

Unlike the God of the Patriarchs, who spoke directly with Noah, Abraham, and Moses, the God of the Prophets dispatches most of His messages indirectly through His chosen representatives:

> [God told Jeremiah,] "Before I formed you in the womb I knew you, and before you were born...I appointed you a prophet to the nations." (Jeremiah 1:5)

> The Lord God does nothing without revealing his secrets to his servants the prophets. (Amos 3:7)

We will consider prophets as people with whom God speaks, giving them instructions either for themselves or to pass on to others. God holds His prophets responsible for carrying out His will. He tells Ezekiel that He has made him, "a watchman for the house of Israel," that he must pass on all of God's warnings, and if a man sins when Ezekiel has not passed on the warning God will kill the man, but, "his blood I will require at your hand." (Ezekiel 3:18)

One would think therefore that life should not be too complicated; it is only necessary to listen to the prophets and behave accordingly. But the difficulty lies in not knowing whom to believe. All the time that Jeremiah was thundering his warnings, other prophets were reassuring Jerusalem that everything was going to be fine. How does one know whom to believe?

> [Jeremiah said] "God, behold... the prophets say to them, 'You shall not see the sword...I will give you assured peace in this place." And the Lord said to me, 'The prophets are prophesying lies in my name; I did not send them.'...." (Jeremiah 14:13, 14)

> Your prophets have been like foxes among the ruins....they have spoke falsehoods....they say, "Says the Lord," when the Lord has not sent them, and yet they expect him to fulfill their word. (Ezekiel 13:4–6)

Ex post facto we have learned who was God's authentic representative, but while the debate was going on, the public must have been somewhat confused. Evidently they listened where they pleased. There's nothing new in the following attitude:

> [They say] to the prophets, "Prophesy not to us what is right; speak to us smooth things...." (Isaiah 30:10)

How many people today select their preachers or mentors on this same basis?

In Jeremiah, chapters 17, 18, and 19, God continues to instruct Jeremiah where to go and what to say, but has already warned him that the people will not listen to him. The words offered by the false prophets are more alluring. Consequently, the Lord Himself became disgusted and sent the armies of the king of Babylon to wreak His wrath on His stubborn people. It finally got to the point:

> Thus says the Lord concerning the prophets who lead my people astray....the sun shall go down upon the prophets and the day shall be black over them.... (Micah 3:5, 6)

> ...I will remove from the land the prophets and the unclean spirit. And if anyone again appears as a prophet, his father and

mother who bore him will say to him, "You shall not live, for you speak lies in the name of the Lord." (Zecheriah 13:2, 3)

Manifestly, Zecheriah got the word, and God, considering the gullibility of His people, put an end to the age of the prophets. After the end of the Old Testament and the Apocrypha, the Bible has no more prophets as such; the God of the Prophets lives on, but is no longer active in people's lives through the prophets.

The image of a God delineated by men who believed that God should communicate with them persisted through the era of the great prophets—Moses, Samuel, Elijah—who were powerful enough to overwhelm any countercurrents without difficulty. But when events amplified the confusion of claims and counterclaims of a profusion of prophets, the people became disillusioned with the idea that God actually did talk with some of His chosen messengers and abandoned the hypothesis completely.

The separation of Israel from the rest of the world was decreed by God, especially through prohibition of mixed marriages, and underlined by the admonitions of the prophets:

> For they have taken some of their daughters to be wives...so that the holy race has mixed itself with the peoples of the lands....sat appalled. (Ezra 9:2, 3)

With the weeping and the desperate pleading of Ezra, the Israelites relented, relinquishing their foreign wives and children. These must have been heart-wrenching times, but the people of Israel felt their holiness more deeply than their family ties, and obeyed Ezra.

Thus Ezra carried the Israelites back in time to Joshua's admonitions:

> For if you turn back, and join the remnants of these nations left here among you....you marry their women and they yours, know assuredly that the Lord your God will not continue to drive out these nations before you; but they will be a snare and a trap for you...till you perish from off this good land which the Lord your God has given you. (Joshua 23:12, 13)

Ezra followed Joshua's lead, despite the fact that a hundred years or more before Ezra's time, Isaiah had practically declared the universality of God:

> ...for my house shall be called a house of prayer for all peoples. (Isaiah 56:7)

When Zerubbabel began the reconstruction of the temple, the people who had occupied the land during the Exile approached him and offered to help, but Zerubbabel brusquely refused:

> We will build together with you, for we likewise...obey your Lord and sacrifice to him....then Zerubbabel...said...it is not for us and you to build a house together unto the Lord our God."
> (1 Esdras 5:68–70)

The reconstruction of the destroyed temple had been initiated by Cyrus as a result of God's inspiration:

> ...the Lord stirred up the spirit of Cyrus king of Persia so that he made a proclamation....God of heaven has given me all the kingdoms of the earth ,and he has charged me to build him a house at Jerusalem....whoever is among you of all his people...let him go up to Jerusalem.... (Ezra 1:1–3)

Most of the Jews took this opportunity to leave Babylon, and this was the beginning of the end of the Exile.

Generally, the "choosing" of the Jews by God is presented as strictly for their benefit and for God's. God for some unexplained reason took a fancy to Abraham and promised to remain faithful to him and to his descendants, from time to time stipulating the condition that they remain faithful and obedient to Him. However, the scriptures also present this relationship in the light of a mission, so the Jews can provide examples to the rest of the world in the ways of faith:

> It is too light a thing that you should be my servant to raise up the tribes of Jacob....I will give you as a light to the nations, that my salvation shall reach to the end of the earth. (Isaiah 49:6)

Despite this view, for some reason never explained, the Gods of the Old Testament never made any overt efforts to convert anyone outside of Israel or even to present Himself to anyone other than the Hebrews, even forbidding alien entry into the Israelite assemblies. God has no basic objections to taking converts into the fold; He will accept the conversion of a sojourner in Israelite country on the condition that the sojourner consent to be circumcised.

The Jews themselves have followed in the footsteps of God, and most seem to be satisfied with their position as a "light to the nations," for it is generally against their philosophy to proselyte or to act as missionaries. God's original intentions seem, however, to have been carried out in the long run. With the help of Saint Paul and Mohammed the ends of the earth have been reached, and nearly half of humanity is under the influence of a God who is anchored firmly in the Jewish Bible/Old Testament.

The God of the Patriarchs was conceived as being stern and imperious, but also just. Retribution was inevitable; the good received their just rewards and the wicked were punished. To the ancient Jews, this was one of the prime functions of God after the Creation had been accomplished. At first, this was also true of the God of the Prophets, but He evolved still further. Some improvement in the application of justice had already surfaced; no longer were the sins of the fathers to be visited on the children of the third and fourth generation:

> In those days they shall no longer say: "The fathers have eaten sour grapes, and the children's teeth are set on edge." But every one shall die for his own sin. (Jeremiah 31:29, 30)

Even though this was a step forward for those who believed in fundamental justice, how was this justice enacted? When the Hebrews realized that God was not always stepping in to punish evil-doers, they began to ask themselves:

> Why dost thou stand afar off, O Lord? In arrogance the wicked hotly pursue the poor.... (Psalms 10:1)

> Why does the way of the wicked prosper? (Jeremiah 12:1)

> Why dost thou look on faithless men and art silent when the wicked swallows up the man more righteous than he? (Habakkuk 1:13)

The wicked still seemed to be prospering at the expense of the righteous. Gradually there came a rethinking of the whole problem. Certainly no one could deny that God was just and must therefore dole out rewards and punishments. If they were not obvious to us, it must be because they were meted out on some other plane. Originally it was thought that when man died, that was all there was to it.

> The living know that they will die, but the dead know nothing, and they have no more reward....there is no work or thought or knowledge or wisdom in Sheol, to which you are going. (Ecclesiastes 9:5, 10)

> But man dies, and is laid low...till the heavens are no more he will not awake. (Job 14:10, 12)

> For the fate of the sons of men and the fate of beasts is the same; as one dies, so dies the other....all are from dust, and all turn to dust again. Who knows whether the spirit of man goes upward and the spirit of the beast goes downward to the earth? (Ecclesiastes 3:19–21)

A tremendous pressure begins to build, both from the side of those demanding justice, and from those who cannot endure the feeling that the end of this life is the end of everything. Finally the dam bursts, and we are flooded with vistas of the resolution of the problem: Judgment Day, the Millennium, the Kingdom of God. All is not lost. There will be retribution, after all, and the souls of men will not be cast into Sheol when their bodies go to the grave. The God of the Prophets has evolved into His final form as truly a just God; the execution of justice is only delayed.

Some of the prophets envision a picture of a better earth:

> He shall judge between many peoples and shall decide for strong nations afar off; and they shall beat their swords into plowshares and their spears into pruning hooks. (Micah 4:3)

> ...I will remove from your midst your proudly exultant ones....I will leave...a people humble and lowly....they shall do no wrong and utter no lies. (Zephaniah 3:11–13)

Others envision a day of justice on earth, when the righteous are rewarded and the sinners, punished.

> For the windows of heaven are opened and the foundations of earth tremble....on that day the Lord will punish the host of heaven, in heaven, and the kings of earth on the earth. (Isaiah 24:18, 21)

> And I will give portents in the heavens and on the earth, blood and fire and columns of smoke. The sun shall be turned to darkness and the moon to blood, before the great and terrible day of the Lord comes....there shall be those who escape....those whom the Lord calls. (Joel 2:30–32)

> There shall be seen earthquakes and uproars...and everyone shall be saved...by his works and by faith....shall be preserved from the said perils....they...that have abused my ways shall dwell in torment. (2 Esdras 9:3, 7–9)

These ideas have not been developed to the extent they will be in the New Testament, but the kernel is there, and the seed will grow. Although we find little more in the Old Testament, the ideas did seem to spread. The Essenes, a monastic brotherhood of Jews which sprang up in Palestine two centuries before Christ, developed a moral system somewhat stricter than their Jewish orthodox neighbors. The system included an eternal soul, a blessed Paradise as a reward for the righteous, and a place of eternal punishment as a penalty for the wicked life. It is interesting to note in passing that evidence indicates the highly moral Essenes to be the first society in history to condemn slavery.

The entire idea of God's kingdom on Earth was inextricably intertwined with the predicted coming of a Messiah, who was expected to rectify everything, to bring the Jubilee for the Israelites and for the rest of the world if it was salvageable. The title Messiah comes from a Hebrew word signifying "anointed" and harked back to the times of the Israelite kings, who were anointed by God through the intermediacy of the prophets. The anointment signified that he had been approved by God, and was under God's special protection, and was responsible to God for carrying out His mission. The Greek word *Christos*, from which we derive "Christ," has the identical meaning. Jesus was originally called "Jesus, the Christ," or Jesus, the anointed one, but what was originally a title came to be used as another name, as when we speak today of "Christ" instead of "the Christ." We are interested at this point in discussing the Anointed One under the title of Messiah, as that is the concern of the God of the Prophets; the Anointed One under the Greek title of the Christ we will leave for the next chapter.

The concept of the coming of the Messiah is a very important one in both Jewish and Christian religions, but on completely different grounds. For the Christian, he has come; for the Jew, he has not. It was the God of the Prophets' intention to direct everything toward that glorious day when His kingdom would reign supreme on earth. The concept was definitely a part of that of the approaching Judgment Day, to compensate for a fading faith in the original idea of swift retribution as part of God's justice. Since it was inconceivable that God could be other than just (in this sense of His having been created in the image of ideal man), the apparently missing justice must only have been postponed. There was a faint dawn of the idea of heaven, but for most part, the presumption was that the kingdom of God would be established right here on earth. The nations that had persecuted Israel would be judged and punished, and the wicked amongst the descendants of Jacob would get their just deserts.

In this new utopia, when the world would be under the direct control of God or of His Anointed One, everybody would live happily ever after. Swords would be beaten into plowshares and spears into pruning hooks. The tribes that had been scattered in the captivities of Assyria and of Babylon would return to Zion, and the whole of the world that remained after disposing of the sinners and the enemies of Israel would coexist peacefully. Some of the prophets saw the coming as accompanied by splendiferous fireworks, earthquakes, whirlwinds, thunder and lightning, and a sky full of apocalyptic visions of cavalry, chariots, and archers. God would be seen radiant on His splendid golden throne, surrounded by heavenly hosts singing hallelujahs. Others expected a simple unannounced coming that would develop as it went along.

Haggai, for instance, was convinced that Zerubbabel, who reorganized the people and rebuilt the temple after the return from the Exile, was the Messiah, but his predictions (Haggai 2) fizzled. Isaiah foresaw a quiet coming:

> For to us a child is born...and the government will be on his shoulders, and his name will be Mighty God, Everlasting

> Father, Prince of Peace....of peace there will be no end....with justice and righteousness....forevermore. (Isaiah 9:6, 7)

> I will raise up for David a righteous Branch, and he shall reign as king....Judah will be saved, and Israel will dwell securely. (Jeremiah 23:5)

> There shall come forth a shoot from the stump of Jesse....with righteousness he will judge the poor, and decide with equity for the meek....the wolf shall dwell with the lamb, and the leopard shall lie down with the kid...and a little child shall lead them. (Isaiah 11:1,4, 6)

Jesse was David's father, and the Messiah was expected to be a descendant of David and, like David, a great military king who could take the reins of government in mighty hands, lay low the enemy, and rule with justice and mercy.

Daniel, too, had his apocalyptic visions, including the perfect ruler and the good days to come:

> ...there came one like a son of man...and to him was given dominion and glory and kingdom, that all peoples, nations and languages should serve him...an everlasting dominion which shall not pass away.... (Daniel 7:13, 14)

Esdras' vision was more in accord with our picture of Paradise. He had a vision of the Son of God:

> And in the midst of them there was a young man of high stature....and on every one of their heads he set crowns....these be they that have put off the mortal clothing and put on the immortal, and have confessed the name of God. (2 Esdras 2:43–45)

Besides being a descendant of David, there were other signs for recognizing the Messiah:

> But you, O Bethlehem...from you shall come forth for me one who is to be ruler in Israel....and they shall dwell secure, for now he shall be great to the ends of the earth. (Micah 5:2, 4)

> Lo, your king comes to you; triumphant and victorious is he, humble and riding on an ass....and he shall command peace to the nations; his dominion shall be from sea to sea. (Zecheriah 9:9, 10)

The differences between the Jewish and Christian concepts of the Messiah cannot be overemphasized. Most Christians understand the Messiah as having some supernatural origin, and in Christian doctrine, the titles of Messiah and Christ have both been elevated to a transcendence far beyond their original meaning. To avoid a misunderstanding of the God of the Prophets, and His promise of Messianic deliverance, we must keep in mind that the Jewish Messiah is basically a natural man, with absolutely no supernatural origins. This is no more than a natural consequence of the purity of Jewish monotheism.

It would be a mistake to consider the air of holiness that accompanies the Jewish Anointed Ones to indicate a supernatural origin. They are holy in the sense that the man-made altars and the vessel consecrated to the use of the temple are holy—because of their contact with God or because of their consecration to God's use. In the case of David and Saul, they were anointed and consecrated by Samuel at the direction of God:

> Then Samuel took a horn of oil, and anointed him in the midst of his brothers, and the Spirit of the Lord came mightily on David from that day forward. (1 Samuel 16:13)

The holiness felt by the people in the presence of the anointed is expressed time and again:

> Shall not Shimei be put to death for this, because he cursed the Lord's anointed? (2 Samuel 19:21)

> David said, "The Lord forbid that I should...put forth my hand against him, seeing he is the Lord's anointed"....(1 Samuel 24:6)

We find in Psalm 2 a hymn which was evidently written on the occasion of the coronation of a new king:

> The Lord...said to me, "You are my son, today I have begotten you...." (Psalms 2:7)

The new king is speaking, and indicates thus his belief that the ceremony of anointment has put him on a new plane in his relations to God.

The fact that the kings were regularly anointed and that the yearned-for Messiah was in reality nothing beyond an especially anointed representative of God, although on a higher level of capability, with whom God could work more intimately and effectively, led to the acceptance from time to time of certain individuals as the anticipated Messiah. His responsibility was to be a leader of the people of Israel, a good and just man, capable of reigning righteously and concurrently destroying the enemies of Israel.

We have already mentioned Zerubbabel as one of these whom the prophet Haggai perceived as the Messiah, because of his ability in organizing the people and rebuilding the glory of the temple. But this was the limit of his achievement, and afterwards he was no longer considered to be the Messiah. Judas Maccabeus, because of his organizing ability and his military genius in defeating the enemies of Israel, even when far outnumbered, was considered by many to be the Messiah, but was unfortunately slain in battle before everything was put in order. Many followed who either claimed Messiah-ship for themselves, or had it attributed to them by others, but in no case did the hoped-for utopia materialize.

The man who probably came the closest to realizing the dream of Judaism in the eyes of the people, and who was accepted as the Messiah during his lifetime, was Simon bar Kozeba. He raised an army of 200,000 men and in a very short period was said to have conquered fifty fortified cities and 945 towns and villages. He temporarily succeeded in lifting the foreign yoke of oppression, and reigned for two and a half years as the invincible king of Zion, holding the mighty Roman Empire at bay. But the Romans could not allow such a stain on their escutcheon. He was finally vanquished by Julius Severus in 135 A.D., but it took fifty-two battles to accomplish the feat.

Others arose from time to time. As recently as the middle of the seventeenth century, Sabbathai Zewi was able to attract a wide following as the expected Messiah, and there was great rejuvenation of Zionist hopes. But this too faded away when he was captured by the Turkish authorities and became a Moslem—probably to save his skin, but definitely to the disenchantment of his followers.

We are hard-pressed to find a passage amongst the Old Testament prophecies that really predicts the concept of the Messiah as it is presented in the Gospel according to St. John. The God of the Prophets, evolved as He has, is still a simple God, alone except for His angels. He allows the human race to proceed on its own, with infrequent interference, but He does have definite plans for future amelioration, and we are only now beginning to see them unveiled.

The translators of the Old Testament have studiously avoided the use in English of the title Messiah, speaking practically always of "the anointed," but the meaning is the same, and we must remember this.

In short, we find that the God of the Prophets has lost the characteristics of a tribal god, has become somewhat less bloodthirsty, but is still jealous and vengeful, is still simple and serious. In two ways, He is radically different from the God of the Patriarchs: He prefers right to rite, and, recognizing that His administration of justice and retribution to date has not been satisfactory, He has consequently made plans for future redressing of evils. Commensurate with the development of a people who have more leisure for philosophic meditation, He has discernible plans for the continued existence of the soul after the body has perished.

# Chapter 6: The Father God

> Our Father, who art in heaven, hallowed be thy name. Thy kingdom come, thy will be done, on earth as it is in heaven....
> (Matthew 6:9, 10)

We now come to the next step in the evolution of God: the appearance of the Father God. The change was neither gradual nor slight; the differences we find are definitely in the character of a mutation. Certainly, many of the characteristics of the Father God were foreshadowed in the lives and philosophies of the Essene sect a century or two before the advent of Jesus, but this was a small, isolated group; their ideas were not shared by the rest of Judea, and they had no connection to Jesus himself, who is central to the concept of the Father God. Further, our sparse knowledge of the Essene thought is shrouded in the mists of history, with only recently a bit of clarification resulting from the discovery of the Dead Sea scrolls.

The scriptures of the New Testament, which present our picture of the Father God, cover a very short period in comparison with the periods covered in what Christians refer to as the Old Testament. Beginning in the year 4004 B.C. or 3761, B.C. (depending on whether you want to take Archbishop Ussher or Jewish tradition as the authority for the date of Creation), the God of the Patriarchs was preeminent for three millennia, or approximately until the time of David, between about 950 and 1000 B.C. There was some overlap in influence, but the God of the Prophets was more prominent on the stage of history from about this time until the end of the Old Testament times, about six hundred years.

The periods mentioned are the times covered in the history of the Hebrews, as written in the Bible. The largest part of this was the subject of oral tradition, and reduction to writing was done generally quite some time after the happenings described. It is true that tradition ascribes the books of Moses to Moses himself, in which case they could have been composed about 1200 B.C. or slightly later, but most evidence indicates that they were the product of several authors, not including Moses. It is thought by some that Moses was capable of writing, and if so probably used the Babylonian cuneiform script; he may have written some laws and history which were later used as part of the basis for the Pentateuch. But the most likely origin was the oral tradition, which is subject to alteration from the memory of one oral historian to another, unless one believes that inspiration of God actually produces word-for-word authenticity in the Scriptures.

The rest of the Old Testament, while it conflicts with some other historical sources, is confirmed by history as well as might be expected from our experience with historians, their sources, and their prejudices. Best evidence indicates that the writing of the Old Testament spread over a period of some eight centuries, from around 850 or 950 B.C. till around 150 B.C., when it is believed the Book of Esther was written, and the Book of Psalms reached its present form. The final selection of the books to be included in the Jewish Bible was made by a group of Jewish scholars in Jamnia around 90 A.D.

In contrast, the story covered by the New Testament developed over a comparatively short period. Except for the story of the Virgin Birth and a few tales of young Jesus, the period of history covered is from about 27 A.D., around the time of the baptism of Jesus, to about 67 A.D., the time of the execution of Paul. The time span during which the writings themselves were recorded was only about fifty years, from the first epistles of Paul to the writing of the Gospel of St. John. Two centuries had lapsed from the last writings of the Old Testament to the first of the New. It will be another five centuries before another widely accepted scripture appears on the scene, the Koran.

Thus, the period covered by the New Testament—also the period during which the concept of the Father God arose—was short but influential. The 1973 Britannica Book of the Year shows 1,024,106,500 followers of the Christian faith in the world, as compared with 13,989,650 Jews. There are also over 500,000,000 Muslims. Still, Jews who might feel in the minority can console themselves with the fact that both Christianity and Islam have firm roots in Judaism, and would not have existed without Judaism as a foundation. In this sense, the seed of Abraham might be said to have multiplied in marvelous abundance.

The Father God made His appearance in a hostile environment. Still, His amazing stamina and vitality were such as to enable Him to survive through an adverse period, till He found an environment more suitable, after which He thrived and outgrew all competition. It was inevitable that with such growth and expansion, there would develop several sub-species of the Father God, as we find many sub-species of cattle resulting from Darwin's evolutionary processes. Each of the sub-species—Orthodox, Roman Catholic, Protestant—has its varieties, but all can readily be traced back to the original Father God of the New Testament, just as we can trace the origin of the Father God back to His antecedents.

The identifying characteristics of the Father God are in many ways different from those of the God of the Prophets. To begin with, He is no longer bloodthirsty, and His sternness has greatly mellowed. His inclination toward ruthless vengeance has almost disappeared. He no longer makes personal appearances, nor do we even hear the words so common in the Old Testament, "Says the Lord." The Father God has no interest in burnt sacrifices, complicated rituals, or fancy ceremonies. His exclusive posture toward the Chosen People falls away, and He becomes a God ready to receive the entire world, without any restrictions or limitations. Almost no trace of legalism remains in the Father God.

The most outstanding characteristic of the Father God is that He is a God of Love, to the extent that many Christians follow John in saying, God is love:

> God is love, and he who abides in love abides in God, and God abides in him. (1 John 4:16)

It is true that both the God of the Patriarchs and the God of the Prophets expressed love for their people, and demanded love from them, toward themselves, and toward others:

In clarification—and possibly oversimplification—we can say that the basic characteristic of the New Testament God is Love; that of the Old Testament God is Holiness.

> You shall not take vengeance or bear any grudge....but you shall love your neighbor as yourself.... (Leviticus 19:18)

The admonition was there, but it was subordinate to an avalanche of other laws, regulations, and ordinances. And the idea of loving one's enemies was entirely new. The point is that there is a qualitative difference between a God who loves and a God who is love. One feels comfortable with the assertion that the Father God is Love. Certainly no one could feel as comfortable with an assertion that any of the other Gods we have mentioned—Ra, Zeus, Jehovah—is love.

What did John actually mean by affirming that "God is Love"? There are many different kinds of love: sexual love and brotherly love—which have been expressed by some writers as Eros and Agape—are two important varieties. The love of the Gods of the Old Testament seemed to be that expressed by a Creator for His creation. This love was a jealous love, fearful of the competition of other gods and idols. It could readily change if the people did not behave according to God's strict standards, and the resulting punishments could be extreme. Yet, when His people had thus been alienated for a while, God began to feel His loss, and He was again ready to express His love and take them back into the fold. Thus, one sometimes cannot avoid the impression that this sort of love is essentially a desire for possession, given in order to solidify the bond between Creator and creation.

That "God is Love," on the other hand, means that love is God's very nature, rather than something He does. In this way, love itself, rather than possession, is most essential to the bond between God and His creation. This does not, however, exclude punishment or the threat of punishment. In this way, the relationship between God and His people is closer to that between a father and His children; a wise and loving father will both threaten and punish His children, knowing that the results will make them better adapted to life.

The love of the Father God, expressed in modern theology by the Greek word "agape," is a form of brotherly love. It is a charitable love which some people have naturally. Will Rogers expressed it well when he said, "I never met a man I didn't like." When Christ was asked which was the greatest commandment, he said:

> You shall love the Lord your God with all your heart, with all your soul, and with all your mind....you shall love your neighbor as yourself. On these two commandments depend all the law and the prophets. (Matthew 22:37–40)

Or as one great religious philosopher expressed it, "These are the commandments. All else is commentary."

It has been claimed that those who have faith in Jesus will be visited by the Holy Spirit, and will then presumably be able to love their fellow beings. Perhaps this is the answer; unfortunately there is little solid evidence to support this affirmation. Most of us know a neighbor or so that we would find extremely difficult to love.

Though the above may seem to digress from a discussion of the characteristics of the Father God, I hold that it is important, in order to be able to understand Him, to understand the nature of the Love that is His most distinguishing characteristic. Here are some words of Paul on the importance of love:

> If I speak in the tongues of men and angels, but have not love, I am a noisy gong or clanging cymbal. And if I have prophetic powers, and understand all mysteries and all knowledge, and if I have all faith, so as to remove mountains, but have not love, I gain nothing. Love is patient and kind; love is not jealous or boastful; it is not arrogant or rude. Love does not insist on its own way....it does not rejoice at wrong, but rejoices in right. Love bears all things, believes all things, hopes all things, endures all things... (1 Corinthians 13:1–7)

It would be difficult to add anything meaningful to that.

It is necessary to go at length into the story of Jesus the Christ, not only in that he is an integral part of the Trinity that later evolved, but also to show that there is absolutely no doubt of his position as God's representative. This, because we must draw our picture of the Father God almost wholly from the testimony of Jesus, since God no longer either appears or speaks in the New Testament:

> In many and various ways God spoke to our fathers by the prophets; but in these days he has spoken to us by a Son.... (Hebrews 1:1, 2)

Another important aspect of the Father God, at least as He is worshiped by many groups today, relates to the issue of the Trinity. From the evolutionary point of view, we can say that there are actually two Father Gods, the Unitarian and the Trinitarian. As far as concerns most of the attributes and characteristics of God, especially God's relations to the world and its people, they are essentially identical. They are identical in their loving character, in their seriousness, in their promises of retribution and eternity. Both of them have their sub-species and varieties, but the variations are not dependent on whether the God is unitarian or triune. We might say that the difference is as between white rabbits and black rabbits. The Unitarian God is cultivated in one environment, the Trinitarian in another, but except for the preference of one or the other, the environments are quite similar, and the two Father Gods fit well into either.

There is little in the New Testament to warn of the advent of the triune God. The idea did not come from Jesus' teachings, but arose from interpretations of his teachings, which identify Jesus as the literal son of God, and therefore a portion of the composite Godhead. Besides God the Father and God the Son, Trinitarians believe in a third element, God the Holy Spirit. The Unitarians object, calling this three-in-one conception of God polytheism.

This issue gives rise to another important question in Christianity: Who is Jesus? Is he human or divine? Is he a part of God, or is he a separate deity? In the scriptures themselves, Jesus often presents himself as a messenger of God, but he also uses expressions such as "Son of God" and "Son of Man." There are references to his sitting on a throne at the right hand of God which definitely imply a separate identity.

> [God] raised him [Jesus] from the dead and made him sit at his right hand in the heavenly places. (Ephesians 1:20)

The statement by John that he was there from the beginning does not absolutely prove divinity, for the Bible refers also to angels as having been there from the very beginning. It is true that at one point, John quotes Jesus, saying:

> I and the Father are one. (John 10:30)

Jesus has been considered everything from a great rabbi, a great teacher; a prophet; a representative of God with powers evolving from a virgin birth conceived by the Holy Spirit; to a part of God Himself. And at the other extreme, considered an impostor and a heretic. Sufficient evidence exists in the scriptures, depending upon interpretation, to support all these views. Consequently, the various views of Jesus and his relation to the Father God continue to coexist. For purposes of the remainder of this discussion, we focus primarily on the view of the singular God, as that is how He is largely presented in the scriptural texts.

It seems rather strange that a story which has subsequently been elevated to such paramount importance, that of the Virgin Birth of Jesus, is mentioned only at the beginnings of the books of Luke and Matthew; it is completely ignored in both Mark and John, and never again referred to anywhere else in the New Testament. It seems inconceivable that something that is to gain such tremendous significance could be ignored to the extent that only Luke elaborates on the original story. One is tempted to wonder if there is validity to the assertion of those, amongst whom are modern Christian theologians, who claim that the story is a legend invented to impress people with the authenticity of Jesus' mission.

Mohammed also felt this way. He based Islam completely on the Judeo-Christian tradition, but does call for a few "corrections" here and there of what he considers errors that have crept into the Scriptures:

> Allah forbid that He Himself should beget a son! When he decrees a thing He need only say: "Be," and it is....those who say: "The Lord of Mercy has begotten a son," preach a monstrous falsehood....it does not become him to beget one. (Koran, Sura 19: 88)

Paul, who was appointed by Jesus himself to carry his message, is quite specific about it:

> ....the gospel concerning his Son, who was descended from David according to the flesh and designated as Son of God in power.... (Romans 1:3, 4)

Matthew says of the Virgin Birth:

> All this took place to fulfill what the Lord had spoken by the prophet: "Behold, a virgin shall conceive and bear a son, and his name shall be called Emanuel." (Matthew 1:22, 23)

Matthew, however, evidently had not read his Scriptures carefully. In the original reference in (Isaiah 7:14), the prophet was responding to the problems of King Ahaz. The virgin birth mentioned was a sign promised by God to Ahaz personally, not a reference to an event that would happen 730 years later and be of no help to Ahaz.

This was not the only occasion in our studies that God was credited with an improbable birth:

> The Lord visited Sarah as he had said, and the Lord did to Sarah as he had promised. And Sarah conceived, and bore

Abraham a son in his old age. (Genesis 21:1, 2)

....Elizabeth in her old age has also conceived a son....her who was called barren. (Luke 1:36, 37)

For with God nothing will be impossible. It was only several centuries later that the developing doctrine of the Trinity claimed that the Holy Spirit was part of God. In this case, the proper interpretation seems to be that the Spirit was the instrument of God, and as Mohammed expressed, when God said, "Be" it was done.

As for the expression "Son of God," often used in referring to Jesus, this is not to be interpreted in the literal sense, any more than it is when men in general are referred to as sons of God:

All who are led by the Spirit of God are sons of God. (Romans 8:14)

For in Christ Jesus you are all sons of God....(Galatians 2:26)

Christ is also referred to as the Son of man, without a literal meaning behind the figurative speech. (Matthew 16:28, 25:31; Mark 13:26; Luke 12:40, 22:22)

When the Son of man shall come in his glory, and all the holy angels with him, then shall he sit upon the throne of his glory. (Matthew 25:31)

We also see that:

...He has spoken to us by a Son, whom he appointed heir of all things, through whom he also created the world...when he had made purification for sins, he sat down at the right hand of the Majesty on high.... (Hebrews 1:2, 3)

Although the implication is that Jesus is of heavenly origin, he is definitely represented as being a separate personage from God. Further evidence that the expression "Son" is either figurative or could be construed to be something like an adopted son is found later in the same book:

...Jesus, the apostle and high priest of our confession. He was faithful to him who appointed him, just as Moses also was faithful in God's house. (Hebrews 3:1, 2)

So also Christ did not exalt himself to be made a high priest, but was appointed by him who said to him, "Thou art my son, today I have begotten thee. (Hebrews 5:5)

The identical words were used when God spoke to his newly anointed king:

> ....the Lord said to me, "You are my son, today I have begotten you." (Psalms 2:7)

This is evidently a formula used by God to denote the official assumption of a responsibility on the part of an Anointed One, a Messiah, whether he be a king or Jesus.

There is of course room for doubt as to the proper interpretation, and it is just this room for doubt that subsequently opened the door for the appearance of the triune God. The Bible in all its parts has always been open to interpretation. As James Branch Cabell said, "The true test of a church member is that, when the Bible says something that is inconvenient, he assumes that it really means something else."

Still, the preponderance of evidence in the New Testament presents Jesus as a Messiah, an Anointed One. For Jesus, the anointing ceremony was performed when John the Baptist baptized him, when:

> ...he saw the Spirit of God descending like a dove, and alighting on him; and lo, a voice from heaven, saying, "This is my beloved Son, with whom I am well-pleased." (Matthew 3:16, 17)

Again, we hear the formula for confirmation similar to that given in Psalm 2.

In passing, we should also add that there is no significance in Jesus referring to God as "my Father" since he also refers to Him often as "your Father" when addressing his disciples or his congregations. Note also Jesus' admonition:

> ....love your enemies....so that you may be sons of your Father who is in heaven.... (Matthew 5:44, 45)

It is important to remember in this connection, that Jesus is recognized by many as a Messiah, and makes the claim himself:

> The woman said to him, "I know that Messiah is coming...."
> Jesus said to her, "I who speak to you am he." (John 4:25, 26)

Even with all the support for Jesus being the son of God and of the predicted birth, his actions do not totally fulfill the prophecy envisioned in the Old Testament. This is not the Messiah who would take the reins of the government in hand and bring the era of peace and prosperity to the Jews:

> "Behold, the days are coming," says the Lord, "when I will raise up for David a righteous Branch, and he shall reign as a king and deal wisely....Judah will be saved and Israel will dwell securely." (Jeremiah 23, 5, 6)

Even his own apostles were of like mind about the Messiah they themselves expected. After Jesus had arisen from his tomb and had spent forty days with them:

> ....they asked him, "Lord, will you at this time restore the kingdom to Israel?" (Acts 1:6)

They obtained their answer rather quickly. As he was talking, he was "lifted up, and a cloud took him out of their sight." And that was the last anyone heard of Jesus, until he appeared to Saul on the road to Damascus and made a Christian out of him. Then nothing more was heard from him, at least as far as the Biblical Scriptures are concerned.

No wonder the majority of the Jews, still under the grinding Roman heel, could not conceive of Jesus as their promised Messiah.

Whether or not he was part of the Divinity, there still remains the question of whether Jesus was of heavenly origin. On this question, the synoptic Gospels (those that are in essential agreement with each other: Matthew, Mark, and Luke) differ somewhat from the Gospel of John. It may be well to remember that from the style and mode of address, the synoptic Gospels are evidently written for the Jewish public, while that of John is quite obviously addressed to the Gentiles. John feels he needs a different, perhaps more impressive approach to make an impact on an audience for whom the whole story is new and foreign. In addition to the previously cited assertions referring to the eternally pre-existing presence of Jesus as the Word, John quotes Jesus:

> I have come down from heaven, not to do my own will, but the will of Him who sent me. (John 6:38)

> He said to them, "You are from below, I am from above; you are of this world, I am not of this world." (John 8:23)

> Truly, I say to you, before Abraham was, I am. (John 8:58)

The closest we come to this view in the synoptic gospels is in:

> He said to them, "But who do you say that I am?" Simon Peter replied, "You are the Christ, the Son of the living God." And Jesus answered him, "Blessed are you, Simon bar-Jona! For flesh and blood has not revealed this to you, but my Father, who is in heaven." (Matthew 16:15–17)

From this we observe a special relationship between Jesus and God, including the inspiration from God which enabled Peter to recognize the Christ, the Anointed One, without having been told. This special relationship is used to communicate the message of God, as well as for exercising other aspects of his God-given authority:

> "But that you may know that the Son of man has authority on earth to forgive sins"—he said to the man who was paralyzed—"I say to you, rise, take up your bed and go home." And immediately he rose before them....(Luke 5:24, 25)

This special relationship is thoroughly demonstrated not only by prolific miracle-working, but also by the miraculous end of the story, and the fact that Jesus knew it was coming.

> From that time Jesus began to show his disciples that he must go to Jerusalem and suffer many things from the elders and chief priests, and scribes and be killed, and on the third day be raised. (Matthew 16:21)

> ....Jesus said, "Truly I say to you, one of you will betray me, one who is eating with me." (Mark 14:18)

> He said, "I tell you Peter, the cock will not crow this day, until you three times deny that you know me." (Luke 22:34)

The subsequent story of the resurrection and assumption to heaven in a cloud is well known, and it underscores the nature of this special relationship.

We have already seen the evolution from the God of the Patriarchs, who placed so much emphasis on rites and sacrifices, to the God of the Prophets, who emphasized obedience to the laws more than in the rites and sacrifices. Now we evolve one step further with the Father God, who is perceived to be more interested in His people doing good, being loving, and being charitable.

This characteristic of the Father God contributes to adaptation to the environment of intellectually developing humankind. Erich Fromm said, "Authoritarian ethics denies man's capacity to know what is good or bad." (Fromm, *Man for Himself*). Humans want to feel ethically and morally responsible, rather than being slavishly obedient to a strict, dictated set of arbitrary rules.

Christ's message is first and foremost love, as we have discussed. Next, it presents a relaxation away from the strict, detailed legal code of Moses into a freer ethical code. The scriptures show Jesus himself confusing the Pharisees with his relaxed attitude toward the Sabbath and toward the cleanliness laws.

This is just the beginning of the appearance of the Father God, and as we mentioned, He appeared in a hostile environment. The sects of the Pharisees and the Sadducees who together constituted the large majority of the people, had practically complete control of the priesthood as well as what administration was allowed by the Roman overlords. To them for whom strict observance of the law was an unquestioned necessity, Jesus was a heretic, a rabble-rousing disturber of the peace. They were mortally afraid of the power he was exerting over the people through his personality, his preaching, and his miracle-working.

Thus, after Jesus' crucifixion, the Father God's existence was itself threatened. The apostles were on the point of disbanding in disillusionment, but rallied at the resurrection. Still, their influence in the community was inconsequential; the church was weak and threatened by hostile forces on all sides. Had it not been for Saul of Tarsus—who, from being one of the foremost persecutors of this new sect, became one of its most ardent supporters after his vision of Jesus on the road to Damascus—the world might never have heard of the Father God.

Saul, who changed his name to Paul, owed the success of his enterprise to the fact that he brought the Father God into an environment to which He was much better adapted, and in which He began to thrive. The area Saul covered—Asia Minor, Greece, and later Rome—was occupied by a society of people who were not focused on legality. Their manner of life was founded on Hellenistic philosophy, with its prodigious variety based on the all-encompassing studies of Aristotle. It ranged from the followers of Epicurus, who considered pleasure and pain to be the chief good and evil; to the Stoic school, founded by Zeno, who disparaged pleasure, believed in the control of nature by God, and was convinced that the highest good was to live in accordance with nature. Here was fertile ground for the nourishment and growth of the new Father God.

It is probable that Paul chose to carry out his mission by bringing the message to the Gentiles because he did not feel comfortable among the Jews, after having changed his views so radically. Whatever the reason, Paul spent most of his days with the Gentiles. He personally relaxed legalism even further, supposedly with the approval of the Father God who had approached him through Jesus. With the support of Peter, he declared freedom both from the demands of circumcision and from the dietary laws. In so doing, he met with opposition from the mother church in Jerusalem, but ultimately was able to convince them that it was more important to amass followers of the ethic of Jesus, than to risk alienating them by insisting on adherence to rigid rules which had no evident logical basis and upon which Jesus himself had never insisted.

Hence, we find that the Father God ultimately abandoned the legalistic approach, and His focus became the commandment to love already mentioned and the Golden Rule:

> So whatever you wish that men would do to you, do so to them; for this is the law and the prophets. (Matthew 7:12)

The relationship of the Father God to His people is characterized by grace, in contrast with the contractual relationship of the Old Testament Gods arising from the covenant. The attitude of God may be inferred from the fact that Jesus almost invariably refers to Him as "the Father," "my Father" or "your Father," implying a relationship between God and His people more like a loving parent with His children than that of an autocratic Creator with his creations. The occasions when he mentions "God" as such are quite rare, and made only where the appellation Father would seem inappropriate. For instance, when the Pharisees asked about divorce, Jesus quoted the Bible:

> God made them male and female....the two shall become one. So they are no longer two but one. What therefore God has joined together, let not man put asunder. (Mark 10:6–9)

Later, when again the Pharisees sought to trap him in heretical answers, he says:

> Render unto Caesar the things which are Caesar's and unto God the things that are God's. (Mark 12:17)

In general, Jesus refers to "God" when disputing with the doctrinaire Pharisees, but to "Father" in talking with the apostles and in preaching to the people.

The Pharisees objected when the disciples plucked grain on the Sabbath; Jesus reminded them that David had eaten the bread of the Temple, and given some to his associates when they were hungry.

> The Pharisees said...."Why are they doing what is not lawful on the Sabbath?"....And he said to them, "The Sabbath was made for man, not man for the Sabbath." (Mark 2:24, 27)

Jesus harks back to when God told Noah that all living things that breathe were food for him, in abrogating the dietary laws:

> "....whatever goes into a man from outside cannot defile him, since it enters, not his heart but his stomach, and so passes on." Thus he declared all foods clean...."What comes out of a man is what defiles a man....evil thoughts, fornication, theft, murder, adultery, coveting, wickedness, deceit, envy, slander, pride...." (Mark 7:18–22)

This teaching was reinforced later from heaven by Peter's vision in a trance:

> ....the heaven opened, and something descending, like a great sheet....in it were all kinds of animals and reptiles and birds of the air. And there came a voice [Christ's] to him, "Rise, Peter; kill and eat." But Peter said, "I have never eaten anything that is common or unclean." And the voice...."What God has cleansed, you must not call common." (Acts 10:11–15)

Paul, in writing to his Gentile converts, summarizes it very plainly:

> God....having canceled the bond which stood against us with its legal demands; this he set aside, nailing it to the cross....Therefore let no one pass judgment on you in questions of food and drink or with regard to a festival or a new moon or a Sabbath. (Colossians 2:14, 16)

And the same applies to circumcision:

> Circumcision indeed is of value if you obey the law; but if you break the law, your circumcision becomes uncircumcision...He is a Jew who is one inwardly, and real circumcision is a matter of the heart, spiritual and not literal. (Romans 2:25, 29)

Though legalistic rules and practices were abandoned, the Father God still had important conditions. Jesus indicated that the commandments to love God and one's neighbor were all that was required, but on the assumption that the hearer would understand what that signified and act accordingly. For those that did not, the meaning was spelled out. In addition, faith and a belief in Jesus himself was required. The requirement of faith we will discuss later. For the rest, it was a question of a proper moral and ethical life, and a contempt for materialism and the wealth of this world. To the young man who asked what he must do to deserve eternal life, in addition to keeping the commandments:

> Jesus said, "If you would be perfect, go, sell what you possess and give to the poor, and you will have treasure in heaven; and come, follow me...." the young man....went away sorrowful; for he had great possessions. (Matthew 19:21, 22)

Jesus watched him go, murmuring sadly, "It is easier for a camel to go through the eye of a needle than for a rich man to enter the kingdom of God."

For the Old Testament, in the absence of heaven or hell, punishment and reward must be earthly, and the righteous could be rewarded by riches— especially Solomon. But Christianity allows for the conflict of poor versus rich, and possessions are deemed evil. We are told of the rich man in hell, who in anguished thirst asks Father Abraham to have Lazarus dip his finger-tip in water and cool his tongue. Abraham refused:

> But Abraham said, "Son, remember that you in your lifetime received your good things, and Lazarus in like manner evil things; but now he is comforted here, and you are in anguish." (Luke 16:25)

For Jesus, worldly possessions were of no consequence; the important thing was how one would spend eternity.

As one great philosopher observed, in Christianity, "all deeds are to be looked upon solely with respect to their supernatural consequences, not with respect to their natural results." (Nietzsche, The Joyful Wisdom)

> ....whatever a man sows, that he will also reap....let us not grow weary in well-doing, for in due season we shall reap [eternal life]. (Galatians 6:7, 9)

Despite Jesus' attitude toward wealth and his concentration on the rewards of the afterlife, it would be a mistake to think that the Father God wants people to live lives of complete asceticism. The idea of drawing away from life, giving up all comforts, and concentrating only on prayer and meditation, which appeared about the time of the Trinitarian God and lasted through the Middle Ages, had absolutely no foundation in the teachings of Jesus. Love and charity were the decrees of the Father God; this was not the focal point of the life of the hermit.

Jesus himself was extremely sociable, visiting with people in all walks of life, from harlots to wealthy citizens. Even his first miracle was performed when attending a wedding feast, where he turned water into wine to keep the festivities jolly. Jesus compared himself with John the Baptist, who was an anchorite:

> For John the Baptist has come eating no bread and drinking no wine....the Son of man has come eating and drinking.... (Luke 7:33, 34)

Another of the Father God's characteristics was that He detests hypocrisy and pride:

> Beware of practicing your piety before men in order to be seen by them; for then you will have no reward from your Father who is in heaven. (Matthew 6:1)

> God opposes the proud, but gives grace to the humble. (1 Peter 5:5)

> Judge not, and you will not be judged.... (Luke 6:37)

For the rest, there are catalogs of what God likes and what He disapproves:

> Now the works of the flesh are plain: immorality, impurity, licentiousness, idolatry, sorcery, enmity, strife, jealousy, anger, selfishness, dissension, envy, drunkenness....those who do such things shall not inherit the kingdom of God. But the fruit of the

> Spirit is love, joy, peace, patience, kindness, goodness, faithfulness, gentleness, self-control.... (Galatians 5:19–23)

It is to be particularly noted that one's good actions are not to be simply for the benefit of those one likes, but for everyone with whom one comes in contact, enemies as well as friends:

> ....love your enemies and pray for those who persecute you....for if you love those who love you, what reward have you? Do not even the tax collectors do the same? (Matthew 5:44, 46)

People in those days evidently did not have a high regard for tax collectors, which is not to be wondered at, as they operated by keeping an arbitrary part of what they collected.

One's credit in heaven was the same whether you treated a beggar or Jesus himself well:

> Truly, I say to you, as you did it to the least of these my brethren, you did it to me. (Matthew 25:40)

St. Paul was specific about the change from legalism:

> ....the law was our custodian until Christ came....But now that faith has come we are no longer under a custodian; for in Christ Jesus you are all sons of God.... (Galatians 3:24–26)

In abandoning a strictly detailed set of authoritative rules and replacing it with a general ethic, the Father God is responding to advancement of humans as individuals, with their ability to assume personal responsibility, to decide for themselves whether an act is morally right, to select their own paths. People could no longer clear their conscience simply by following the rules for the Sabbath, the rules for tithing, and the rules for cleanliness, while closing their hearts to the needs of those around them. In a way, this made life more difficult, requiring that people make personal decisions and a psychological effort rather than blindly following a rigid track, but it was more personally rewarding and more satisfying to one's self-respect.

It is expedient at this point to insert the observation that this approach is neither unique, nor does it originate with Christ. Buddha's teaching, five centuries before Jesus, was a moral and ethical teaching unencumbered by either strict ritual or a detailed catalog of legal codes. Neither the pagan gods of the Greeks and Romans nor the transcendent gods of Plato and the Stoics demanded blind adherence to a complicated regimen of law. Modern Reform Judaism follows a moral and ethic that is almost indistinguishable from the morals and ethics preached by their fellow-Jew, Jesus. Even the atheistic communists preach brotherhood.

Accounting is done by the Father God, not through earthly retribution, but after one's life has been lived. It is not made clear whether one will go directly to heaven or hell, or will sleep in the tomb until Judgment Day, but in relation to eternity, the difference is minor. Rewards and punishments will be meted out. The drawback is that there are only two possibilities, everything is either black or white, guilty or not guilty, heaven or hell. Early Christian theologians were unable to accept that a little lie, a bit of envy, or a touch of gluttony would put a person on the same level as murderers and adulterers, relegated to hell fire. They developed the idea of purgatory, "all who die in peace with the church, but are not perfect, pass into purgatory," where the souls of those guilty only of venial sins can spend some time being cleansed before passing on into Paradise.

Very little in the Bible substantiates the idea of purgatory, unless one wants to stretch one's imagination based on a couple of brief references to praying for the dead. (1 Peter 4:6; 2 Maccabees 12:44, 45) Still, it seems more probable that here the dead are considered to be sleeping, waiting for the Day of Judgment. The Father God presented in the New Testament has no half-way measures. We can only comment that the Father God who administers purgatory is a later variation on the concept of reward and punishment in the afterlife. When the time comes:

> For the trumpet will sound, and the dead will be raised imperishable. (1 Corinthians 15:52)

> When the Son of man comes in his glory....he will sit on his glorious throne....he will place the sheep at his right hand, but the goats at the left....and the [sinners] will go away into eternal punishment, but the righteous into eternal life. (Matthew 25:31, 33, 46)

> When the Lord Jesus is revealed from heaven with his mighty angels in flaming fire....those who do not know God and....those who do not obey the gospel of our Lord Jesus shall....suffer the punishment of eternal destruction.... (2 Thessalonians 1:7, 8)

Presumably, the Father God must allow for some straying from perfection. There are two escape hatches—faith and repentance:

> For this is the will of my Father, that everyone who sees the Son and believes in him shall have eternal life....(John 6:40)

The message in this passage is clear. It carries with it the assumption that those who believe in Jesus will automatically become righteous.

The one thing we do clearly discern in the New Testament's promise about the future is the imminence of Judgment Day. It is clear that the time is short, and not in just relative terms:

> Truly, I say to you, there are some standing here who will not taste death before they see the Son of man coming in his kingdom. (Matthew 16:28)

> Children, it is the last hour....many antichrists have come, therefore we know it is the last hour. (1 John 2:18)

And Paul cautions his followers to change their ways of life and prepare, "for the form of this world is passing away." (1 Corinthians 7:25–31)

We may wonder whether God thought to increase the chance of His people living righteously by threats of imminence of the Last Judgment. There is unfortunately no answer in the Scriptures. We are told to expect fireworks, so it is not surprising that people caught up in earthquakes and volcanic explosions think that the end of the world is coming:

> For nation will rise against nation....there will be famine and earthquakes....the sun will be darkened, and the moon will not give its light, and the stars will fall from heaven....and they will see the Son of man coming on the clouds of heaven.... (Matthew 24:7, 29, 30)

After nearly two thousand years, we are still waiting.

Like the previous Gods, the Father God could be called a male chauvinist. Woman's function was to produce enough babies to make up for the high rate of infant mortality, and to stay home taking care of the household chores and her brood. In these days before contraceptives when usually women became pregnant while still breast feeding their infants, there was just no way that most could fully partake in life outside the home. Women could not be expected to keep up with politics or other planning. We learn that women were subordinate to men in the following passage:

> Just then his disciples came. They marveled that he [Jesus] was talking with a woman. (John 4:27)

Jesus did not hesitate to talk with women, but also did not endeavor to liberate them. He had no female apostles, and he and his apostles evidently led celibate lives. Their attitude was obviously the origin of clerical celibacy in the Roman Catholic church:

> The unmarried man is anxious about the affairs of the Lord; but the married man is anxious about worldly affairs, how to please his wife. (1 Corinthians 7:32, 33)
>
> Now a bishop must be above reproach, married only once....manage his household well....for if a man does not know how to manage his own household, how... can he care for God's church? (1 Timothy 3:2, 5)

We must assume that the teaching of the apostles was either through what they learned from Jesus, or through inspiration from the Father God. At least we are heartened by the fact that although women were accounted as second-class citizens, they were accorded due respect and proper treatment:

> I permit no woman to teach or to have authority over men; she is to keep silent. (1 Timothy 2:12)
>
> You wives, be submissive to your husbands....Likewise you husbands, live considerately with your wives, bestowing honor on the woman as the weaker sex....(1 Peter 3:1, 7)

The Father God, though He does not make Himself manifest, does keep everything under control. Not only does Jesus repeatedly affirm that his authority comes from the Father, but it is also evident to those who listen to him:

> On the Sabbath, he entered the synagogue and taught. And they were astonished as his teaching, for he taught them as one who had authority, and not as the scribes. (Mark 1:21, 22)

Jesus was not only given the power to perform miracles in order to invest him with sufficient authority in the eyes of the public, but he was also empowered to transfer his authority and miracle-working ability to his disciples, so that they in turn could capture their audience and impart their message.

> And he called his twelve disciples and gave them authority over unclean spirits, to cast them out, and to heal every disease and every infirmity....[Jesus charged them] "do not be anxious about how you are to speak....for it is not you who speak, but the Spirit of your Father speaking through you." (Matthew 10:1, 19, 20)

The divine supervision even included the selection of the itinerary:

> [Paul and Timothy were] forbidden by the Holy Spirit to speak the word in Asia...they attempted to go to Bithynia, but the Spirit of Jesus did not allow them... (Acts 16:6, 7)

This was followed by a vision sending them to preach in Macedonia.

It is interesting to note that most of the miracles were performed among the Jews, and the mission to the Gentiles was concerned principally with sermons and preaching. This was a result of the realistic discernment of the difference between the Jews and the Gentiles that Paul understood so well:

> For the Jews demand signs and Greeks seek wisdom....(1 Corinthians 1:22)

The miracle-working of Jesus and his disciples showed nothing on the grand scale of the military victories of the Old Testament. This is hardly surprising, for the Jewish nation was living at peace with its neighbors under the Pax Romana during the short period of the disciples' activities. By far the greater part of the miracles were acts of mercy, casting out of unclean spirits, healing diseases, and raising people from the dead. Not only was this impressive to the people, but inherent benevolence of this sort of miracle induced a sympathetic feeling amongst appreciative bystanders.

There were a few miracles that did not come under this category. The changing of water into wine at the wedding feast did not even serve the purpose of a sign, since neither the host nor the guests knew that Jesus had brought it about, although the disciples were aware of it (John 2:1–11). The same applies to the withering of the unfortunate fig tree, caused by Jesus simply out of pique in not finding figs on the tree, even though it was out of season (Mark 11:13, 14, 20). Essentially they served as lessons to aid in convincing the disciples, as did the two occasions when Jesus fed the multitude from a few loaves of bread and some small fish (Matthew 14:15–21; 15:32–38).

As for the rest, the four gospels are replete with the healing miracles performed by Jesus, and Acts presents a long list of miracles wrought by the apostles, and for them by angels.

> And when this had taken place, the rest of the people on the island [of Malta] who had diseases also came and were cured [by Paul]. (Acts 28:9)

It would be superfluous to list further the multitudinous miracles reported; it is enough to comment that they are plentiful enough to establish that miracle-working was an important facet of the Father God.

Of course, the great miracle—the axis around which the whole narrative of the New Testament revolves—is the resurrection. Without it, the apostles would probably have disbanded after the crucifixion, and without any shadow of doubt it is the principal foundation for belief in the minds of the majority of the followers of the Christian religion, the ultimate guarantee of the authenticity of the Christ story. In the words of Peter:

> ....we preach Christ crucified. (1 Corinthians 1:23)

Unlike the raising of Lazarus or other cases of raising from the dead, this was not a miracle produced by a miracle-working man, but came directly from the machinations of heaven. Although Jesus himself had predicted it, his disciples had not believed his predictions. As a matter of fact, after they had seen Jesus raise others from the dead, and had heard his statement that he would return, there is something strangely puzzling about the stories of the return: the disbelief, the failure to recognize him, his appearance and disappearance on occasion. The performance was more what one might have expected from a ghost than from a physical body raised from the dead.

> And when they saw him, they worshiped him, but some doubted. (Matthew 28:17)

> But their eyes were kept from recognizing him....[later] their eyes were opened and they recognized him; and he vanished out of their sight. (Luke 24:16, 31)

> The doors were shut, but Jesus came and stood among [the disciples], and said, "Peace be with you." (John 20:26)

Still, after the first shock, they did accept him, and he remained with them for forty days, long enough to convince even doubting Thomas (John 20:24–28), before his ascension into heaven on a cloud (Acts 1:3–9). And from this we have the crowning accomplishment of the miracle-working Father God.

Miracle-working both inspires and demands faith. We have seen previously asserted by John the primary importance of faith:

> For this is the will of my Father, that everyone who sees the Son and believes in him should have eternal life.... (John 6:40)

Everyone, he says, without exception. This is all that is necessary to put one on a par with the saints for, as we have noted, there is nothing intermediate between heaven and hell. Perhaps John was extravagant in his enthusiasm, but such statements underscore the undeniable importance Jesus and his disciples placed on faith and belief.

Probably in no other aspect of the Father God is it so obvious that He was made in the human image. People through the ages have constantly felt a need to be appreciated, respected, and accepted by others as they see themselves. From a purely logical point of view, a unique, all-powerful being should realize His powers—what He is and what He can do—so that it would seem irrelevant whether or not His creatures recognize His omnipotence or His existence. Lack of recognition in no way changes the facts about God. But humans, who are far from perfect, yearn for this type of recognition and so ascribe this need to God.

Related to this need is pride: a need to assert one's self and demonstrate to others one's capabilities and preeminence. In this, the Father God is no different from His predecessors. More than just accepted, God must be glorified:

> Christ became a servant....in order that the Gentiles might glorify God for His mercy. (Romans 15:8, 9)

> This illness [of Lazarus]....is for the glory of God, so that the Son of God may be glorified by means of it. (John 11:4)

Not only does God allow humankind to be disobedient but provides the mercy to allow an opportunity for Jesus to demonstrate the glory of the Father God, but:

> For God has consigned all men to disobedience, that he may have mercy on us all. (Romans 11:32)

The understanding then as now is the same as Paul exclaims in the next verse, "how inscrutable his ways!"

Both Jesus and his disciples emphasize belief in Jesus himself:

> I am the way, the truth and the life; no one comes to the Father, but by me. (John 14:6)

And God must have authorized this conduit, for:

> The words I say to you I do not speak on my own authority; but the Father who dwells in me does His works. (John 14:10)

Since Jesus said:

> He who has seen me has seen the Father....Believe me that I am in the Father, and the Father in me.... (John 14:9, 11)

This is about as close as the New Testament comes to proclaiming divinity for Jesus. These statements, plus the continued insistence on the importance of the belief in Jesus rather than stipulating a belief in God, can well have been the foundation that led to the development of the doctrine of the Trinity. If that were accepted, the continued insistence on a belief in Jesus becomes more nearly reasonable:

> ....for you will die in your sins unless you believe that I am he. (John 8:24)

> ....if you confess with your lips that Jesus is Lord and believe in your heart that God raised him from the dead, you will be saved. (Romans 10:9)

Fortunately for the desirability on the part of humanity for ethics and morals, from time to time a demand for something besides faith creeps in:

> What does it profit....if a man says he has faith but does not have works? Can his faith save him?....faith by itself, if it has no works, is dead. (James 2:14, 17)

One thing the Father God does not allow for is the limited capability of the human mind. He demands love and belief, but in creating humans, He has so designed us we cannot ourselves resolve to love or to believe. Both love and belief are elusive; neither can be commanded. No matter how much someone reasons and argues with one person that they should love a particular other person, no amount of oratory will convince them. All the good intentions in the world will not change the fact of love either positively or negatively. A person may be willing to believe, if someone will present arguments acceptable to him; yet, if his mind does not accept the validity of the arguments, there is absolutely nothing that he can personally do about it.

As long as there is some small lingering doubt in the back of our minds, regardless of whether or not reason supports it, as to the validity of Jesus' claims, we have an insurmountable obstacle to belief, and no amount of urging and reasoning can change this. Nor are we helped any by a statement of Jesus, which only adds to the confusion:

> I thank thee, Father...that thou hast hidden these things from the wise and understanding and revealed them to babes...for such was thy gracious will. (Luke 10:21)

In short, God seems to allow people not to believe, and then condemns them to eternal damnation because they did not believe. One cannot help but feel that there is something wrong here, and yet Paul accepts this state of affairs. To the question "Is there injustice on God's part?" he replies:

> Has the potter no right over the clay, to make out of the same lump one vessel for beauty and another for menial use? (Romans 9:21)

Certainly there are a few pronouncements and allegations in the New Testament that seem to conflict with the assertion that God is Love. How can a loving God endure the thought of the tortured and tormented souls in hell? How can He expect a man to be blissful in heaven when the man knows that his brother is roasting in hell? Ideal love does not make demands. It does not say, "I will love you as long as you come up to my expectations." Some contemporary thought no longer adheres to the idea of hell because of these considerations. But we are not describing the present God, we are presenting the Father God of the New Testament, who is still alive in many congregations.

In another context, a relevant idea is contained in the parable of the prodigal son. After his father had given him his share of the inheritance, he left home and squandered his property in riotous living, but when he came home penniless, he was given a royal reception. Hurt by the lavish accolade, his brother complained that, though he had served his father well for many years, he had never been given even a kid to have a party with his friends, but for the son who devoured his living with harlots, the father killed the fatted calf (Luke 15:11–32). It hardly seems fair to the faithful son, but such is human nature. Hence the Father God, created in the human image, is credited with the same propensity, and it is scarcely surprising to find Jesus saying:

> I tell you, there will be more joy in heaven over one sinner who repents than over ninety-nine righteous persons who need no repentance. (Luke 15:7)

Our characterization of the Father God, drawn solely from the Scriptures of the New Testament, is based on an assumption that it is the authentic word of God. Although God Himself does not speak, Jesus told us that, "I do not speak on my own authority, but by [that of] the Father" and, "it is not you [the disciples] who speak, but the spirit of the Father speaking through you." Hence we do have God's word relayed to us through intermediaries who are presumably reliable.

Despite this, there are a few inconsistencies that make it difficult to accept every word of the New Testament as literal. As a written record of what Jesus and his disciples said which was reduced to writing some years after it was spoken, we are not surprised that thus its accuracy is sometimes subject to the erosion of memory. Viewpoints differ; anyone who has sat on a jury and listened to the conflicting evidences of several witnesses, all under oath, knows that it is almost impossible to obtain a precise, consistent report of details of any occurrence, especially where bias exists.

In any event, the story holds together as well as one might expect on reading accounts written by several independent reporters. We will, however, provide a few examples of inconsistencies to illustrate, none of which are really significant enough to affect the narrative as a whole.

In spite of the fact that all four gospels attest to the crucifixion of Jesus, Peter said, in talking to the high priest:

> The God of our fathers raised Jesus whom you killed by hanging him on a tree. (Acts 5:30)

In Matthew and Mark, referring to the two robbers crucified alongside Jesus, it was stated that both robbers railed against him, but in Luke, when one railed at him:

> ....the other rebuked him, saying, "....we are receiving the due reward of our deeds; but this man has done nothing wrong." (Luke 23:40, 41)

There is also some confusion about who carried the cross:

> So they took Jesus, and he went out, bearing his own cross.... (John 19:17)

> And they compelled a passer-by, Simon of Cyrene....to carry his cross. (Mark 15:21)

There is also some discrepancy over Judas' end:

> And throwing down the pieces of silver in the temple, he departed; and he went out and hanged himself. (Matthew 27:5)

> Now [Judas] bought a field with the reward of his wickedness; and falling headlong he burst open in the middle and all his bowels gushed out. (Acts 1:18)

The Father God, like the other Gods, is presented as being omnipotent and omniscient. The mission, resurrection, and the miracles of Jesus are all examples. In addition:

> "I am the Alpha and the Omega," says the Lord God, who is and who was, and who is to come, the Almighty. (Revelation 1:8)

Although the Father God expects man to exercise his free will, He is able to intervene from time to time:

> God....will not let you be tempted beyond your strength, but with the temptation will also provide the way of escape.... (1 Corinthians 10:13)

And He knows what is going on:

....what we are is known to God.... (2 Corinthians 5:11)

And before him no creature is hidden., but all are open and laid bare to the eyes of him with whom we have to do. (Hebrews 4:13)

As was mentioned before, one of the principal differences between the Father God and the Gods of the Patriarchs and of the Prophets, is His evolution as an international God, not only the God of the Jews. This is the next logical evolutionary step, beginning with the strictly tribal God we first found in the God of the Patriarchs, and following the appearance of the monotheistic God of the Prophets, who while claiming uniqueness and an absence of rivalry, still remained isolated among His chosen Israelites.

As the Jews began to mingle with other nationalities, hear other philosophies, and listen to other viewpoints, it became inevitable that the image of the God of the Prophets would be reconstructed on a grander scale. They had from time to time relapsed into worship of other strange gods, but they had always returned to the God of their inheritance.

This is still true of Jewish people today. They cling with indomitable tenacity to Jehovah, to Elohim. While it is true that both Reform and Conservative Jews have recast their Gods—especially in reference to shifting from Mosaic legalism to morals and ethics—and it is true that the first "Christian" church was a strictly Jewish church, modern Jews are definitely not followers of the Father God. They cannot accept the divinity of Christ, or even the representation of a relation with the divine any closer than that which characterized the ancient prophets. The depiction of Paradise and Hell have no counterpart in their religious beliefs. Their God has evolved from the God of the Prophets to sustain itself in the conditions of the modern environment.

When Jesus first began preaching, he considered that his mission was strictly for the Israelites. When he first sent out his disciples to spread the word, he cautioned them:

Go nowhere among the Gentiles....but go rather to the lost sheep of the house of Israel. (Matthew 10:5, 6)

Yet we could see signs of the Father God even before the New Testament:

What shall I do unto thee, O Jacob? Thou, Judah, would not obey me; I will turn to other nations, and unto them will I give my name.... (2 Esdras 1:24)

Jesus eventually did make contact with a non-Jew: a Roman centurion whose slave was desperately ill. His Jewish friends recommended him to Jesus because of the Roman's sympathy for them, and because he had helped in the building of the synagogue. Not desiring to trouble Jesus, he requested that the healing be done at that distance, and it was. Jesus commented, "Not even in Israel have I found such faith." (Luke 7:2–10)

Still, Jesus was not yet ready to deviate from the narrow Jewish path. When a Canaanite woman who believed in him plead to have the demon cast out of her daughter:

> He answered, "I was sent only to the lost sheep of the house of Israel." (Matthew 15:24)

But as she continued her pleas, she impressed Jesus with her faith, and he acceded to her wishes. Later, on the way to Galilee he passed through Samaria and spent some time preaching to the Samarians, gaining some believers amongst them. Finally, he reached the point where he recognized that his mission should include others as well as Jews:

> And I have other sheep, that are not of this fold; I must bring them also, and they will heed my voice. (John 10:16)

It is finally confirmed that being one of the Chosen People implies a duty as well as a privilege:

> You are a chosen race, a royal priesthood....that you may declare the wonderful deeds of him who called you out of darkness into his marvelous light. (1 Peter 2:9)

> I have set you to be a light for the Gentiles, that you may bring salvation to the uttermost parts of the earth. (Acts 13:47)

Thus the significance of being chosen by the Father God is far different from being chosen by the God of the Patriarchs. Peter himself, with the help of visions, is convinced:

> Truly, I perceive that God shows no partiality....anyone who fears him and does what is right is acceptable to him....can anyone forbid water for baptizing these people who have received the Holy Spirit just as we have? (Acts 10:34, 35, 47)

And Paul was easily persuaded:

> Is he not God of the Gentiles also? Yes, of the Gentiles also, since God is one.... (Romans 3:29, 30)

So they went their way preaching to Greeks, Romans, and to anyone who would listen. And, they declared the equality of all persons, as far as their relations to Jesus were concerned, on one occasion even including women:

> Here there cannot be Greek and Jew, circumcised and uncircumcised, barbarians, Scythian, slave, free man, but Christ is all, and in all. (Colossians 3:11)

> There is neither Jew nor Greek, there is neither slave nor free, there is neither male nor female, for you are all one in Christ Jesus. (Galatians 3:28)

So in the sight of the Father God, one person is equal to another, as long as he has faith and does good works. For the Father God, the only valid labels are "sinner" and "righteous."

Before leaving the New Testament we will include as a lagniappe some citations that indicate the origin of some familiar sayings and some practices. While these may not contribute much to the fundamental characterization of the Father God, they do throw some light on certain aspects of His nature that differentiate Him from other Gods.

For instance, the idea of the "born-again" Christian derives from the following source:

> Therefore, if anyone is in Christ, he is a new creation; the old has passed away, behold, the new has come. (2 Corinthians 5:17)

The terrible practices of the Inquisition, and especially of the Spanish Inquisition were based on the altruistic theory that it was the duty of the Church to protect the souls of men through whatever means were available, since the soul was eternal and the flesh only briefly transient. Because Jesus had declared unequivocally that faith was required for salvation, any means that could be used to induce faith or a statement of belief, even the most horrendous tortures, were considered to be rendering a beneficial service to the soul. For Biblical support for their theory, the Inquisitors could turn to:

> ....with the power of our Lord Jesus, you are to deliver this man [who lived with his father's wife] to Satan for the destruction of the flesh, that his spirit may be saved in the day of our Lord Jesus. (1 Corinthians 5:4, 5)

We find the origin of some of the more peripheral sects which demonstrate their faith by handling poisonous snakes:

> And these signs will accompany those who believe....they will speak in new tongues; they will pick up serpents, and if they drink any deadly thing, it will not hurt them. (Mark 16:17, 18)

The person who manages to get bitten by a rattlesnake has insult added to his injury, for his brethren may easily explain the incident by simply accusing him of not having had enough faith.

And we find that Paul was responsible for the quotation that is often used in churches when the collection plate is passed around:

> ....for God loves a cheerful giver. (2 Corinthians 9:7)

# Chapter 7: Allah

Praise be to Allah, the Lord of the Creation
The Compassionate, the Merciful,
King of Judgement Day!

You alone we worship, and to You alone we pray for help.

Guide us to the straight path
The path of those whom you have favored,
Not of those who have incurred Your wrath
Nor of those who have gone astray.
(Koran, Sura 1: The Exordium)

In considering Allah as having been made in the image of the Arab, we must consider not only the Arab himself, but also his ideals, that is, what he thinks a God should be; what he himself would be, if he were God. This image is affected not only by the Arabian people, but especially by the personality and background of the man who originally drew the portrait of Allah, the architect of Islam, the Prophet and Messenger of God, Mohammed.

The word Arab itself—of Semitic origin—signifies desert, and was applied also to the nomads who inhabited the desert lands of what is now called the Arabian peninsula. This was a harsh, inhospitable land: a barren country with occasional oases, and with some areas towards the southwest and the north a bit less forbidding than the land as a whole. Water was scarce, necessitating reliance on irrigation in some areas; in others, the streams would periodically dry up, forcing the nomadic movements of tribes from one area to another, to take advantage of what water could be found. Camels, who had already evolved to adapt to their surroundings, had the capacity to store appreciable quantities of water, so that they could go for many days without refueling. The camel thus became the Arab's beast of burden, the only animal capable of days-long crossing of the arid desert.

With the camel as the ship of the desert and the rugged personality of the Arab aboard, a partnership was formed uniquely suited to maintain the trade routes between the civilized centers of Ethiopia, Egypt, Byzantium, and the Indus valley. No other team could withstand the hardships and privations inherent to desert travel, and the ocean-going ships of the times were not up to the trade requirements. Thus the Arabs, characterized by traits of tenacity, endurance, and self-reliance, became the masters of the trade-route monopoly.

Most of them were poor, even by the standards of those days. Certainly, their nomadic lifestyle did not allow for the accumulation of material wealth. Where mobility was imperative, one could not accumulate many possessions. A limited wardrobe, a few cooking utensils, weapons, and some items of personal gear were all that a nomad could carry.

One of the most striking verifications of this condition was the custom of abandoning or burying alive unwanted girl babies. Not only was the demand for women limited, because of the limited demand for what a woman could contribute to the communal life, but the constant concern of scavenging food meant that each superfluous mouth to feed contributed to what could become an intolerable burden. Poverty was simply a way of life.

Of course, trading does require capital, and certain tribes who maintained the principal trading centers became in essence the bankers of the trade: wealthy merchants and owners of trains of camels.

One of the most important trading centers was Mecca, under control of the tribe of the Quraysh, and located near the middle of the western coast of Arabia.

The early Moslems designated the era immediately preceding the advent of Mohammed the "time of Ignorance." Although Mecca had become a great trading center during this period, and with the presence of the Kaaba—a sort of pagan pantheon—a center of pilgrimage, it had not developed what we might consider a culture in the sense of those of Persia, Greece, Rome, or Egypt. Trade was at the core of Arabic life, and although the Arab people could not avoid absorbing ideas here and there from those they met while traveling, there were no Arabian schools or important developments in Arabian philosophy that compare to those of these other cultures.

The vast majority of the Arabs, including Mohammed, were illiterate. This meant that any knowledge they retained must be retained mentally, and they did broadly develop both their own individual memories and the vocation of professional memorizers, who could recite history and genealogies accurately at great length.

Although the Arabs, like the Hebrews, felt their tribal and kinship ties very strongly, to the extent that anyone establishing kinship with a group could count on the protection of the group, and of no one else, their mobile life modified this to a great extent. They were able to accept as normal, relations with other than their own tribes, and had a more complex view of foreigners than as enemies to be feared and hated, as something to be exterminated, or from whom they might expect extermination. They had no horror of being contaminated by the stranger, especially because they were themselves protected by their rugged individualism from external contamination; they were always ready to exchange ideas, if only to pass the time. Travelers themselves, they appreciated the problems of travelers, and were thus by nature a hospitable people.

Not all of Meccan wealth came from bankrolling the caravans. There were also the trade fairs, which brought visitors from all surrounding countries, and the Kaaba, which was a magnet for the religious pilgrims. Thus the tourist trade was an important source of income to the Meccan merchants. It was said that at one time, there were as many as three hundred and sixty-seven different idols in the Kaaba, each of which attracted its share of pilgrims. Tradition alleges that the central structure of the Kaaba was built by Abraham himself, and that its embedded sacred Black Stone was set there by Abraham.

The presence of the Kaaba had two effects on the people of Mecca. First, it was incumbent on them to protect the integrity of this pantheon of pagan gods as a tourist attraction and a source of wealth. At the same time, its proximity and the confusion of myriad religions induced in them a certain disdain, an apathy that bordered on cynicism. They had had their fill of paganism and were mentally ready for something else, but they could not afford to relinquish a lucrative source of income.

The seeds of change were there. Allah was already recognized in the pantheon as the dominant God, in a manner similar to the position of Zeus in the religion of ancient Greece. Furthermore, they were surrounded on all sides by religions that had developed into monotheism and had discarded all superfluous gods. The Jewish people were everywhere and comprised a large fraction of the population of the city of Yathrib (which later changed its name to Medina after the arrival of Mohammed). In Persia, the Zoroastrians had Ormazd and had eliminated all others but the god of evil, Ahriman—and he was being pushed into the loser's role.

Arabia itself was characterized by lack of overall organization. Each tribe was a rule unto itself, with no codified laws, controlled rather by custom invoked when necessary by the sheikh. Mecca had no highly formalized government, but was guided by an oligarchy of the more prominent merchants. The Bedouins had a strong distaste for authority, a fundamental characteristic that has persisted to this day among these highly self-reliant people.

It was into this world that Mohammed was born, a member of one of the less-important clans of the prominent Quraysh tribe. His father died before he was born and his mother died when he was six. Most of his upbringing was in the house of his uncle Abu-Talib. While still young, he became engaged in the service of a wealthy Quraysh widow, Khadijah, and was occupied with handling her camel caravans in trading over a wide area. Although Khadijah was fifteen years his senior, there was evidently a strong mutual attraction, and they married when Mohammed was about twenty-five.

During the more than fifteen years of their marriage, Mohammed had no other wives. He and Khadijah worked together, and she became very supportive of the beginning of his mission.

Mohammed had developed a habit of going to a certain cave on Mount Hira for the isolation needed for his meditations. It was there that, one memorable night, he was visited by the angel Gabriel, either in a dream or a vision, who commanded, "Recite." After Mohammed had three times asked what he should recite, Gabriel began to dictate to him the words of Allah, which Mohammed was later informed came from a book extant through all eternity which Allah maintained in heaven. Mohammed, like his compatriots who could not read, had a well-developed memory, remembered what was told him, and in a series of visions spread over the next twenty years, received the words which became the Glorious Koran, the fundamental Scriptures of one of the world's major religions.

At first concerned that he was falling under the influence of a jinn, one of the invisible spirits of Arabia, who among other pastimes occupy themselves with inspiring poets, Mohammed hesitated for some time before declaring any of his visions to anyone besides Khadijah. She listened, encouraged him and—along with her cousin Waraqa—became convinced of their validity.

In his travels, Mohammed had had contact with both Jews and Christians. At home, Mohammed had known family members of a monotheistic bent. There was therefore nothing new in the principles presented to him by Gabriel, but the idea that he should himself become a prophet, a Messenger of God, was a bit overwhelming. The gravity of the situation, the dangers of the life of a self-declared prophet weighed heavily on him, but the inner drive from his inspiration and the reinforcement and encouragement he received from Khadijah and Waraqa decided him. He began preaching on a small scale to those in Mecca who would listen.

Most of Mohammed's converts came from the deprived classes, who are always open to a word of consolation or a promise of something better. As long as Mohammed preached quietly, he was allowed to proceed undisturbed. However, when he began preaching against idol-worship and expanded his field to the pilgrims that came to worship the idols, the reigning Quraysh became apprehensive. Their opposition mounted, and Mohammed eventually had to escape to Yathrib with some of his followers.

He continued his preaching in Yathrib (later known as Medina). Soon, he had an appreciably larger following than he had had in Mecca. During a period of several years, there were a few armed clashes between Mohammed's supporters and their opponents, with the results favorable first to one group, then the other. In the end, Mohammed, who proved himself an effective diplomat as well as a capable military leader, returned to Mecca with a large following of several thousand, obtained permission to enter the city, and soon won many converts to Islam. The time was ripe for a religious revolution. The promise of Islamic pilgrimage to the Kaaba could well replace any loss in pagan pilgrim traffic resulting from conversions. Mohammed's internal opposition gradually faded. In the surprisingly brief passage of twenty years, Islam became the accepted religion of Arabia.

Islam. The word signifies submission—submission to the will of God. How was it that a nation characterized by rugged individualism assumed a religion of submission in such a short period of time? It can only be explained by an evident readiness on the part of the Arabs to consider something different from that in which they were gradually losing faith, plus the positive claims of the religion itself on their ideals, their way of life, and its promises for an eternal blissful future for those who believed. The predestination it preached allowed acceptance of the bitter blows of fate so frequent in their harsh land. There was a potent appeal in the feeling that one could relax and leave all responsibility in the hands of God.

Before going on to see what that God, Allah, was like, we will for a moment consider the Scriptures which declare the religion of Islam and paint the portrait of Allah.

Mohammed accepted in general terms the Scriptures of the Jews and the Christians, which he believed consisted essentially of the Pentateuch (the books of Moses), the Psalms, and the Gospels. For Mohammed, the other books of our present-day Bible were incidental and not part of the primary Scriptures. The Koran was dictated to him at the command of Allah by the angel Gabriel from the heavenly Book that contained all of God's word, and which had existed before Time. It was now being dictated in Arabic for the benefit of Mohammed and his people.

> We have revealed the Koran in the Arabic tongue that you may grasp its meaning. It is a transcript of Our eternal Book, sublime, and full of wisdom. (43:2)

> Yet before it the Book of Moses was revealed, a guide and a blessing to all men. This Book confirms it. (46:12)

> We sent forth Jesus....and gave him the Gospel, in which there is guidance and light....and to you We have revealed the Book with the truth. (5:46)

It is important to keep in mind that not only the Koran—but also the books of Moses and the Gospels—were believed to have derived from the eternally existing heavenly Book. It is from this that Mohammed drew his term "People of the Book" for Jews and Christians alike, and counted them among those who believe in Allah. Mohammed fervently believed in all the prophets who preceded him; only with the reservation that errors had been made in the transcription of the words of God, and that it was his mission to make the necessary corrections and additions to complete the story.

> The relationship between myself and the Prophets can be compared with a house which a man built carefully, but left one brick unlaid. Those who visited the house admired it, except for the empty space for the one brick. Then I laid the brick. I am the Seal of the prophets. (T:1785)

The Koran is a faithful mirror of the character and accomplishments of Mohammed himself. Not only does it express his theology in terms of his experience, it also shows the lacunae in his knowledge of the previous Scriptures, which was acquired essentially in discussions with Jews and Christians whom he respected. Although the sources were principally monks and rabbis, their own knowledge may also have been incomplete.

In arranging the Sura—the chapters of the Koran—in their probable chronological order, we often find that revelations are made to order; Gabriel obligingly dictating new revelations or changes in older ones that were appropriate to the occasion.

> If We abrogate any verse or cause it to be forgotten We will replace it by a better one or similar. (2:106)

This admittedly is somewhat difficult to reconcile with the statement that the Koran is being dictated from a Book which has existed throughout eternity. We will not attempt an explanation.

The Hadith are traditions of Mohammed which present in the main something he said or something he did that will clarify or elaborate on the Koran. After Mohammed's death, it was found necessary to collect these. The Moslems based even the detail of their everyday life and their "law" on the Koran, but Mohammed could not possibly include in it the answer to every question that arose, especially since so many arose after his death. The Hadith began to be collected during the Prophet's lifetime, and continued for a few centuries afterward. Until the Musnad of Al-Tayalisi, the first known written collection, begun nearly two hundred years after Mohammed's death, the collections were all oral. The individual Hadith commenced with a list of names giving the chain of passage from the person who had heard it directly from Mohammed, to the latest, each one considered strictly genuine only if transmission was personal. Some collectors of Hadith are claimed to have been able to recall accurately as many as 200,000 Hadith. The most highly considered written collection is that of Al-Bukhari, who was said to have considered 600,000 but accepted as certainly genuine only 7,397, and after eliminating duplications found 2,762 distinct ones.

If Al-Bukhari accepted only a bit over one percent of those that he considered, obviously many must be suspect, and non-Moslems especially consider many fraudulent, invented for the purpose of supporting some religious, moral or political view.

> The vast flood of traditions soon formed a chaotic sea. Truth and error, fact and fable mingled in an undistinguishable confusion. Every religious, social and political system was defended, when necessary to please a Khalif or an Ameer to serve his purpose, by an appeal to oral traditions. The name of Mohammed was abused to support all sorts of lies and absurdities....(quoted from an Indian Moslem author) (G, 97)

Still, the Hadith were carefully screened by their collectors, being judged first on the authority of the transmitters, then on the character of the Hadith themselves whether they were consistent with the Koran, with history, with circumstances, with reason, and with each other. What remains in the literature presents a portrait of Allah as He is seen by the Moslem, so for our consideration what is accepted is more important than any question of whether it is pure and unadulterated. Its importance derives from the Koran-declared infallibility of Mohammed:

> Whatever the Apostle gives you, accept it; and whatever he forbids you, forbear from it. (59:7)

Mohammed himself is quoted in the Mishkat as saying, "When I order you anything respecting religion receive it, and when I order anything about the affairs of the world I am no more than a man."

We must remember that the Koran itself is, unlike the Pentateuch and the Gospels, a book which was assembled very shortly after the revelation it presents, from existing written scraps as well as from the fantastic memories of Mohammed's Companions and Followers. It is the only scripture till its time of which we have no doubt about the author. Outside of the Pentateuch, there is no certain historical confirmation of Moses and his predecessors. Outside of the New Testament and some of the discarded gospels the only historical reference to Jesus is a quotation in the works of the Jewish historian Flavius Josephus, and that is questioned by many who consider it an insertion made much later.

Thus we have the effect of Moses, Abraham, and Jesus under spotlights on the stage of history, while Mohammed arrived with full floodlights on the stage. It is not surprising to discover that those who wished to promote the cause of the Prophet did at a later date recount some tales of miracles performed by Mohammed, trying to raise him to the level of Jesus, despite the fact that Mohammed himself disclaimed all ability to perform miracles. Some other accounts of exploits and expeditions are questioned, but that is normal in any part of history. There is no doubt whatsoever that Mohammed is a concrete historical figure.

The evolution of Allah, despite Mohammed's acceptance of Jesus as a prophet, is not as an offspring continuing the line of the Father God. Rather, it is a branching line of evolution based on origins in the God of the Patriarchs and the God of the Prophets. The Father God line evolved instead into the Trinitarian God, and subsequent changes will be considered later. In no way can we consider Allah related to the Trinitarian God, other than through common historical ancestry.

There are fundamental differences between Allah and his heavenly ancestors. Although Allah loves a good fight, He is not bloodthirsty to the extent of the God of the Patriarchs; nowhere does He demand extinction, and He is always ready to forgive the enemy and accept Him if he will embrace Islam. Allah is not basically jealous, as is Jehovah; rather, He is aloof, never showing Himself. He has a concrete Paradise and Hell ready for the deserving. One cannot consider Him more abstractly, as has been done with the Father God, as "God is Love." He cares little for sacrifices, and has long learned that miracles are valueless. Let us look more in greater detail at the characteristics of Allah.

Perhaps we can accept more readily the picture of Allah if, instead of considering Him as the identical God, as did Mohammed, we can think of Him as a reincarnation of the Gods of Moses and of Jeremiah. Then we can accept the differences without feeling that God Himself has changed. For as a matter of fact, as we have mentioned before, the God of the Patriarchs and the God of the Prophets as a species have themselves changed little, and are still with us in the congregations of the fundamentalists for the former and Reform Judaism and other less dogmatic sects for the latter. Differences in other Gods are evident all around us, yet these are all variations of the originals, and will continue to exist as a result of improved adaptation to their environment.

Allah, for the Arabs, is a designation equivalent to God, as was Elohim for the Jews. To become a Moslem, it is only necessary that one accept, "La ilaha illa 'l-Lah; wa Muhammadan Rasul-al-Lah"—generally translated as, "There is no God but Allah and Mohammed is His Prophet." This emphasizes the fact that Mohammed admitted of no distinctions in identity between the God of Judaism and the God of Christianity. Where he did differ from the Jewish or Christian concept of God, he believed that some errors had cropped up in their understanding, not in the identity of God Himself.

In considering the character of the God of Islam, one must bear in mind that an accurate theological depiction of Allah is of minimal importance to the Moslem. After the preeminence of the emphasis on belief, submission to the will of Allah is the chief tenet of Islam. What is most important to a believing Moslem is thorough knowledge of the law, of God's will. That said, we will proceed to try and paint His portrait, especially as it compares to the Jewish and Christian Gods.

One of the most striking characteristics of Allah is that, in spite of His detailed knowledge of the world and His far-reaching control of humankind and the universe, He remains aloof. Al-Ghazali, the pre-eminent Moslem theologian, insists that He is transcendental—beyond human comprehension. He is never seen or expected to be seen; even after His arrival in Paradise, He will be seen only by a privileged few. Still and all, an accurate theological depiction of Allah is unimportant to the Moslem. Islam being submission to the will of Allah, all that is important is thorough knowledge of the law, of God's will.

While it is true that also the Father God was never visible (other than His manifestations as the Holy Spirit), His voice was heard on a couple of occasions, as when He was pleased with Jesus after his baptism. Jesus is also presented as a special emissary from God, with a direct line to the Father. In contrast, Mohammed had no direct line to God. He had only the angel Gabriel as an intermediary, and not once in his life did he hear a word directly from God. It is true that the words of the Koran often sound as if Allah were addressing Mohammed directly, but this is due to the manner in which they were relayed by Gabriel.

> He [Mohammed] does not speak out of his own fancy. This is an inspired revelation. He is taught by one who is powerful and mighty [Gabriel]. (53:2)

Although the Old Testament Gods were originally very active and each had a long series of prophets, within the last two centuries before Christ and for nearly six hundred years afterward, there were no prophets worthy of the name, and none from whom any canonical records exist until Allah sent Gabriel to inspire Mohammed. As real prophets were rare, many people wanted something more than Mohammed's word alone to authenticate his experience: signs were requested, miracles demanded, and angels asked for.

But Allah remained aloof, except for the dictation of the Koran through Gabriel. Allah was disgusted with the lack of results of signs and miracles in His previous incarnations:

> The unbelievers ask: "Why has no sign been given him by his Lord?" (13:28)

> Let him show us some sign, as did the apostles in the days gone by. Yet though We showed them signs, the nations We destroyed never believed in them. (21:5)

Allah holds that, though He has already piled miracle on miracle in His past incarnations, the world is still no better than it was. Why should He continue with these second-rate miracles when the really impressive signs are there for everyone to see if they just open their eyes?

> Surely in the heavens and the earth there are signs for the faithful; in your own creation, and in the beasts that are scattered far and near....in the alternation of night and day, in the sustenance Allah sends down from heaven, and in the marshaling of the winds....signs for men of understanding. (45:2)

> Do you not see how the ships speed upon the oceans by Allah's grace, so that He may reveal to you His wonders? (31:31)

> We made the son of Mary and his mother a sign to mankind.... (23:48)

> It was Allah who raised the heavens without visible pillars....forced the sun and moon into His service...spread out the earth and placed upon it rivers and immovable mountains....Surely in these there are signs for thinking men. (13:2)

Allah wants man to have his chance of the rewards of Paradise, but it is up to man himself whether he earns them. Man needs Allah, but:

> Allah does not need his creatures' help. (29:5)

So Allah remains aloof. He does not even require of Mohammed that His Prophet make any special effort. Allah intends to be known as being just; He will not condemn anyone without a warning, but once that warning has been given He does not intend to brood over it, nor should His Prophet do more than just pass the message on:

> Never have We destroyed a nation whom We did not warn and admonish beforehand. We are never unjust. (26:208)

> If they give no heed, know that we have not sent you [Mohammed] to be their keeper. Your only duty is to warn them. (42:48)

In accepting the theologically important fact that Allah forbore to produce miracles as signs, we must accept that some of the Hadith are unreliable, because they contradict Mohammed's denial of Allah's inclination to miraculous demonstrations. Such stories—such as the feeding of seventy or eighty men with a few loaves of bread (G, 136) or the poisoned shoulder of goat's flesh which called out that it had been poisoned before Mohammed could eat it (G, 134)—were evidently invented to enhance Mohammed's reputation amongst those who had difficulty accepting his words without some positive proof.

Yet perhaps we should consider as miraculous two Koranic passages in which Allah, like Jehovah before Him, sent divine assistance to Mohammed's battling forces:

> ...when you were attacked...we unleashed against them a violent wind and invisible warriors.... (33:9)

# Mitchell's Motel & Cottages

P.O. Box 1717 • Hwy. 28 & 106
Highlands, NC 28741-1717
(704) 526-2267
1-800-522-9874 - Reservations only

> I am sending to your aid a thousand angels in their ranks....I shall cast terror into the hearts of the infidels....it was not you, but Allah, who slew them. (8:10, 12, 18)

But note the difference between these two cases and the miracles of the Bible. They were not done as signs; in fact, the miracles themselves were invisible, both to Mohammed and to his enemies. They might not even have become known had not Allah afterwards related through Gabriel what He had done. It is for this reason that we do not classify these in the same category as the miracles of Jehovah or the Father God. Rather, they evidence the tight control Allah maintains over His creation.

Those who are congenitally unable to accept any sort of miracle might argue that the fact that Mohammed's Koran was composed in the glare of historical floodlights and during his lifetime made it difficult or impossible to inject myth into the principal Islamic scriptures. On the other hand, the fact that the Gospels were written half a century after the crucifixion of Jesus allowed more time for legend to develop and made cross-checking of the facts impracticable. This does not, however, affect our discussion of the God of Islam, as our primary concern is how different religions portray God. What we can draw from this that is significant to our exploration is that the Father God was a God who relied on miracles as signs, while Allah was not.

With the first glance into Islam, one is immediately struck by how deeply laws, rules, and restrictions penetrate into Moslem life. The first impression is that Allah must be even more legalistic than was the God of the Patriarchs. Yet there is a fundamental difference. Jehovah dictated a complete set of laws to Moses on Sinai which were used as the basic legal code for the Hebrews, with some later additions in the Talmud and other traditional sources. While Allah did dictate an assortment of laws through Gabriel for inclusion in the Koran, these are not organized into any formal code and are scattered throughout the Book. A large part of Moslem law is found in the Hadith, arising from the traditions of the Prophet. The centrality of Moslem laws springs from a desire to know and to submit to the Will of God, rather than an imposed set of rules. The difference is that between the subject of an autocratic dictator on the one hand, and on the other, a yes man who tries to find out what his boss wants, and behaves in a manner that he thinks will please him. The Moslem submits because he wants to, not because he feels that he is being forced to.

Islamic law covers both spiritual and temporal aspects of life. The fundamental desire of the Moslem is submission to the Will of Allah as completely as possible. Not only were there generally accepted laws against adultery, theft, and idolatry, plus positive admonitions to take care of widows, orphans, and wayfarers; there were also dietary laws, prohibitions concerning intoxicants, strict rules concerning times of prayer, manner of praying, and preparations for prayer; rules for ablutions after contact with dead bodies, menstruating women, and nocturnal emissions; details of how to behave when on pilgrimage, dress and jewelry for women, treatment of diseases, manner of greeting believers and non-believers, witnessing of contracts. The Hadith covers such minute details as requiring three stones and the left hand to wipe the anus after evacuation and which foot should be advanced on entering and which on leaving the mosque.

Several things are repeatedly enjoined or forbidden. Care of orphans and their property is stressed. Mohammed, himself an orphan, had first-hand knowledge of the orphan's plight. Aid to wayfarers is enjoined time and again—in a land peopled with nomads and travelers. Rules for contracts and witnesses are frequent, in a country where probably the majority of the people, at least most of the wealthy, make their livelihood from trade.

Guillaume and others have contended that the Koran presents transgression not so much as sin from the point of view of a moral offense, but as violations of legal code with proper terms dictated for a business-like correction and expiation of the misdeed. This interpretation is supported historically. For example, the following law:

> The adulterer and the adulteress shall each be given a hundred lashes… (24:2)

was evidently based on the pre-Islamic notion of adultery not so much as a moral wrong, but as an injury to the property rights of others.

Carrying out the following injunction:

> For the man or woman who is guilty of theft, cut off their hands to punish them. (5:37)

would obviously make thievery more difficult in the future. This has even been represented as an act of mercy on Allah's part, by deterring the culprit from further sin.

As with the God of the Patriarchs, retaliation is an accepted form of punishment:

> …break teeth of a woman who broke those of a slave girl. He who kills a man intentionally must be given up to the relatives of the slain. if they wish, they can kill him, and if they will, they can accept blood money. (G-M, 108)

But the Koran enjoins the person in whose hands the right to punish exists to be merciful:

> In the Torah we decreed a life for a life, an eye for an eye…a tooth for a tooth….But if a man charitably forbears from retaliation, his remission shall atone for him. (5:45)

Further, the vast majority of offenses carry no specific punishment in the Koran. Allah is presented as a great record-keeper, preparing the evidence to put on the scales on Judgment Day: the standard treatment for moral offenses.

> We are the witnesses of all your thoughts and all your prayers and all your actions. Not an atom's weight escapes your Lord....but is recorded in a glorious book. (10:61)
>
> If a man greets you, let your greeting be better than his, or at least return his greeting. Allah keeps count of all things. (4:86)
>
> [On Judgment Day] Their book will be set down before them, and you shall see the sinners dismayed at that which is inscribed in it....it omits nothing, small or great.... (18:49)

This could of course be considered as a "businessl-like" means of treatment of sins, and certainly the lives of the Arabs as traders makes a business-like Allah conceivable. Still, the overall tone of the Koran leans in the moral direction, and there is no reason why even the most serious business man should not feel that his religion can carry the burden of ideals and morals for him, without contractual overtones.

With all the myriad laws, rules and regulations, the record-keeping, the warnings that these records will be used against the sinner, neither good nor evil works will affect whether a person will go to hell or paradise. These scales that weigh sins and good actions serve only to determine the time exposed to torture or the relative rewards of Paradise. The only cardinal sin that determines whether a soul will go to hell or heaven is unbelief. This is an irrefutable aspect of the Muslim faith; it is repeated time and again both in the Koran and in the Hadith:

> The basest creatures in the sight of Allah are the faithless who will not believe.... (8:54)
>
> He that chooses a religion other than Islam, it will not be accepted from him and in the world to come he will be one of the lost. (3:85)
>
> He that fears Allah shall be forgiven his sins and richly rewarded. (65:5)

The line is drawn. No matter if you lead an exemplary life, if you try to believe and cannot, you will roast in hell. Those who do believe, will have their sins forgiven. The only really significant sin, therefore, is disbelief.

So we find that Allah, like the Father God, had a need for recognition that far surpassed His desire for obedience. Disobedience could be overlooked; it was forgivable if one only repented and asked for forgiveness. But disbelief was the unforgivable sin. There was no way of repenting disbelief other than by believing.

An interesting twist on this emphasis on belief is that Allah already knows that belief or non-belief is not up to the individual, but is decided by Allah Himself.

> Had your Lord pleased, all the people of the earth would have believed in Him. None can have faith except by the will of Allah. (10:99)

> We have cast veils over their hearts, lest they understand our words, and made them hard of hearing. (18:58)

> You cannot help a man if Allah seeks to mislead him. Those whose hearts He does not please to purify shall be rewarded with disgrace in this world and a grievous punishment in the next. (5:41)

It is a complete waste of time to search the Koran or the Hadith for the reasoning behind this. Allah claims to be just, but His justice is according to His, not human, standards. From a human vantage-point, Allah appears completely arbitrary. His commands are to be obeyed without question and without any reference to their moral implications. He may often demonstrate forgiveness and mercy, but He acts on no principles we can fathom. We have neither the knowledge nor the insight to understand Allah's plans, nor as His creations, do we have the right to question them.

We have established the character of Allah as a God who maintains complete and continuous control over all His creation. Where gods are omniscient and omnipotent, there always arises the question of predestination. This is, in fact, one of the most important concepts of Islam: a concept of Allah as a God who holds the reins tightly in His hands, a Deity who maintains complete and continuous control over all His creation. How much control does God exercise; does man really have any say-so after all? All religions with a personal god concede that God can at the very least answer prayers. How far does He carry His control? All the way down the line, say some adherents of Islam, and they quote at length from the Koran to prove their point. Unfortunately, in this respect, the Koran indicates the possibility of a schizoid character, a split personality that sometimes claims full control, sometimes calls on man to decide his destiny by his own choice of actions.

Mohammed is quoted as saying: "The first thing which Allah created was a divine pen, and He said to it, 'Write'; it said, 'What shall I write?' And Allah said, 'Write down the fate of every individual thing to be created,' and accordingly, the pen wrote all that was, and that will be, to eternity." (Farah, *Islam*) A more absolute statement would be difficult to find.

We are from this point of view mere actors on a stage, playing out our little comedy as Allah has written it, not only for the brief time we spend on earth, but also for the space of eternal bliss or eternal damnation. Allah particularly warns us against presuming to have control over our destinies:

> Do not say of anything, "I will do it tomorrow," without adding: "If Allah wills." (18:23)

And yet there is another side to this coin. If He intends to maintain a meticulous control and follow each word written by the primordial pen precisely, why does He bother to warn His subjects? Why should it be necessary to require belief, to set tests, to bend His messenger to instruct mankind? We begin to find an easing of the rigid picture in a Hadith of Al-Bukhari:

> [The Prophet was asked,] "Are those destined for Paradise known from those destined for Hell?" "Yes," replied he. The man answered, "Then of what use are deeds of any kind?" He answered, "Everyone does that for which he was created or that which was made easy for him." (G, 172)

It cannot be denied that this is still a statement of predestination, but there is a fissure in the inevitability of what has been written. One does good deeds or evil deeds because they were made easy—not impossible. The person standing outside of Islam can readily see that a belief in this variety of predestination will inspire the believer to salutary action. None but a completely debauched individual wants to believe God has made him a sinner headed for hell. It is only natural to want to believe that Allah has made him for better things, and to demonstrate it to himself by following the path he believes that Allah has set out for him, at least to the best of his ability. We find that Allah sometimes even denies strict predestination. This is first implied by the frequent warnings passed on by Mohammed:

> I have been sent to warn you plainly. Those that accept the true faith and do good works shall be forgiven and richly rewarded; but those that seek to confute Our revelations shall be the heirs of Hell. (22:49)

An emphasis is also placed on the idea that Allah has set out to test humankind:

> We shall put you to the proof until We know the valiant and the resolute among you.... (47:30)

Both good and bad treatment are used to test mankind, but the fact of the test itself indicates that humans possess at least certain amount of free will. One consequence of such an approach is that Moslems are likely to accept either fortune or misfortune as the will of Allah, and neither can logically be expected to have an impact on their faith. Whether a Moslem has been personally convinced of predestination or not, the inscrutable Will of Allah and its machinations will not dislodge him from his position. And for a final nod at free will itself:

> ...by the soul and Him that moulded it and inspired it with knowledge of sin and piety: blessed shall be the man who has kept it pure, and ruined he that has corrupted it! (91:5)

So predestination and free will continue to exist in dynamic equilibrium with one another—both sides can find their answers in the Koran and the Hadith, but Allah Himself has not settled in one way or another. He remains, as far as this characteristic is concerned, a split personality. In a way, Allah can be compared with the author of a grand historical novel. Fortune and misfortune, wealth and poverty are distributed among the actors without any regard to whether the distribution is fair to each and every one. Tragedy, romance, adventure, and comedy abound, and none of the players has any right to request anything for himself. The grand design is woven with each thread where Allah himself wants it. And as we often find in the novel, those that have been given of the best in the beginning, get their "comeuppance" in the end, while those that have had more than their share of trials and tribulations finally arrive at the happy ending.

Concerning Allah's relation to humankind, He has something in store for everyone. Those who have successfully passed the test of afflictions and temptations and still believe will go to Paradise, and those that are destined for Hell will be given their share of comforts on earth. Allah considers that the wealth and pleasures given on this earth are payment to the unbelievers for their good deeds, so that no good deeds will remain to their credit in the ledger when Judgment Day arrives.

> The unbelievers rejoice in this life; but brief indeed is the comfort of this life compared to the life to come. (13:28)

Again we note that the accent is on belief or nonbelief. The believers are reassured by Allah:

> Did you suppose that you would go to Paradise untouched by the suffering which was endured by those before you? (2:214)

> That which Allah has in store is far better than any merchandise or merriment. (62:12)

Paradise itself has benefited from the evolution of God. The God of the Patriarchs had no after-life. The God of the Prophets had planned some sort of afterlife, but was extremely vague about it. The Father God made it somewhat more definite, at least to the extent of announcing Hell as a place of eternal torture and Paradise of eternal bliss; yet one is left on one's own to imagine them. Not so with Allah. He draws a picture of exactly what is in store for you; He lets you know exactly what it will be like so that a man can decide for himself whether the game is worth the proverbial candle.

It is not surprising to find that Allah's Paradise and Hell are well adapted to the environment, experiences, and desires of the Arab. For a person living in a hot, barren, dry climate, the worst punishment imaginable is still more heat, with no chance to slake his desperate thirst. The sand storms of the desert are magnified into scorching winds and pitch-black smoke. The condemned, who has been hungry for a great part of his life, is offered poisonous fruits. Hell is made to order to fit the worst that the desert dweller can imagine.

> ...They shall dwell amidst scorching winds and seething water, in the shade of pitch-black smoke, neither cool nor refreshing....shall drink boiling water...as the thirsty camel drinks. (56:39, 55)

> He shall be cast into the raging Fire; he shall neither live nor die. (86:12)

> ...flames...throwing up sparks as huge as towers, a bright as yellow camels. (77:28)

> When they cry out for drink they shall be showered with water hot as molten brass, which will scald their faces. (18:30)

> ....let them taste their drink; scalding water, festering blood and other putrid things. (38:55)

> The fruit of the Zaqqum tree shall be the sinner's food. Like dregs of oil, like scalding water, it shall simmer in his belly. (44:45)

It is assuredly difficult to imagine that anyone who would sincerely believe in the words of the Koran would even take a minimal risk of exposure to these tortures of the damned, no matter how difficult it might make earthly life.

Even greater is the incentive for one who believes in the rewards of the Garden of Delights which Allah has prepared for believers. In contrast to Hell, the hardworking desert dweller is presented with a spectacle of cool clear streams bubbling through shady green gardens, while the believer relaxes on soft couches, dressed in elegant brocades and surrounded by luscious dark-eyed houris and bright young serving boys. He entertains himself with profound conversations with his friends, who recline on nearby couches. His thirst is slaked by fine wines which had been forbidden him on earth, but they are not intoxicant, and do not interfere with his enjoyment of repose and intercourse. The Arab, who had previously held no such belief in Paradise, must have found a great incentive for conversion to Islam in this depiction.

It is interesting to note that the scene of Paradise is designed exclusively for the male believer chauvinist, of which the Arab is the prime example. Nowhere does Allah depict a Paradise for the ladies, with the male equivalent of the voluptuous houris. To add insult to injury, the male believer, on arriving in Paradise, will not even have his wife to greet him, but a company of ravishing, dark-eyed beauties who are presumably never shrewish or carping; ever-acquiescent and loving.

> They shall recline on jeweled couches....shall wait on them immortal youths with bowls and ewers and a cup of purest wine that will neither pain their heads nor take away their reason; with fruits...and flesh of fowls that they relish. And theirs shall be the dark-eyed houris, chaste as hidden pearls....they shall hear no idle talk, no sinful speech, but only the greeting "Peace, peace!"....We created the houris and made them virgins, loving companions. (56:15)

> Whenever a woman vexes her husband in this world, his wife among the houris of Paradise says: "Do not vex him...for he is only a guest with thee. He will soon leave thee and come to us." (G-M, 125)

The houris, we observe, are virgins; but it does not state whether this virginity is maintained throughout eternity, or whether it is periodically renewed. In any event, for a people who knew nothing of fast cars, sleek yachts, and color TV, it would not be easy to imagine a more desirable mise en scene. The pagan Arab, who had no such belief in Paradise, must have found in this depiction a great incentive for conversion to Islam.

If there is a section of Paradise for believing wives, Gabriel has not bothered to tell Mohammed of it. In view of the subordinated role of the female—beginning in pre-Islamic and continuing to the present time—this seeming oversight, which may seem surprising from the viewpoint of other cultures, was not even considered worthy of notice by the Arabs. Arabic men were accustomed to keeping their women out of sight of all but the immediate family and the wealthy were privileged to have as many as four wives and all the slave concubines that they could afford. For the poor, the demand for women was limited, because there was little demand for what a woman could contribute to the communal life, but each additional mouth that needed to be fed compounded the constant struggle to scavenge food. Women were seen as property of little more consequence than beasts of burden. Consequently, the girls born to poor families were often buried alive in their infancy.

The Koran also contains many rules regarding marriage, dowry, and divorce that bear strongly on the treatment of women in a Moslem household. While Allah expresses concern for the compassionate treatment of women, women are subject to the often arbitrary will and sense of justice of their fathers, husbands, and brothers in much the same way that devout Moslems are subject to the arbitrary will of Allah. Men are allowed to have plural marriages, to keep their women isolated from non-family members, and to beat recalcitrant wives. They may also divorce an unwanted spouse by a simple oral declaration of divorce.

Allah Himself places small value on women. In discussing the unbelievers who worship female deities, like the three idols that reside in the Kaaba and are said to represent daughters of Allah, Allah becomes highly indignant:

> Would Allah choose daughters for Himself and sons for you? When the birth of a daughter is announced to one of them, his face darkens and is filled with gloom. Would they ascribe to Allah females who adorn themselves with trinkets and are powerless in disputation? (43:15)

Allah goes on to explain His position:

> Men have authority over women because Allah has made the one superior to the others....Good women are obedient....for those from whom you fear disobedience, admonish them and send them to beds apart and beat them. (4:34)

> Women are your fields; go then into your fields as you please. (2:223)

Quantitatively, women are worth just half as much as men. When inheritances are divided, the woman's share in the same relative position in the family is just half that of the man's. If witnesses are required for the signing of contracts, and enough men are not available, one male witness may be replaced with two female witnesses. For certain types of witnessing, the witness "must have the quality of veracity, and thus be neither a slave nor a woman." (Williams, *Islam*)

When one considers that most of Mohammed's adult life was spent with one woman, first in the employ of the rich widow Khadijah, subsequently in monogamous union with this evidently capable woman fifteen years his senior, his and Allah's attitude only serve to underscore the position of women as a whole in Arabia. It is possible that Mohammed's teachings did have some positive influence on the relative roles of women, for the Prophet said:

> In the Time of Ignorance, we did not consider women, nor did we let them interfere in any of our affairs. Then God brought us Islam and gave the women the place He gave them, together

> with rights, without permitting them to interfere in our affairs.... (T:23)

Mohammed did adjure decent treatment of wives and proper treatment of women on divorcing, when their dowry was to be given them.

> A Moslem must not hate his wife. If he dislikes her for one trait, let him find pleasure in another. (G-M, 125)

This would be good advice even today. And the Prophet did, on some level, appreciate women, for he said:

> The best property in the world is a virtuous woman. (G-M, 124)

There can be absolutely no doubt of the pro-masculine character of Allah, nor any question of whether this masculinity was adapted to the environment. Mohammed recorded:

> I have not left behind me a source of discord more injurious to men than women. (G-M, 124)

The Equal Rights Amendment and the Women's Liberation Movement would alike be completely incomprehensible to Allah as He evolved in the heyday of the camel caravan.

By the time of the birth of Mohammed in the year 570, the Unitarian Father God had generated a new form: the Trinitarian Father God, with God the Father, God the Son, and God the Holy Ghost somehow mystically united into one Godhead. The theologians evidently could understand how three could be one, even though to the average man it remained a bit confusing, and made it difficult for the missionary to convince his converts that they were not really talking about polytheism. As is true today, at that time both forms of the Father God existed, each in His own environment, but the predominant form was the triune God.

Among those who could not understand or accept the three-in-one idea was Mohammed, probably because he was exposed to as much or more Jewish thought as Christian. Although Mohammed could not read, and thus had only oral access to the Torah and the Gospels, he was undoubtedly aware that the three-in-one idea was not actually posed in the original gospels. Further, in attempting to steer his compatriots away from pagan worship, he had the problem of eliminating the influence of al-Uzzah, al-Lat, and Manah, who, excepting Allah, received the most wide-spread reverence of the Arabs, and whose idols resided in the Kaaba at Mecca. These three were believed to be daughters of Allah. If it were acceptable that Allah could have a son in Jesus, there might be no reason not to admit also daughters. In insisting that Allah was not simply pre-eminent, He was unique,

Mohammed not only simplified his theology, he also simplified the problem of dealing with Allah's "daughters."

For Mohammed, the awesome power of a deity who could create the universe and all that it contains, and could maintain a constant supervision over the thoughts, words, and deeds of all its people, jinn, and beasts, must be of such a nature as to transcend all need for assistant deities. It was inconceivable that such a power could be subdivided. Allah was responsible for everything that existed, had existed, and would exist, and had no intention of dividing that responsibility.

> [Allah is]...the Lord of the heavens and the earth, who has begotten no children and has no partner in his kingdom.... (25:2)

Allah insisted on belief in Him. Unlike the God of the Patriarchs, who called Himself a God jealous of other tribal deities, Allah is not by nature jealous. He has no reason to be—there is nothing to be jealous of. In the Koran, Gabriel quotes Allah as referring to idols as useless bits of wood or metal.

> The idols whom you invoke....have power over nothing. (35:15)

> They are but names which you and your fathers have invented. (53:20)

Allah Himself is disdainful of idolatry; His concern is to lead His people to the truth about Him. Rather than forbidding the idols themselves, it is worshipping the idols and believing in their powers that Allah abhors.

Still, Mohammed, inspired by Allah, realized the dangers of temptation presented by the mere existence of anything that could serve as an idol. He had seen not only the examples of the plurality of gods worshiped in the Kaaba, he had observed the deification of Christ on the cross and the veneration of Mary and the various saints. The Prophet wanted nothing available that could by the remotest possibility detract from the pure worship of Allah. The safest procedure was to remove the temptation by removing the objects that could incite it. So Mohammed exhorted against any sort of representation of nature, distorted or otherwise. In one story, Mohammed refused to enter a house containing pictures:

> Aisha [one of Mohammed's wives] relates that she bought a cushion on which were pictures, and when the Apostle of God saw them, he stood at the door and would not enter. (G-M, 128)

Thus the devout Moslem will have no pictures, even of Allah or of Mohammed, in either his home, or his mosque. As a result, the decoration by abstract forms and lines that we have come to know as "Arabesque" was developed into a high art form in Islam. Mosques and public buildings are covered with the exquisite intricate designs and radiant color combinations that we recognize instantly as being of Islamic origin.

Allah's contempt for idolaters was greater than He held for atheists. Rather than being jealous of something that did not exist, Allah was angry that the unbelievers refused to be convinced of what did so obviously exist.

Nor does He express jealousy of Jesus, for it was He who sent Jesus down to serve as a prophet. He is, however, furious with men who insist on misrepresenting the truth. Allah states specifically:

> Jesus was no more than a mortal whom We favored and made an example to the Israelites. (43:58)

> "Jesus...did you ever say to mankind: worship me and my mother as gods beside Allah?" "Glory to You," he will answer, "How could I say that to which I had no right?" (5:116)

> Those who say, "The Lord of Mercy has begotten a son," preach a monstrous falsehood....it does not become him to beget one. (19:88)

Alongside the solitary Allah, even Satan has nothing of the power of evil deities, as has Ahriman in the dualistic Zoroastrian religion. Allah considered man His greatest creation, superior even to the angels:

> Your Lord said to the angels., "I am creating man from clay....Kneel down and prostrate yourselves before him [Adam]." The angels all prostrated themselves except Satan, who was too proud...."I am nobler than he. You created me from fire..but him from clay." (38:69)

This act of disobedience enraged Allah, who cursed Satan and threw him out of heaven. From then on, Satan has it in for mankind, and does his best to take his evil revenge. But his only power is to tempt man, to seek to lead him astray from the right path. This falls right in with Allah's design, since Allah wants man to be tested before he is allocated a soft couch in Paradise.

Moslems give Allah ninety-nine "names" besides, which are in reality attributes, such as the Almighty, the Merciful, the Compassionate, the Invincible One, the Most High. He is omnipotent, omnipresent, and omniscient.

> He need only say "Be," and it is. (40:68)

Nor does he suffer from human limitations:

> Neither slumber nor sleep overtakes Him. (2:255)

> In six days We created the heavens and the earth and all that lies between them; nor were We ever wearied. (50:37)

We note that this is in contrast with Jehovah, who needed rest on the seventh day at the end of His labors. The difference is recognized in Islam, which does not take the Sabbath as seriously as do the orthodox Hebrews. Allah, who requires daily prayer, does indeed require special observances once a week, on Friday, but once these are dispensed with, the Moslem is free to do as he chooses:

> When [Friday] prayers are ended, disperse and go in quest of Allah's bounty. (62:10)

Obviously there is no need to commemorate the resting of a God who never tires. Indeed, it would be difficult to imagine a God doing all that Allah does, seeing all, keeping up with all, if He could tire.

> He has knowledge of all that land and sea contain; every leaf that falls is known to Him. There is no grain of soil in the darkest bowels of the earth, nor anything green or sear, but is recorded in His glorious Book. It is He who makes you sleep...by night then rouses you.... (6:59)

Had Mohammed known about modern science, he would have said that Allah steered each electron in its orbit, guided the billions of stars in their far-flung galaxies, for Allah reigns supreme.

> He created man from a little germ....He created the beasts which provide you with warm clothing, food and other benefits....he has given you horses, mules and donkeys which you may ride....He who sends down water from the sky....He brings up corn and olives, dates and grapes....He has forced the night and the day, the sun and the moon into your service....He has subjected to you the ocean, so that you may eat of its fresh fish and bring up from it ornaments....the ships ploughing through it....set firm mountains on the earth lest it should move...rivers, roads and landmarks, so that you may be rightly guided.... (16:3ff.)

Not only has all this been created by Allah, but it is He who supervises it continuously. Allah does not require the aid of humans,

> ...know that Allah does not need you. Yet the ingratitude of His servants does not please Him. If you are thankful, your thanks will please him. (39:7)

Certainly it is to be expected than an almighty God will not need His creations. But the idea that He evidently does feel the need of appreciation and gratitude—can that be a sign that He was created in the image of man?

Repeatedly, Gabriel passes on the word that Allah resents the ingratitude of humankind:

> Confound man!! How ungrateful he is! (80:18)

Throughout the Islamic texts, the only contacts of either Allah or any of His heavenly forces that was perceptible to the senses were the visitations of the angel Gabriel to Mohammed for the purpose of transmitting the Koran. Even the angel forces sent to aid in battles remained invisible to both sides. Yet Allah is everywhere—transcendentally.

> Whichever way you turn, there is the face of Allah. He is omnipresent and all-knowing. (2:115)

> If a man draws near me by the space of a span, I draw near to him by the space of a cubit; and if he draws near me by the space of a cubit, I draw near him by the space of a fathom. (T:1967)

He is everywhere at once, controlling the winds, the rains, the destinies of man. He is invisible to the senses, but the Sufi mystics of Islam can feel His presence. And Allah requires a response to this presence, felt or unfelt. The obligations are both moral and ceremonial. Sacrifices and burnt offerings are of little or no interest to Him; the main rites expected of the Moslem worshipper are prayer and pilgrimage. He has Gabriel tell Mohammed that to the "spot where Abraham stood":

> Pilgrimage to the House is a duty to Allah for all who can make the journey. (3:97)

This is required at least once in a man's life if a man is physically and financially capable of making the trip, even though it means severe hardship. Once at Mecca, there is a vastly complicated ritual observance requiring several days: turns about the Black Stone; visits to the holy spots, including the well of Zamzam; throwing stones at the devil. The important effect of this journey, or Hajj, is the deep sense of brotherhood in Islam generated by becoming part of this grand performance. All participants must wear a simple white seamless robe, so that all people meet on the same level in their relations to Allah.

The same feeling of brotherhood is engendered by taking part in the ritual prayers five times a day. When the muezzin calls from the top of the slender minarets (these days, the call is issued electronically via a taped message and a loudspeaker installed on a high platform), the faithful gather in the mosques or at certain locations in the streets, face in the direction of Mecca, and pray according to the prescribed ritual. This serves as a constant reminder of the presence of Allah and brings men closer to Allah and to each other. The discipline inherent in this ritual derives from strict adherence to ritual series of prayer formulae, hand movement, kneeling, bowing, and prostrating one's body, the meaning of which is nullified if words are confused or gestures made improperly. Recital of parts of the Koran is included, especially in the more formal religious ceremonies held each Friday in the mosque:

> When the Koran is recited, listen to it in silence so that Allah may show you mercy. Remember your Lord deep in your soul with humility and reverence and without ostentation, remember Him morning and evening and do not be negligent. (7:205)

The original requirements for morning and evening prayer gradually expanded both in the Koran and in Mohammed's preaching until, at the time of Mohammed's death, the requirements had reached five prayers a day. When these prayers should occur was at first general. Later, it was made more specific and announced by the call of the muezzin, wherever the group or community was large enough. A hadith of Tayalisi gives a guide:

> The time of zuhr is when the sun begins to decline from the meridian until the shadow of a man corresponds to his height, until the time of the 'asr. And the time of the 'asr is until the sun becomes yellow. The time of the mahgrib is until the twilight disappears....and the time of the isha is between that and the half-way point of the night. The time of subh is when the dawn rises until the time of sunrise. (T:2249)

Prayers are not offered during the actual rising or setting of the sun, presumably due to an ancient belief that at those times, the sun was between the horns of the devil—certainly an inauspicious time. This may have also been the result of an effort to discourage people from relapsing into sun-worship.

Nowhere does Mohammed refer to Allah as a "Father," probably to avoid any possibility of thinking of Him as having a son. Nor does Allah behave with a typical father's interest and love. He does, however, have some of the traits of a good father. He claims to be stern and just, but His justice is mitigated by compassion and mercy. Far from being simply a strict judge, He looks for opportunities to forgive and approves forgiveness in others. He approved of Joseph who forgave his brothers after being sold into slavery in Egypt by them (12:97), and the Prophet tells us that:

> There is no man who receives a bodily injury and forgives the offender, but God will exalt his rank and diminish his sin. (G-M, 101)

Never forgetting that the first requirement, the absolute commandment is belief, next comes the importance of forgiveness and good works. And Allah promises to practice what He preaches. If you are good and forgiving, He will be good and forgiving to you. Just be sure not to forget that:

> ...whoever...dies an unbeliever, his works shall come to nothing in this world.... (2:218)

If you remember that, and believe:

> As for the faithful who do good works and believe in what is revealed to Mohammed...He will forgive them their sins and ennoble their state... (47:2)

> Good deeds make amends for sins. (11:113)

> He that does a good deed shall be repaid many times over. (42:24)

Every Sura except the first, the Exordium, is begun with "In the name of Allah, the Compassionate, the Merciful." All through the Koran, we are reminded of Allah's forgiving character. But even the innate willingness of Allah to forgive everyone is limited. Unlike the Father God, who joyously accepts death-bed repentance:

> Allah forgives those who commit evil in ignorance and then quickly turn to Him in repentance; But Allah will not forgive those who do evil all their lives and, when death comes to them, say: "Now we repent!" (4:18)

And there is the unforgivable sin:

> Nor will He forgive those who die unbelievers....Allah will not forgive idolatry. (4:18, 116)

Part of the phenomenal success of Islam in the years following Mohammed's ministry is due to the forgiving nature of Allah. He, unlike the bloodthirsty God of the Patriarchs, never instructed His people to invade enemy territory and to massacre all of its inhabitants, even thought they might have been idolaters worshipping other gods. The Jews and the Christians—the

People of the Book—were considered to be already believers in Allah, even though they might have strayed slightly into error. They were accepted into the Islamic community, although they were in certain ways treated as second class citizens if they did not themselves embrace Islam. Belligerent destruction of Jews and Christians did occur, but only as political expediency, and if they surrendered, they were well treated.

Wherever the forces of Islam met with military victory, those who surrendered were spared. They had discovered that humanitarian treatment of enemies often turned them into friends, or at the very least, made their absorption into the growing Islamic empire manageable. A sympathetic reception, as opposed to the violent massacres which had often been the custom of the times, convinced many grateful people in all the countries invaded by the conquering Moslems to convert to Islam. The Moslem Empire at its height stretched from the Iberian peninsula across North Africa and the Middle East into India and beyond. With the exception of Spain and Portugal, most of the area of that abandoned empire is still predominantly Moslem.

Undoubtedly, the conviction of the faithful that Allah would reward them for fighting on His behalf turned the Arabian army into a better organized, more disciplined military organization with a sense of purpose. Allah's promise of Paradise made the already war-like Bedouin an even more valiant and determined fighter. With the thought of the soft couches, the cool shady gardens threaded by clear, bubbling creeks, and dark-eyed, voluptuous houris waiting for them, it could almost be disappointing not to be killed in battle. But a warrior could not simply expose himself to death—the reward was not for suicide, but for those who fought bravely for Allah.

> As for those slain in the cause of Allah...He will admit them to the Paradise He has made known to them. (47:7)
>
> Paradise lies in the shadow of the swords.... (T:530)
>
> He that fights in the way of God but the time between two milkings of a camel, Paradise is his due. (G-M, 111)

This lays the basis for the Jihad, or Holy War of the Moslems. War against unbelievers is not only permitted, it is encouraged. Allah suggests that it is sometimes desirable to wait for an attack, but often His declarations of war are belligerent. The wars Allah desires are efforts to convert the world into believers, so that others too may some day enjoy the pleasures of Paradise. Similar to the reasoning upon which the perpetrators of the Spanish Inquisition grounded their activities, Muslim wars were represented as being for the benefit of the souls of the infidels. If one listens to the propagandists, all wars are either defensive or altruistic. In following Allah's exhortations, they are altruistic.

> Make war on them until idolatry is no more and Allah's religion reigns supreme If they incline to peace, make peace with them, and put your trust in Allah. (8:39, 60)

> Believers, make war on the infidels who dwell around you. Deal courteously with them. (9:123)

The bellicose Bedouin—brought up in an atmosphere of tribal raids based both on economic necessity and on continual tribal vendettas in which the balance of blood never came out even—did not lose his warlike spirit. Islam banned the internecine warfare, and Allah strictly forbade the killing of believers:

> The believers are a band of brothers. Make peace among your brothers and fear Allah.... (49:10)

The militant character of the desert Arab was not subdued, but in building the solidarity against outsiders, could be channeled through the Jihad into the successful wars of expansion that built the fantastic might of the Moslem Empire of the Middle Ages.

With all of Allah's mercy and compassion, He is anything but a peaceful God. He is definitely martial and militant, but for what He considers a good cause. He does not visualize a Utopia on Earth—especially since He marks His subjects in the womb, with some destined for misery and the torments of Hell—but He does desire a world united in a brotherhood of believers, who, being believers, will all be eligible for admission to the Garden of Delights.

> Say, "We believe in Allah and that which is revealed to us; in what was revealed to Abraham, Ishmael, Isaac, Jacob and the tribes; to Moses and Jesus and other prophets by their Lord. We make no distinction amongst any of them, and unto Allah, we have surrendered ourselves." (2:136)

# Chapter 8: The God of Mormon

> And also those to whom these commandments were given, might have power to lay the foundation of this church, and to bring it forth out of obscurity and out of darkness, the only true and living church on the face of the whole earth, with which I, the Lord, am well pleased... (Doctrine and Covenants, 1:30)

The concept of God as we have considered Him thus far, is based on scriptures that have been commonly accepted by the believers in each particular faith. It is believed by the followers of each of these faiths that these scriptures were inspired by God Himself through one means or another. They became a part of what is known as "revealed" religion, because of the idea that the knowledge of God and the principles of the religion were revealed to the human race by God Himself acting either directly or indirectly through individuals selected by God.

The first of these in the series we selected was the Torah, or Pentateuch; the so-called Books of Moses. Some traditions assert that they were written by Moses himself, though the story of his death at the end at least must have been by some survivor. No evidence exists in these books to support this claim. We must remember that many of the older scriptures were reduced to writing long after they had persisted as oral tradition; perhaps all of them, including a fair part of the Koran and the New Testament Gospels. It is assumed by many that the Pentateuch was assembled in its present written form after the Babylonian exile, and was influenced to a large extent by Babylonian mythology, with its stories of creation from Chaos, of universal flood, and the Babylonian seven-day week. Be that as it may, for our purposes, we may assume that the Old Testament was in large part written after the Pentateuch, over a period of several centuries, ending about two centuries before the birth of Christ.

The fact that several groups of believers use the same scripture, and each perceives a different interpretation is a basic reality in religion. This book itself is an interpretation of various scriptures as understood by its author; undoubtedly, many will disagree with the interpretation.

From the Torah and other Jewish books and from the traditions of the Talmud, there arose in ancient times a variety of sects, such as the Pharisees, the Sadducees, and the Essenes. From the Gospel of Christ, we have a dozen principal Christian religions and hundreds of minor variations. The Koran has its Sunni, its Shi'ites, and its Sufi mystics, as well as a number of minor groups.

Several centuries passed between the revelations of Moses and other Old Testament prophets before the appearance of a new prophet-revealer in the form of Jesus the Christ. Then, another half-dozen centuries elapsed before another prophet appeared who was able to assemble a large, permanent following—Mohammed. Following the advent of the Koran, a number of variants of religion developed that showed enough strength to remain important into the nineteenth century. These included the Jewish forms that abandoned strict orthodoxy, and the Methodist, Baptist, and Presbyterian branches of Protestantism that followed upon Martin Luther's break with the Roman Catholic church.

While it might be said that these religions were inspired by God's influence on their founders, still, in each case, the founders of these new religions used the same basic scriptures. Although they presented their various views in a large body of literature, none of it is considered "scripture" by the followers of these new variants, and little is read today by anyone other than students and theologians.

Thus, from the time of the Koran till the nineteenth century, no prophet appeared who was accepted by a sufficiently wide following to produce writings considered to be scriptures. Mohammed had called himself the "Seal of the Prophets," and after twelve centuries, it was beginning to look as if his self-applied title had some foundation in fact.

This state came to a sudden end in the first half of the nineteenth century with the appearance of three completely different new writings that have been accepted as a form of scripture by enough followers to become important worldwide religions. All three claim to have their roots in the Old and New Testaments, and one includes also the Koran (which, as we will recall, is itself based on the religion of the Old and New Testaments). Yet without going back to polytheism, it would be difficult to imagine a set of three religions starting with Jehovah and winding up as diverse as are Mormonism, Christian Science, and the Baha'i Faith.

What is the reason for this sudden, unheralded appearance on the stage of religion of three such different faiths, each with its own following of dedicated and thoroughly convinced believers, after such a long period of relatively insignificant, scriptureless variations? No one has offered a satisfactory explanation. One suggestion that the three parts of the Trinity each decided to present its own view can hardly be taken seriously, even if one were to assume the position that Mormonism concentrates on Jesus Christ, that the Baha'i faith focuses on a

Father God who created a world and wanted to see it develop, while Mary Baker Eddy's Christian Science God might be seen as focusing on the Holy Ghost.

The world had for some time gone on with gradual evolutionary changes in God, characterized by the splitting, branching, and redividing of the three basic religions of Judaism, Islam, and Christianity. Suddenly, it was faced with three individuals who attained the fundamental status of prophets—Joseph Smith, Mary Baker Eddy, and Husayn 'Ali (Baha'u'llah), each of whom produced writings accepted as scripture by their followers. Could there have been a sudden surge of cosmic rays that caused mutations resulting in the evolution of three new God-species almost simultaneously?

Mormonism is the common name of the religion of a church known officially as the Church of Jesus Christ of Latter-day Saints. Mormons themselves accept and use the term "Mormon," derived from their principal scriptural work, the "Book of Mormon." This name comes in turn from one of its divisions, also entitled "the Book of Mormon," said to have been written by one of the figures of the church history by the name of Mormon. The church today claims a worldwide congregation of some four million people, and is very active in missionary work, most of which is performed by men in their early twenties whose expenses are mostly paid for by themselves or their families.

The texts that may be considered the scripture of the Church of Jesus Christ of Latter-day Saints include the Book of Mormon, the Doctrine and Covenants, the Pearl of Great Price, and the Articles of Faith, all produced by Joseph Smith. Smith asserted that he was shown by the angel Moroni, who appeared to him in a vision, where to find the gold and brass plates that were the records of a group of Israelites who came to America around six hundred B.C., about the time of Jeremiah and just before the Babylonian exile. These American colonists underwent a continual round of belief and doubt, incessant internecine wars and other vicissitudes which first led to a large increase in numbers, but ultimately ended in practically wiping out all concerned by the fourth century after Christ. They had their prophets, who predicted in accurate detail the coming of Jesus, even to the details of His future preachments. Subsequent to Christ's resurrection, He appeared to these immigrants in America for a short season. The power of His preaching initiated a great revival, which later disintegrated, and ended with the virtual annihilation of the people in one last great Armageddon.

All this history was translated by Smith with the help of the "Urim and Thummim," a pair of crystal balls set in a breastplate and buried along with the inscribed plates. This translation became the Book of Mormon. (Students of the Bible will remember that the Urim and Thummim were instruments, not fully described, used by the ancient Hebrew priests to determine the will of God, probably in a system of casting lots.)

Among other things, the records tell of the building of a great ship and the design of a compass under God's instructions, and recount the voyage which eventually terminated with a landing on the coast of what is now North

America. The originally small group multiplied, building great cities, and from battle casualty descriptions, the group population must have reached several million.

> There had been slain by the sword already...two millions of mighty men, and also their wives and their children. (Ether 15:2)

Nowhere in the Book of Mormon are there references which can accurately place any of these cities, and nowhere is there any reference to an indigenous population. One is led to the inference that the Indians found by later explorers either kept themselves well hidden, or were descendants of these immigrants, and thus originally of Semitic origin.

Some of the Israelites in the new continent may have come from another wave of immigration. We find in the Apocrypha an explanation of what happened to the ten lost tribes of Israel that were the victims of the Assyrians:

> ...will leave the heathen and go forth into a further country where never mankind dwelt. (2 Esdras 13:41)

Unfortunately, all we know of them and this country is that it was:

> A great way to go—and the same region is called Arsareth.... (2 Esdras 13:45)

The plates were reburied by Smith when he finished with them. Two documents exist, one signed by three witnesses and one by eight, stating that Smith showed them the plates.

The Doctrine and Covenants were revelations given to Smith by God over the years of his administration of the church, generally when there was some question of church doctrine, church action or organization to be decided. The Pearl of Great Price included a group of revelations and a translation which Smith claimed came from a papyrus written by Abraham.

There is one outstanding difference between the predictions of the prophets of the Book of Mormon and the Biblical prophecies of the coming of the Messiah. While the Biblical prophecies are quite vague in form and often allegorical—typically similar to oracular pronouncements—those of the Book of Mormon are concrete and exact. Even though some were made nearly six hundred years before the birth of Jesus, they contain not only His preachings and the words of John the Baptist as quoted in the Gospels, but also details about Jesus' crucifixion and resurrection. Some detractors of the Mormon religion hold that this exactitude is due to the report of the revelation being ex post facto, but we are nowhere trying to claim validity or invalidity for any of our Gods. We are only trying to trace their evolution and relate them to their environment, as well as seek evidence to enable the reader to determine in his own mind whether man made God in his image or vice versa.

A new sect, claiming to be the only true church, will always have its troubles. The U.S. Constitution can only guarantee the freedom of religion insofar as it ensures that no laws can be made to abridge religious worship. What it cannot prevent is individual hostility. The religion's potential for fomenting hostility was probably furthered by Smith's assertion that, when he was questioning which church he should join, the Christ appeared to him in a vision and told him to:

> ...join none of them, for they were all wrong....all their creeds were an abomination in his sight...(Joseph Smith 2:19)

Even before God revealed to Smith that polygamy was once again acceptable, hostility and mob violence troubled the Latter-day Saints, and forced them to move from New York state, to Missouri, to Illinois, laboriously rebuilding their community wherever they went. This pattern of persecution came to a head when a mob assaulted a jail in which Joseph Smith and some associates were being held, killing Smith and his brother. Under the leadership of Brigham Young, the group finally moved another thousand miles west to the new territory of Utah where the solitude finally afforded them the opportunity to worship in peace. Finally in 1890, the Saints, one of whose tenets was obedience to the law of the land, followed the new U.S. laws against polygamy and outlawed it in their own church. Since then, they have not only become tolerated, but admired by many for their industriousness and their distaste for government welfare.

Since Joseph Smith was brought up in a Protestant Christian environment, where belief in the words of the New Testament was fundamental, one would not logically expect much difference between the Father God of the New Testament and the God of Mormon. And indeed, the differences are not great. We present the God of Mormon as a distinct god essentially because of the existence of the Mormon Scriptures and their unusual character. One of its most unusual aspects is that, except where it is quoting the Bible, nothing in the history of the Hebrew immigrants presented in the Book of Mormon can be found in any other preexisting records. Another unusual aspect is its concentration over a period of a thousand years, both before and after the coming of Jesus, on Jesus Himself as the principal and continuing focus of religion, almost to the point where one gets the impression that God Himself is of merely secondary importance. We even find Enoch, the father of Methuselah and great-grandfather of Noah, preaching redemption to those who believe in Jesus Christ five or six centuries before the Flood (Moses 6:52)! God explains to Adam, who is still alive, His plans of salvation through Jesus Christ (Moses 6:57–62).

This concentration on Jesus in no way downgrades God, since Jesus is part of the Godhead.

Perhaps here we have our widest discrepancy with the image of the Father God. The Gospels present a clear picture of a monotheistic Unitarian God, with the single exception of the beginning of the Gospel of St. John, in which Jesus is referred to as the Word which existed from all time, a reference which is not quite clear and is subject to a variety of interpretations, including that John saw things differently from Matthew, Mark, and Luke, and no one was there to prove who was right. The statement by Jesus that, "I am in the Father and the Father is in me" does not prove the Trinitarian point any more than the statement that "God is in his heart" in reference to good Christians proves pantheism. It is essentially a figure of speech used by Jesus, who loved to use figures of speech, allegories, and parables. God Himself uses the expression, speaking to Enoch:

> Thou shalt abide in me, and I in you.... (Moses 6:34)

And Jesus said of believers:

> They may become...one in me as I am one in the Father.... (D.C. 35:2)

Mormonism, however, flatly affirms the Trinitarian viewpoint.

> Which Father, Son and Holy Ghost are one God, infinite and eternal, without end. (D.C. 20:28)

As Gregg Braden expresses it: "The Trinity is real and separate; their unity is one of purpose and operation and not one of substance." (Braden, *They Also Believe*, p. 440) However, it is not certain that Joseph Smith would have accepted this interpretation.

Throughout the Mormon scriptures, the emphasis is placed consistently on Jesus Christ. When God says one must believe, the emphasis of this belief is on Jesus, the "Only Begotten," rather than in the Father God. It is interesting to note that time, as humans see it, evidently means nothing to God who, in talking to Enoch more than three thousand years before the birth of Jesus, refers to Him as "mine Only Begotten Son," and again requires belief in Him rather than the Father:

> Jesus Christ, the only name...whereby salvation shall come unto the children of men.... (Moses 6:52)

There is no doubt of the godly potency of Jesus, as He is credited with the actual Creation:

> Behold, I am Jesus Christ....I created the heavens and the earth and all things that in them are. I was with the Father from the beginning. (3 Nephi 9:15)

The Latter-day Saints believe that the resurrection of the believers will be not only that of souls, but will include the recovery of the body of flesh and bone.

> They...shall receive the same body which was a natural body. (D.C. 88:28)

This is logical, given that humans were created after the image of God, and:

> The Father has a body of flesh and bones as tangible as man's; the Son also; but the Holy ghost...is a personage of Spirit. (D.C. 130:22)

As a part of God, the principal function of the Holy Ghost is to act, upon occasion, as God's messenger; to inspire certain acts or directions; and to enter into a newly baptized person, bringing an emotion of inspiration and a deep feeling of rebirth in Christ—a realization that something far beyond normal material experience is happening.

> ...he (Aaron) was led by the Spirit to the land of Nephi, even to the house of the king.... (Alma 22:1)

> ...after they had spoken these words the Spirit of the Lord came upon them, and they were filled with joy....(Mosiah 4:3)

At this point, we will take a moment to consider the environment into which the Mormon God was born, and whether we could reasonably estimate His chances of survival.

To begin with, the young nation of the United States of America was largely comprised of a number of individuals and groups who moved to the New World to escape religious persecution or limitations on their religious worship. Hence, they were basically a strongly religious people. They came to avoid the vicissitudes of life on the old continent, not because they were weak and unable to endure them, but because they were strong and capable of fighting their way to a better life in a land free of governmental oppression. With the Declaration of Independence and the new Constitution they reaffirmed their belief in equality before the law, the right to the pursuit of happiness, and the basic freedoms of the Bill of Rights. According to Mormon doctrine, the American Constitution was in fact the work of the God of Mormon.

> And for this purpose have I [God] established the Constitution of this land, by the hands of wise men whom I raised up unto this very purpose.... (D.C. 101:80)

The morals American immigrants brought with them were practically exclusively those of the Christian Church; even more, those of Protestant Christianity. Hosts of them wanted no part of a church controlled by an Italianate hierarchy, any more than they wanted to be taxed without representation by George III. One cannot avoid considering that the repeated references to that "abominable church" must be references to the Church of Rome:

> ...that great and abominable church, which was founded by the devil and his children.... (1 Nephi 14:3)

Thus, the morals and the church mutually reinforced each other, and the Father God, as He was understood by the various Protestant sects, existed in a favorable environment. This was confirmed in the early nineteenth century by a strong religious revival occurring principally among the Baptists, Methodists, and Presbyterians. Though nominally worshipping the same God and His son Jesus, each cherished small differences in doctrine or manner of worship that allowed each preacher to maintain that his church was, "the only true church," and threaten his communicants with hell fire if they left his congregation to take part in a different system of worship.

Such was the religious climate when God told Joseph Smith that all the existing churches were wrong and ordered him to start over. God instructed that this new church was to be based on the translation of the plates and on the direct revelations to Smith by God, Jesus, and the angel Moroni.

Since Christianity was the accepted religion of the majority, it is not surprising to find the new church concentrating more on Christ than on God. God Himself approves, having dictated the name of the church:

> For thus shall my church be called...The Church of Jesus Christ of Latter-day Saints. (D.C. 115:4)

The hard life of the pioneers as they moved westward, breaking new ground and building new communities, was concordant with the concept of a strict God who had no time for levity or diversions. Here again we find the dictates of this evolved God well-adapted to His environment. He cautions His people:

> ...as any man drinketh wine or strong drink....behold, it is not good....strong drinks are not for the belly but for the washing of your bodies....tobacco...is not good for man....hot drinks are not for the body or belly....flesh also of beasts and of the fowls...are to be used sparingly. (D.C. 89:5–12)

> ...cease from all your light speeches, from all laughter, from all. your lustful desires, from all your pride and light-mindedness.... (D.C. 88:121)

Folk who work hard and desist from lust and light diversions at least deserve a rest now and then, and this is awarded to them on God's holy day. Once they have taken care of their duties to offer their oblations, observe their sacraments, and confess their sins:

> ...on this day, thou shalt do none other thing, only let thy food be prepared with singleness of heart.... (D.C. 59:13)

In considering the admonitions, instructions, and commandments of the Mormon God, we pause to remember something we said about the Father God—that we could understand the statement that "God is Love" when applied to Him, but that it was difficult to get such a feeling about other Gods. This applies also to the God of Mormon; He states that He loves and He wants to be loved, but one cannot easily accept a statement that "God is Love" about a God who spends so little time on injunctions such as "love thy neighbor" and stories of the Good Samaritan, and so much on belief, baptism, threats, admonitions, and detailed instructions about church organization and operations.

Although the God of Mormon has much in common with the Father God, such as promising forgiveness and salvation through Jesus, offering baptism and faith, answering prayers and performing miracles, abandoning Mosaic laws, and promising a second coming of Christ with a better earth, followed by a Judgment Day and a division of the sheep and the goats between Paradise and Hell, evangelism, and so on, there are differences. We do not intend to dwell on these similarities, but point out differences.

The theological battle as to whether the wine and the bread of the sacrament are actually the blood and the flesh of Christ or are merely representative does not seem to have been quite settled in the Mormon scriptures. In some references they are accepted as symbolic, in remembrance:

> ....I have broken bread and blessed it...in rememberance of my body....take of the wine of the cup and drink of it...in remembrance of my blood.... (3 Nephi 18:6–11)

> ...meet together often to partake of bread and wine in the remembrance of our Lord Jesus....bread...in remembrance of the body....wine...in remembrance of the blood....(D.C. 20:75–79)

Others present this sacrament as bearing another meaning:

> The manner of their elders and priests administering the flesh and blood of Christ unto the Church.... (Moroni 4:1)

> ...ye shall not suffer anyone knowingly to partake of my flesh and blood unworthily. (3 Nephi 18:28)

So the problem of transubstantiation is still with us, and the God of Mormon has not settled it.

One issue that the Father God did not face squarely was racism as it materialized in America. Slaves in Biblical times were white as well as black, so there was no need for a racist attitude to salve one's conscience for keeping fellow men in bondage by claiming innate superiority of one race over another. Conditions in the new America were different. Black African slaves were claimed to be an inferior race by those who hoped to keep them in bondage. But there was already a strong movement against this racism, and abolitionists were particularly active in the North. Although God did not object to slavery when slaves were white as well as black, many now considered God to be in favor of emancipation and equality. Preachers quoted the Bible at length on both sides of the question, and which side of the question they assumed often depended on whether those who filled the collection plates were slave-owners or not.

We are therefore not too surprised to find the God of Mormon ambivalent. He advocates equality, and Mormon scripture asserts that laws against slavery already existed nearly a century before Christ:

> ....he denieth none that come unto him, black and white, bond and free, male and female.... (2 Nephi 26:33)

> It is against the law of our brethren...that there should be any slaves among them. (Alma 27:9)

But the underlying propensity towards prejudice shows through regardless:

> And he [the Lord] caused a cursing to come upon them...a skin of blackness...that they shall be loathsome unto thy people....and because of the cursing...they did become an idle people, full of mischief and subtlety....(2 Nephi 5:21–24)

> ...for the seed of Cain were black, and had not place among them. (Moses 7:22)

This prejudice yet resides in the Mormon church at the time of this writing. There are black Mormons, but they are excluded from the high offices of the church. Church officials somewhat apologetically explain that God has not yet sent down a revelation saying that the church is ready to have a black president, but that God's revelations are continual, and it could come any day now.

One of the marked differences between the God of Mormon and the Father God is that the former maintains a much closer and more continuous contact with His people on earth through communications (revelations) that are both highly frequent and greatly detailed. These communications are reported as being received almost continually—from either God, Jesus, or the angel Moroni—from the beginning of the history of the Book of Mormon about 600 B.C. into current history. Article 9 of the Mormon Articles of Faith reads: "We believe all that God has revealed, all that He does now reveal, and we believe that He will reveal many great and important things pertaining to the Kingdom of God."

In the first days of the new church, God's revelations served to appoint various church officers by the word of God, and to define for them the work they were to do or where they were to go to preach.

> I give unto you [God says] my servant Brigham Young to be a president over the Twelve traveling council....I give unto you Vinson Knight, Samuel H. Smith and Shadrach Roundy...to preside over the bishopric....(D.C. 124:127, 141)

The Mormons expect revelations to indicate to them who will be chosen for the presidency of the church each time that the position is vacated:

> The president of the church...is appointed by revelation.... (D.C. 102:9)

A further departure from the religions of the Father God is the subject of a revelation to President Joseph F. Smith (October, 1918) which was considered important enough to be included in the "Pearl of Great Price" in 1976. This concerns a vision by President Smith, in which he is shown the righteous dead assembled in Paradise with Christ ministering among them. Among others, he saw Adam, Eve, Noah, Isaiah, Daniel, and the early Mormon church fathers. He saw Christ appointing certain among the righteous to preach to the souls of those who had died in sin or were unbelievers and learned that, "The dead who repent will be redeemed, through obedience to the ordinances of the house of God." We are thus given to understand that, with acceptance of God, repentance, and vicarious baptism, sinners, such as Jesse James and Adolph Hitler, could be redeemed.

This may not, in fact, be as much of a divergence from other Christian religions as it seems. The Bible itself contains a hint that the Father God might act similarly:

> For this is why the gospel was preached even to the dead, that though judged in the flesh like men, they might live in the spirit like God. (1 Peter 4:6)

This hint, not fully clarified in the Bible, may well have been the seed of what was clarified in Joseph F. Smith's vision nineteen centuries later. It may be that the vision of redemption of the dead was God's effort to explain exactly who would and would not be saved. The standard Mormon requirements for salvation include a knowledge of and faith in God, a knowledge of the story of Christ and a belief that salvation comes through Christ, sincere repentance for sins committed, and baptism, followed by keeping of God's commandments. It is repeated time and again that no one can be saved except through Jesus:

> ...men drink damnation to their own souls except they...believe that salvation...is to come in and through the atoning blood of Christ. (Mosiah 3:18)

This clarity still leaves us with the problem of the unfortunate souls who have never heard the story of Jesus, despite all efforts:

> ...God hath sent his holy prophets among the children of men, to declare these things to every nation and tongue, that thereby whosoever should believe that Christ should come...might receive remission of their sins....(Mosiah 3:13)

At first glance, considering what we have heard before, it would seem that it is impossible for a man to be saved in ignorance. One gets the impression that these poor folk will be consigned to the flames of hell through no fault of their own. But there is hope for them. Although a man cannot be saved in ignorance, he will still be given a chance after death, if he did not have one before:

> ...where there is no law given, there is no punishment....(2 Nephi 9:25)

> ...he that knoweth not good from evil is blameless....(Alma 29:5)

> ...and they that knew no law shall have part in the first resurrection.... (D.C. 45:54)

Section 128 of Doctrine and Covenants goes into detail about how the vicarious baptism for the dead should be handled, in consideration of individual cases. The vision of Joseph F. Smith seems to take care of those who were ignorant on earth but will be given a chance to learn in heaven.

Children are a special case. The Mormons do not agree with some Christian churches, including the Catholics, who baptize babies as soon after their birth as possible to be certain they will not be damned. The God of Mormon does not agree that humans are born in sin:

> ...God having redeemed man from the fall, men became again, in their infant state., innocent before God.(D.C. 93:38)

God considers that infants do not have the ability to tell the difference between right and wrong, and therefore cannot sin. The sacrament of baptism is an affirmation of repentance and of acceptance of Jesus, therefore an infant who does not understand sin cannot logically repent; if the child does not understand thoroughly the story of Jesus, it cannot be expected to accept it other than superficially.

> ...wherefore...I know that it is solemn mockery before God, that ye should baptize little children. (Moroni 8:9)

> And he that saith that little children need baptism denieth the mercies of Christ. (Moroni 8:20)

As a result, God will admit unbaptized toddlers into the benefits of heaven without the necessity of baptism, which they are to accept only when they have become of age to be able to understand what they are doing.

> And their children shall be baptized for the remission of their sins when eight years old.... (D.C. 68:27)

The process of redemption through repentance and baptism constitutes being "born again," a birth into the Sprit, a necessity for salvation.

> For, said [Alma], I have repented of my sins....behold I am born of the Spirit. (Mosiah 27:24)

> Ye must repent, and be born again; for the Spirit saith that if ye are not born again ye cannot inherit the kingdom of heaven.... (Alma 7:14)

In order to be able to tell the difference between those whose belief is sincere and those who have merely gone through the motions of belief, God has made a few simple statements that will allow anyone to test his own faith. It is believed that faith will allow anyone to perform miracles, to heal, to cast out devils, to drink poison, to be immune to poisonous vipers, and so on:

> ...Every soul who believeth on your [Christ's apostles] words and is baptized by water for the remission of sins, shall receive the Holy Ghost. And these signs shall follow them that believe....in my name they shall cast out devils....shall heal the sick....open the eyes of the blind and unstop the ears of the deaf; and the tongue of the dumb shall speak....and if any man shall administer poison unto them it shall not hurt them; and the poison of a serpent shall not have power to harm them. (D.C. 84:64–72)

We see that faith has its rewards.

Of course, it might be argued that anyone who feels the need to test his faith does not really have it, so that the ability to perform miracles at will or to drink cyanide with immunity, as in Jonestown, could not be used as a test, but only to prove to others the extent of one's belief. We find that for the God of Mormon, miracles are of primary importance. In comparison with the Father God, the situation is one of increased frequency and of a larger number of miracle-workers, rather than a qualitative difference, so that we will not at this point carry the discussion beyond citing a few examples, to show the variety of miracles attributed to believers in the God of Mormon.

Miracles in the Book of Mormon are plenteous and in wide variety:

> ....God has not ceased to be a God of miracles.(Mormon 9:15)

And so we find that the God of Mormon is generous with His miracles.

> ...after I had prayed, the winds did cease, and the storm did cease, and there was a great calm at sea. (1 Nephi 18:21)

> ...and the earth shook mightily, and the walls of the prison were rent in twain....and the chief judge and the lawyers...were slain by the fall thereof. And Alma and Amalek came forth out of the prison.... (Alma 14:27, 28)

> And their curse was taken from them [after being converted], and their skin became white like unto the Nephites.... (3 Nephi 2:15)

> And [John] said...Lord give unto me power over death, that I may live and bring souls unto thee. And the Lord said...because thou desirest this, thou shall tarry until I come in my glory. (D.C. 7:2, 3)

Some modern religious persons have trouble believing in miracles. This might be an appropriate time to repeat an earlier comment that if one is willing to believe in a personal God capable of creating the whole of the universe and all of its "natural laws," it follows logically that He is capable of suspending the laws He created or using them in ways unknown to us.

Revelations are related to miracles in that they are phenomena under the control of God which we as humans do not understand. As with miracles, the God of Mormon has been generous with His revelations. We first hear of them even before it was known that the God of Mormon was not that of the other Christian churches; when fourteen-year-old Joseph Smith received a vision in answer to his prayer. Two bright and glorious persons appeared:

One of them spake unto me...pointing to the other, "This is My
Beloved Son. Hear Him!" (Joseph Smith 2:17)

It was at this time that the Son, in answer to a question by Smith as to which of the sects he should join, was told that he must join none of them, that all their creeds were an abomination in His sight. Later, the angel Moroni showed Smith the golden plates, and, after a period of some four years, directed him to take them and translate them into what became the Book of Mormon.

The revelations commence on the second page of the Book of Mormon:

...as [Lehi] prayed...there came a pillar of fire and dwelt on a
rock before him; and he saw and heard much....(1 Nephi 1:6)

Not since the time of Moses, with the organization of the plagues of Egypt, the dictation of the legal code, and the minute details given for the construction of the tabernacle and the raiment of the priests, have revelations been given with such frequency and in such detail. With the exception of the revelation of St. John, the appearance of Christ which converted Saul of Tarsus to St. Paul, and the vision of St. Peter at Joppa, the Father God was parsimonious with His revelations, leaving Jesus to pass on His wisdom and His instructions. The Trinitarian God of Mormon was much more communicative, in all three forms: Father, Son, and Holy Ghost all had their contacts with humankind. Since all other creeds are an abomination unto the Lord, His revelations have over the recent past been only to the Mormons, and not to other Christians.

...the only true and living church upon the face of the earth,
with which I, the Lord, am well pleased.... (D.C. 1:30)

The revelations were also frequent during the history of the early immigrants covered by the Book of Mormon, giving visions of heaven and a wide range of instructions. God or His representatives made contact in dreams, or by speech, but there were also many face-to-face appearances. While, amongst others, the story of Moses, affirms that one cannot look on the face of God and live, the corporeal God of Mormon, is not so terrifying. The first face-to-face appearance specifically so designated was to the unnamed brother of Jared—not the grandfather of Methuselah, but another Jared, living at the time of the tower of Babel:

And never have I showed myself unto man whom I have created, for never has man believed in me as thou hast.... (Ether 3:15)

There were other face-to-face visits:

> And I, Enoch, saw the Lord....and he talked with me, even as a man talketh one with another, face to face....(Moses 7:4)

> Thus I, Abraham, talked with the Lord, face to face, as one man talketh with another. (Abraham 3:11)

as well as Joseph Smith's vision previously mentioned. During the time of religious history covered by the Book of Mormon, there were very frequent and widespread relations between God and humankind:

> And there are many among us who have many revelations, for they are not all stiff-necked....as many as...have faith, have communion with the Holy Spirit.... (Jarom 4)

> ...Nephi and Lehi, and many of their brethren...having many revelations daily...did preach unto the people.... (Helaman 11:23)

Some of these resulted in the conversion of men who thus became great preachers and missionaries:

> For I went about with the sons of Mosiah, seeking to destroy the church of God, but behold, God sent His holy angel to stop us by the way....And he said unto me...seek no more to destroy the church of God. (Alma 36:6, 9)

This was analogous to the story of Saul of Tarsus, with a similar result; Alma became one of the greatest preachers of the Book of Mormon.

Jesus, on His brief visit to the Nephites, called and commissioned twelve disciples:

> ...he stretched forth his hand unto the multitude...saying, Blessed are ye if ye shall give heed unto the words of these twelve whom I have chosen from among you....(3 Nephi 12:1)

God, in preparing His plans for men, realized that they would be more effective if men had at least some knowledge of the status quo and of His intentions, and it was from this idea that the revelations came:

> And after God had appointed that these things should come unto man...he saw that it was expedient that man should know concerning these things....therefore he sent angels to converse with them...and...God conversed with men, and made known to them the plan of redemption.... (Alma 12:28–30)

Visions of heaven were included, to divulge what God's promises had in store for the righteous:

> Yea, methought I saw, even as our father Lehi saw, God sitting upon his throne, surrounded with numberless concourses of angels, in the attitude of singing and praising their God; yea, and my soul longed to be there. (Alma 36:22)

Joseph Smith was also permitted a vision of the celestial kingdom, related in the Pearl of Great Price:

> I saw the transcendent beauty of the gate...and the blazing throne of God, whereon was seated the Father and the Son...and the beautiful streets of that kingdom, which had the appearance of being paved with gold....

The question of plural marriage—which for so long a time haunted the Church of Latter-day Saints and was by some considered synonymous with Mormonism—was a subject of revelation. Originally, it was contrary to church doctrine:

> Wherefore I the Lord will not suffer that this people shall do like unto them of old....there shall not any man among you have save it be one wife; and concubines he shall have none. (Jacob 2:26, 27)

Somehow or another God reconsidered. A little less than a year before the martyrdom of Smith, God tells him of the difference between secular marriages and those made for eternity, and continues:

> ...if any man espouse a virgin, and desire to espouse another, and the first give her consent...he is justified; he cannot commit adultery for they are given unto him...and if he have ten virgins given unto him by this law...he is justified. (D.C. 132:61, 62)

Beginning with this revelation, polygamy was legitimized for the church's communicants, and remained so until its official revocation in 1890.

Some of God's revelations were concerned, as in the Vine of Moses, with the choice of a Promised Land for this group of His people. In this case, the Promised Land was the continent of North America, which was not only a luxuriant, delightful land, but also did not require being cleared of hostile inhabitants, as was necessary in the land of Canaan. Since the Cherokees, the Seminoles, the Algonquins, and others are never mentioned, we can only assume that the Book of Mormon implies that these people did not exist at the time, and could well be the descendants of the remnants of the Hebrews that came over with Nephi. Any discussion of this point or attempt to resolve the question is outside the purview of this work.

> ...ye...shall be led to a land of promise...which I have prepared for you; yea, a land which is choice above all other lands. (1 Nephi 2:20)

By the time of the development of the Church of Latter-day Saints, the location of the promised land became more specific, but by then we return to a situation more like the land of Canaan—there are indigenous populations to be dealt with:

> ...the land of Missouri...this is the land of promise and the place for the city of Zion. (D.C. 57:1,2)

> ...ye shall assemble yourselves together to rejoice upon the land of Missouri, which is the land of your inheritance, which is now the land of your enemies. (D.C. 52:42)

Fortunately, these pioneers were able to purchase the land from their "enemies," avoiding a military confrontation of the nature of the battles guided by Joshua against the Canaanites. But unfortunately, the newcomers' attitude of being among enemies subsequently aroused a fierce hostility, and they were finally forced to move further west as a result of mob violence. It was only after the death of Joseph Smith, when Brigham Young led the Mormons on a thousand-mile trek westward to the uninhabited areas around Great Salt Lake that the Mormons finally found peace. For a while, this peace was troubled by the U.S. hostility to polygamy, but at long last stabilized after Church President Wilford Woodruff closed the issue with an official declaration in September 1890 forbidding further plural marriages.

The move to Utah Territory was inspired by a revelation of the word and will of God, given in 1847 to Brigham Young, who had taken over as president. This is one of the very few parts of Mormon scripture that did not come directly from the hands of Joseph Smith, the prophet, and is the closing section (No. 136) of the Doctrine and Covenants.

In the early part of the Book of Mormon, as we have seen, revelations were frequent, and given to many. However, by the time of the appearance of the Prophet Smith, God has become a little more particular with whom He speaks. Through Smith, God announced that He will henceforth be exclusive:

> ...verily I say unto thee, no one shall be appointed to receive commandments and revelations in this church excepting my servant, Joseph Smith.... (D.C. 28:2)

With Smith, God's revelations are detailed and in depth, many of which are concerned with the organization and operation of the church, and who would be chosen for what assignments. Through Moroni (the son of Mormon, not the angel Moroni), Christ had already dictated the manner of ordination of priests and elders, the mode of administering the sacramental bread and wine, of baptism, and of church discipline (Moroni, chapters 2–6). Now, fourteen centuries later, God goes into more detail. In D.C. 20, instructions for the sacraments are again given, the duties of the elders, priests, teachers, deacons, and members of the church and their interrelations are given by Jesus. D.C. 107 gives further detailed directions for the organization of the church. Yet, even after having provided the general detailed description of church organization, God in the latter half of the D.C. 124 names the individuals chosen by God for the high church offices, the members of the council of Twelve, the high council, the leaders of the quorum of seventies, various other councilors and priests, naming a total of nearly fifty individuals for the various positions. Likewise, dozens of individuals are named by God or by Jesus for missionary or ministerial work in D.C. 52, 75, 79, and 80.

Certainly these dictates of God have their advantages; undoubtedly a man will work diligently and with more inspiration in his position in the church when he is told that God Himself has selected his name for a specific assignment.

Further, we find the God of Mormon specifying provisioning for elders, priests, and the Prophet Smith (D.C. 42 :71 and 43:13), as well as:

> ...it is meet that my servant, Joseph Smith, Jr., should have a
> house built, in which to live and translate. (D.C. 41:7)

In D.C. 124: 62–82, God felt it expedient to give detailed directions for the formation of a stock company to construct a boarding house, to be called Nauvoo House, including naming the officers of the corporation, price of the shares of stock, limits of stock purchases allowed giving the names of several church members who are to put stock into the house.

Evidently, the Lord at one point wearied of this detailed administration:

> For behold, it is not meet that I should command in all things;
> for he that is compelled in all things, the same is a slothful and
> not a wise servant.... (D.C. 58:26)

What brought this on was probably God's exasperated feeling that He had to remind His people to do such as:

> Pay the debt thou has contracted with the printer. (D.C. 19:35)

And yet He persisted, in considerable detail from time to time, concerning organization, duties, assignments, financial matters, and the like through the lifetime of Joseph Smith, and on into the details of the organization of the westward trek led by Brigham Young.

Two characteristics appear in the God of Mormon that are readily understandable in a modern context. One relates to a view of the universe with which churchmen before Galileo disagreed:

> And worlds without number have I created....many worlds that have passed away....and there are many that now stand.... (Moses 1:33, 35)

The God of the Mormons recognizes modern astronomy.
And is there not something with a familiar ring in:

> Now these lawyers were learned in all the arts and cunning of the people; and this was to enable them that they might be skillful in their profession....Amulek...perceived their thoughts, and he said...O ye wicked and perverse generation, ye lawyers and hypocrites.... (Alma 10:15,17)

> Now the object of these lawyers was to get gain.... (Alma 10:32)

Earlier in this chapter, we mentioned the absence of vagueness and allegory in the concrete predictions of the coming of Jesus presented in the Book of Mormon, as compared with the poetically obscure predictions of the Old Testament. The exactitude of the God of Mormon is far more compatible with modern man, who is not used to the enigmatic language of ancient oracles, and this may well have helped this God adapt to His environment.

The records of the Book of Mormon show that the first prediction of the coming of Jesus, quite near the beginning of the Book, was made nearly six full centuries before the coming, and was indeed accurate in its estimate of the time to elapse:

> Yea, even six hundred years from the time my father left Jerusalem, a prophet would the Lord God raise up among the Jews—even a Messiah, or in other words, a Savior of the world. (1 Nephi 10:4)

Subsequently the whole story emerged in detail in Nephi's vision:

> ...and in the city of Nazareth, I beheld a virgin....and he said...the virgin whom thou seest is the mother of the Son of God....the virgin again, bearing a child in her arms....Behold the Lamb of God, yea, even the Son of the eternal Father....and

> I also beheld the prophet who should prepare the way before him. And the Lamb of God was baptized of him; and after...I beheld the heavens open, and the Holy Ghost come down...in the form of a dove...and he went forth ministering....and the multitudes gathered to hear him....and I also beheld twelve others following him....and I beheld multitudes of people who were...afflicted with all manner of diseases, and with devils and unclean spirits....And they were healed by the power of the Lamb of God....I...saw that he was lifted up upon the cross and slain for the sins of the world. (1 Nephi 11:13–33)

Thus, six centuries before the birth of Jesus, we have a vision that was so accurate it might almost seem to have been copied from St. Luke's gospel. The God of Mormon continues with other revelations and visions which confirm and flesh out the story:

> ...yea, the God of Abraham, and of Isaac, and the God of Jacob, yieldeth himself...as a man...to be crucified...and to be buried in a sepulchre.... (1 Nephi 19:10)

> ...God himself shall come down among the children of men....and because he dwelleth in the flesh he shall be called the Son of God.... (Mosiah, 15:1, 2)

> Behold, they will crucify him; and after he is laid in a sepulchre for the space of three days he shall rise from the dead.... (2 Nephi 25:13)

We are even provided with such specific details as the correct names of Jesus and His mother:

> ...his name shall be Jesus Christ, the Son of God. (2 Nephi 25:19)

> And behold, he shall be born of Mary, at Jerusalem....she being a virgin.... (Alma 7:10)

Here a couple of minor slips enter the picture. Jesus was born in Bethlehem, not in Jerusalem—but this is fairly close, as Mary was from Jerusalem. And Christ is not a name, but a title similar to Messiah, meaning the Anointed One. He is referred to generally in the four Gospels as Jesus, or the Christ; only rarely as Jesus or Christ without an article. These slips must have been translator's errors. Still, they must be accepted, for when Jesus finally does arrive in the new continent, He calls Himself Christ and is referred to as Christ and not "the Christ."

Another accurate prediction was that of the signs of the birth of Jesus that would be seen in the new colony:

> ...there shall be great lights in heaven....in the night before he cometh there shall be no darkness....and it shall be the night before he is born...there shall a new star arise.... (Helaman 14:3–5)

> ...in that day that he shall suffer death the sun shall be darkened....there shall be no light upon the face of this land....the earth shall shake and tremble....great tempests....graves shall be opened....many saints shall appear.... (Helaman 14:20–25)

These predictions did come true, and they are described in blazing detail in 3 Nephi chapters 1 and 8.

One further prediction that seems to have come true was Nephi's:

> For it shall come to pass in that day that the churches are built up....when the one shall say unto the other: Behold, I, I am the Lord's, and the others shall say: I, I am the Lord's....and they shall contend one with another; and their priests shall contend one with another.... (2 Nephi 28:3, 4)

This prediction requires no further confirmation than that of our own experience.

The God of Mormon resented His treatment by the Jewish establishment:

> ...they shall be scourged by all people, because they crucify the God of Israel....they shall wander in the flesh...and be hated by all nations. (1 Nephi 19:13, 14)

Yet the God of Mormon is a forgiving God, and this announcement of the coming anti-Semitism is tempered by the promise that they will one day accept Jesus as the real Messiah, and then allowed to return from their wanderings.

> And it shall come to pass that the Jews which are scattered also shall begin to believe in Christ; and they shall begin to gather in upon the face of the land; and as many as shall believe in Christ shall also become a delightsome people. (2 Nephi 30:7)

When this will happen no one knows. The present state of Israel shows no sign of conversion to Christianity. We can only infer from the statements of the God of Mormon that the present status of Zionism is evanescent, and that the real and final return of the Jews to their promised land is still some time in the future.

Still, despite the Mormon God's displeasure with the Jewish establishment, and the failure to date of a large number of Jews to accept Christ, there is evidence in many passages that the God of Mormon is basically a Hebrew God; for instance:

> ...if the Gentiles shall hearken unto the Lamb of God, they shall be numbered among the house of Israel; and they shall be a blessed people.... (1 Nephi 14: 1,2)

We find one phenomenon in the Mormon scriptures that is a bit confusing to a non-theologian: a hint of polytheism. It is not a basic part of Mormonism, and is not in the Book of Mormon, but should be mentioned to complete the picture. This is a reference to small gods in the Doctrine and Covenants, relating to certain of the most righteous individuals:

> ...they shall pass by the angels, and the gods, which are set there....Then shall they be gods, because they have no end...and the angels are subject to them. (D.C. 132:19, 20)

> Abraham...Isaac...and Jacob...because they did none other things than that which they were commanded...sit upon thrones, and are not angels but are gods. (D.C. 132:37)

The origin of this concept is undoubtedly in one of the Psalms:

> God has taken his place in the divine council; in the midst of the gods he holds judgment. (Psalms 82:1)

And in the Book of Abraham, given in the Pearl of Great Price, the reference is carried further. Chapters 4 and 5, in retelling the story of Creation, present it as having been achieved by "the Gods":

> ...the Lord said: Let us go down....and they, that is the Gods, organized and formed the heavens and the earth. (Abraham 4:1 )

In practically every succeeding verse, reference is made to "the Gods." Is this simply a reference to the triune God, or are there others?

God wishes to carry on the old traditions, and selected a place in Missouri to which He gave the name Zion, evidently with the intention of making it the center of His new religion and the true church headquarters.

> Wherefore this is the land of promise, and the place for the city of Zion. (D.C. 57:2)

This is to be the location of the New Jerusalem. The Mormons worked diligently over the next two or three years trying once more to build a new center, with the help of a number of revelations from God, who told them:

> For behold, I say unto you that Zion shall flourish, and the glory of the Lord shall be upon her. (D.C. 64:41)

But something about the Latter-day Saints soon engendered antipathy in their neighbors. Troubles started early, and in a little over two years, mob violence again erupted, and the people lost household goods, livestock, and crops. God blamed this misfortune on their transgressions, but having said that Zion shall flourish:

> Zion shall not be moved out of her place, notwithstanding that her children are scattered. (D.C. 101:17)

Unless there will be a further change in the future, this seems to be another case of the clouded crystal ball. Zion did not flourish, and God finally had to be more patient:

> ...it is expedient in me that mine elders should wait for a little season, for the redemption of Zion. (D.C. 105:13)

So that today, the center of the world of the Saints is a "stake" of Zion, Salt Lake City, and the word from God is that:

> Zion shall be redeemed in mine own due time. (D.C. 136:18)

One characteristic of the God who evolved into the God of Mormon that helped Him adapt towards His environment is His strong inclination toward democracy. We have already noted that He took credit for the U.S. Constitution, and probably inspired the Declaration of Independence as well, although He does not mention it.

One of the Articles of Faith of the Latter-day Saints is:

> We believe in being subject to kings, presidents, rulers and magistrates, in obeying, honoring, and sustaining the law. (A.F. 12)

This implies that the church is not above the law. In a democratic manner, their duty is to select men capable of being proper rulers:

> When the wicked rule, the people mourn. Wherefore, honest men and wise men should be sought for diligently, and good men and wise men ye should observe to uphold.... (D.C. 98:9, 10)

In the beginning, God expressed Himself as strongly democratic:

> And this land shall be a land of liberty unto the Gentiles, and there shall be no kings upon the land....For he that raiseth up a king against me shall perish.... (2 Nephi 10:11, 14)

Like the God of the Patriarchs, the Mormon God could change His mind and did not stand up to His declaration, for only shortly thereafter:

> Nephi began to be old....wherefore he anointed a man..to be king and ruler over his people.... (Jacob 1:9)

God made no move either to prevent Nephi's action or the succession of a new king, and for nearly a thousand years, there were kings aplenty in the land. The same fate met God's declaration against priestcraft:

> He commandeth that there shall be no priestcrafts.... priestcrafts are that men preach...that they may get gain and praise of the world.... (2 Nephi 26:29)

and the rest of the Book of Mormon is as full of priests it is of kings.

In Sce. 84 of Doctrine and Covenants, Jesus expounds broadly on the priesthood. But at least we can find Prophet Smith saying:

> No power or influence can or ought to be maintained by virtue of the priesthood.... (D.C. 121:41)

And the modern church of the Saints has no paid or professional ministry—as a matter of fact, only about half a hundred of the top church officials plus the full-time clerks are paid. Bishops, deacons, elders, and others are volunteers who are self-supported by ordinary labor. The Saints' missionaries follow the example of St. Paul:

> And he lived there [in Rome] two whole years at his own expense...preaching the kingdom of God and teaching about the Lord Jesus Christ.... (Acts 28:30)

Two other Mormon concepts are thoroughly compatible with America as a land of opportunity for the foreign oppressed, and a land with freedom from religious laws:

> Yea, the Lord hath covenanted this land unto me, and to my children forever, and also all those who should be led out of other countries by the hand of the Lord. (2 Nephi 1:5)

> ...now the law could have no power on any man for his belief. (Alma 1:17)

> If a man desired to serve God, it was his privilege....but if he did not believe in him there was no law to punish him. (Alma 30:9)

It is certainly to be expected that the God of Mormon would exhort the faithful to uphold a strict and serious moral attitude, and to help those that had not their abilities to take care of themselves. These self-reliant people believed it when they were told:

> ...they must be brought to stand before God, to be judged of their works.... (1 Nephi 15:33)

> Thou shalt not be idle; for he that is idle shall not eat the bread nor wear the garments of the laborer. (D.C. 42:42)

This included the priests as well:

> ...when the priest had imparted unto them the word of God, they all returned again diligently unto their labors; and the priest, not esteeming himself above his hearers, for the preacher was no better than the hearer.... (Alma 1:26)

Alma goes on at length to show that hard work results in prosperity, while prosperity carries the duty to help other less fortunate neighbors. King Benjamin also says:

> ...succor those that stand in need....ye will not suffer that the beggar putteth up his petition to you in vain. (Mosiah 4:16)

Certainly the charitable requirements set fairly high standards for the Saints. One is not expected to amass wealth for the pleasure thereof, since:

> And if thou obtainest more than that which would be for thy support, thou shalt give it into my storehouse....(D.C. 42:55)

> Verily, thus saith the Lord, I require all their surplus property to be put into the hands of the bishop of my church in Zion. (D.C. 119:1)

After the surplus has been drained off:

> ...those who have thus been tithed shall pay one-tenth of all their interest annually; and this shall be a standing law unto them forever.... (D.C. 119:4)

The church treasury is then in a position to be helpful to the widows and orphans. The Saints have a reputation of avoiding government welfare programs. Those who cannot, with all their best volition, take care of themselves, are looked after by the church, in accordance with God's instructions:

> ...that every man who has need may be amply supplied and receive according to his wants. (D.C. 42:33)

> ...and widows and orphans shall be provided for....(D.C. 83:6)

We find that the Lord is careful about other aspects of the morals of His people:

> Behold, it is...forbidden, to get in debt to thine enemies. (D.C. 64:27)

God was speaking at the time to those who were preparing to go to the new territory where Zion was located, where He had already told the faithful that the land was inhabited by enemies. Whether He was referring to them, or whether He considered anyone to whom one owed a debt an enemy is not quite clear, but the advice is good in either case.

We will close this chapter with references that show the God of Mormon to have an approach to forgiveness similar to that of the Father God. This would be expected, in view of the fact that the Mormon religion is based so strongly on Jesus and His teachings, and one of Jesus' best known admonitions was that of turning the other cheek. The Saints did not fight with equivalent violence the mobs who sought to destroy them, but made every effort to go through the prescribed legal channels to attempt to be allowed to live in peace. God tells them:

> If men will smite you, or your families...and ye bear it patiently and revile not against them...ye shall be rewarded.... (D.C. 98:23)

One is required to bear it patiently at least three times, then, if God has not already punished the offender, he is in the hands of the one he has offended. Still, he should be forgiven. A man is not required to forgive without limit. Elsewhere, God is briefer and more to the point:

> I, the Lord, will forgive whom I will forgive, but of you it is required to forgive all men. (D.C. 64:10)

It is quite obvious from the history of the Latter-day Saints that they are a patient, serious, hard-working people, willing to put out all the efforts required to build a community from scratch, and beyond this, to devote time to missionary work seeking to bring what they considered the benefits of belief in Jesus to unbelievers or those whose belief was distorted by improper influences.

Perhaps the system is not perfect, but the inclination is in the right direction, and the ideas of the God of Mormon are compatible with the environment, helping to ensure His survival.

In summary, the differences between the Father God and the God of Mormon, while definitely present, are not radical enough to disturb anyone with a sincere ecumenical approach.

# Chapter 9: The Healing of God

> The physical healing of Christian Science results now, as in Jesus' time, from the operation of divine Principle, before which sin and disease lose their reality in human consciousness and disappear as naturally and as necessarily as darkness gives place to light... (*Science and Health*, xi:9)

> The scientific fact that man and the universe are evolved from Spirit, and so are spiritual, is as fixed in divine Science as is the proof that mortals gain the sense of health only as they lose the sense of sin and disease. (*Science and Health*, 69:2)

It would be difficult to imagine two religions, both derived from the story of Jesus, appearing within just a few years of each other, as different in sentiment and philosophy as are Mormonism and Christian Science. The concrete, basic, fundamentalist-leaning religion of the Latter-day Saints which was so easily understood and readily accepted by the hardy frontiersmen, finds no parallel in the transcendental beliefs of Christian Science, which developed in the parlors of the already-stable cities of the new country.

The God of Mormon is a concrete, easily pictured God who appeared in person and spoke often to His followers, while the Healing God of the Christian Scientists is a strictly spiritual, metaphysical being who remains aloof and is neither heard nor seen. The Mormon hell has its fire and brimstone; the Mormon heaven, its choirs of angels singing hosannas and praising God, while the Scientists' heaven and hell are conditions, states of mind rather than locations. Both repeatedly affirm that man was made in the image of God. Yet for the Mormons, this means that God must therefore have a corporeal form, while the Scientists look in the opposite direction and assure us that, since God is spiritual, the real man is also spiritual and without a body. The God of Mormon is unequivocally a Trinitarian God, while the Scientists call this polytheism and deny it. For the Mormons, the Second Coming and the Judgment Day are circled in red on God's calendar, though we cannot see it; the Scientists have nothing that could in any way be considered even remotely equivalent. The God of Mormon dictated detailed laws, codes, organizational and missionary instructions; the Healing God does not even concern Himself with mundane life. The God of Mormon requires strict belief—but the healing God says nothing of this, and His followers insist that what is important is not belief, but understanding.

Christ Himself might have difficulty in discerning why both call themselves Christian. The one point on which these religions agree is that the ultimate basis for religion is the Christ.

Both are revealed religions, based on the Bible, each with its own additional revealed Scripture. But even the methods of revelation are eons apart. We remember that Joseph Smith received his word from the voice of God or of God's messengers as was standard practice in ancient days. The revelations came to Mary Baker Eddy, the founder of Christian Science, through inspirations that followed long and assiduous study of the Bible in her own search for a valid interpretation of the Holy Writ. Nonetheless, she evidently felt, as any other prophet, the authenticity of her revelations:

> God had been graciously preparing me during many years for the reception of this final revelation of the absolute divine Principle..... (107:3)

> ....I won my way to absolute conclusions through divine revelation, reason and demonstration. (109:20)

The results of her study and revelations were published as *Science and Health with Key to the Scriptures* in 1875, and serve the Church of Christ, Scientist (the official name of the church) as Scripture on a level with the Bible, both being read in all Christian Science services. She has also written a number of other books and articles, but none occupy the prominent position of *Science and Health*.

> [*Science and Health*] is the voice of Truth to this age, and contains the full statement of Christian Science, or the Science of healing through Mind. (456:27)

Mary Baker Eddy was originally a Congregationalist. Unsatisfied with the liberal approach to religion that typifies Congregationalism, she plunged into a deep study of religion, especially of the Bible. Plagued with poor health, she found her health improving as her ideas developed, and with a claim that the Bible was her sole teacher, by 1866 she felt far enough advanced in her discovery to begin organizing the results of her work. Manuscript copies were circulated beginning in 1867, some were copyrighted in 1870, but *Science and Health* was not published until 1875.

She was very active in the practice of Christian Science (Mind-healing), wrote many articles and books, edited and published the *Christian Science Journal*, established the church organization, and founded and operated for some years the Massachusetts Metaphysical College for instruction in Christian Science.

The product of the activity of this remarkable woman is a world-wide organization of the Church of Christ, Scientist with about 2,200 congregations of dedicated believers. The organization's national newspaper, the *Christian Science Monitor*, has been highly respected in the media field.

In order to be able to improve our understanding of the Healing God, we will start with a brief statement of three basic principles of Christian Science. The wording may not be completely acceptable to a Science theologian, but the general idea will be presented in a few words so that the uninitiated can better follow what is to come.

1. God created humans in His image, completely spiritual, as is God Himself, with no physical or material attributes. The eternal and infinite God has neither beginning, ending, nor passage of time as we feel it on earth, and humankind is eternally coexistent with God.

2. Somewhere, somehow, its origin unknown, man began to experience the unreal phenomena of material life, explained as in a way equivalent to a dream life, in which are found the errors of understanding: sin, sickness, and death; errors, since they do not really exist. A perfect God could not have created evils such as sin, sickness, and death. The situation is worsened by interaction of so-called mortal minds on each other and on each other's ideas.

3. Understanding this will enable man to shake off this dream and return to his rightful spiritual and immortal position as a reflection of God, unencumbered by sin or disease. Complete understanding will yield the perfect existence, removing even birth and death; partial understanding will improve man's lot, permitting healing of disease.

Here we are confronted with an incontrovertible evolutionary mutation of the God species. The Healing God in no way developed gradually from other forms; He appeared suddenly on the scene without any preliminary warning. He may, and probably will, become modified with the passage of time, as have other gods. But His characteristics are as different from previously discussed gods as mammals are from reptiles, feathered birds from scaly fish, reasoning humans from reacting animals. Yet His origin was the same as that of other gods, just as man and bird have common ancestors.

We consider here also another feature of the nature of evolution. Evolution seems to follow no predetermined teleological path—at least, not exclusively. It can produce new species by branching off in various directions. One of these directions may be progressive, one may move sidewise and fill an empty niche in the environment, another may be regressive. The first two will likely survive, the last will probably die out.

In the animal kingdom, we find such successful niche-fillers as the cuddly koala, which feeds solely on the leaves of the eucalyptus tree; and the South American anteater whose diet consists exclusively of ants and termites. Both of these are successful products of evolution, as they occupy environmental niches to which they are adapted, and where they essentially have no competition.

It is inevitable that, in the multiplex heterogeneity of the environment of the gods, namely religious man, there is room for a numerous variety of God-species to survive and thrive, and there will always be niches ready for new forms, just as in nature there is room for a multitude of species of animals, insects, and plants.

While it is not impossible that the Healing God may turn out to be the forerunner of a species that in the dim future could be the predominant one, today He seems to have found His limited niche, as has the koala. Among humans there was a scattered number who were dissatisfied with God as He was presented in their religion, and at the same time concerned with health and the apparent ability of mind to influence health or pain, as had been recently demonstrated with Mesmerism, hypnotism, homeopathy, and related phenomena. These people were, generally, intellectually inclined, more willing to think than simply to believe. Strict law codes and doctrinal creeds had no attraction for them, and complex rites and ceremonies seemed to be devoid of real meaning. The practices that seemed necessary for discipline and for building human relations to each other and to God seemed superfluous to them. Many of these people naturally gravitated toward the new Christian Science, and a following quickly developed.

Since most people today find accepting the precepts of Christian Science difficult, it is unlikely that there will be a rapid expansion of the environment for the Healing God. Still, He can survive quite comfortably in the limited environment available to Him. A certain number of people will always be attracted to the promises of divinely directed health cures and health maintenance.

In the beginning, Mary Baker Eddy had a number of imitators, as well as detractors. However, the strength of the Church of Christ, Scientist became such that the imitators fell by the wayside and the detractors no longer interfere with the work and operation of the church. For the fact must be accepted by the detractors that testimony exists of many thousands of wide-ranging cures that have been effected by the practice of Christian Science. Call them "faith cures" or what you will, they support the validity of Christian Science to Eddy's followers.

One is impressed on reading *Science and Health* with the continual repetitions, theme and variations, which suggest a searching for the final answer. Eddy expresses this herself:

> Today, though rejoicing in some progress, [the author] still finds herself a willing disciple at the heavenly gate, waiting for the Mind of Christ. (ix:16)

> We can, and ultimately shall....avail ourselves in every direction of the supremacy of Truth over error....until we arrive at

> the fullness of God's idea, and no more fear that we shall be sick and die. (406:20)

But she has full confidence that her revelations have put her on the right track and that persevering study will result in complete and effective understanding.

> When the Science of being is universally understood, every man will be his own physician, and Truth will be the universal panacea. (144:27)

Meanwhile, even this incomplete understanding can be highly effective in producing cures such as chronic headaches, rheumatism, tumors, cataracts, digestive disturbance, eczema, consumption, and even fractured bones, according to the testimony of those who have been cured.

As for the detractors, we propose to take the part of Gamaliel, when he spoke to his fellow Pharisees who wanted to kill Peter and the apostles:

> Keep away from these men and let them alone; for if this plan or this undertaking is of men, it will fail; but if it is of God, you will not be able to overthrow them. You might even be found opposing God! (Acts 5:38, 39)

For the uninitiated who are trying to comprehend Christian Science, a background in semantics is helpful. It is necessary to understand that Eddy often uses words to convey ideas far removed from their usual significance to the man in the street. The vocabulary is esoteric, and Eddy complains that:

> English is inadequate to the expression of spiritual conceptions and propositions, because one is obliged to use material terms in dealing with spiritual ideas. (349:15)

> The inadequacy of material terms for metaphysical statements, and the consequent difficulty of so expressing metaphysical ideas so as to make them comprehensible to any reader who has not personally demonstrated Christian Science....the great difficulty is to give the right impression. (115:3)

For instance, in Christian Science, the term "real" is generally used to indicate things spiritual, not material. "Death" and "flesh" are held to be illusions. "Knowledge" is evidence from the senses, the opposite of spiritual Truth (590:4). Some words are even given multiple and conflicting definitions in the Glossary, such as:

> Believing: ....the perception of spiritual truth. Mortal thoughts, illusion. (582:1)

> Wine: Inspiration, understanding. Error; fornication; temptation; passion. (598:17)

It is therefore not simply expedient, but absolutely necessary, before deciding whether one agrees or disagrees with a statement, to be certain that one understands how the words of that statement are being used. Otherwise, one might easily stumble over such assertions as:

> Both the material senses and their reports are unnatural, impossible, and unreal. (551:1)

And we are told by Eddy that:

> She affixed the name "Science" to Christianity, the name "error" to corporeal sense, and the name "substance" to mind. (483:13)

The same care regarding semantics will apply to our exegesis as well as to quotations from *Science and Health*, as we are under the same difficulties.

With this in mind, we will proceed to discuss the Healing God, a God who is overseer of what is in essence a simple religion, with no code of laws, no list of dictated morals, no rites or ceremonies, no priesthood, and a bare minimum of creed and doctrine. In essence, it is an intellectual metaphysics, devoid of the usual characteristics of mysticism.

In considering the characteristics of the Healing God, we must remember that for the Christian Scientist, the Bible is basic, as is *Science and Health*. Still, we also remember that we found three distinct variations of God in the Bible: the God of the Patriarchs, the God of the Prophets, and the Father God; as well as indications of variations of the individual species, such as the Unitarian and the Trinitarian Father Gods. We also find that Eddy was free with her interpretations of the Holy Writ, often seeing it in a completely different light than as seen by the orthodox Jew or Christian. (Jesus Himself did not interpret the Bible in the then-accepted Mosaic sense.) One outstanding example of Eddy's insight is her interpretation of the Adam story, which she sees as a false representation of the "error" of material creation, an allegorical depiction of the falsity of material interpretations:

> The statement that life issues from matter [dust] contradicts the teaching of the first chapter....that all Life is God....this second Biblical account [of the creation] is a picture of error throughout. (526:6)

The Adam story could not possibly be a true picture, for:

> In common justice, we must admit that God will not punish
> man for doing what He created man capable of doing, and
> knew from the outset that man would do. (357:1)

Isn't it surprising that one does not more often find this benign concept of a God said to be a God of love?

We must then seek to infer a great deal about God which is not specifically stated in *Science and Health*, attempting to draw a portrait of the Healing God which is compatible with the implications in Mary Baker Eddy's work. Whatever we do, it will be obvious that there will be no possibility of confusing the Healing God with any of the other Gods we are considering.

As portrayed in *Science and Health*, the Healing God is that great creator who is defined by a list of divine synonyms:

> God: Divine Principle, Life, Truth, Love, Soul, Spirit, Mind.
> (115:13)

It is important that the reader remember these synonyms, for Eddy often uses them interchangeably with the term "God." This God is not an anthropomorphic personality, but is all, and is infinite:

> Even eternity can never reveal the whole of God, since there is
> no limit to infinitude or to its reflections. (517:22)

As an infinite God, He must be incorporeal and transcendental:

> In one sense, God is identical with nature, but this nature, is
> spiritual and not expressed in matter. (119:17)

> The physical senses can obtain no proof of God. (284:21)

We obtain here a nebulous image of a transcendental being beyond the powers of understanding of the mortal brain: an essence unlikely to show itself in burning bushes or pillars of fire and equally unlikely to take part in a military campaign or to give detailed instructions on church organization. Still, we must recognize that many people require a more concrete concept of God, and are unhappy with the vagueness of a transcendental God who leaves them with nothing either to hold on to or to refute. Therefore, God is, practically by Christian Science definition, goodness. Since He is infinite and all-pervading, no room remains for anything that is not good; therefore, evil was obviously not created by God and therefore cannot be real.

We see again that the variations in environments allow for ready survival of these non-competing Gods who have evolved through the ages.

> Whatever is valueless and baneful, He did not make—hence its unreality. (525:21)

> The Christian Science God is universal, eternal, divine Love which…causeth no evil, disease or death. (140:25)

These points are basic to the understanding of Christian Science. It is fundamental that God is both good and spiritual: God is literally incapable of creating anything incompatible with His characteristics; therefore, God cannot have created either sin (evil) or matter, which is material and not spiritual. The principal expressed here is far from original; the same idea was expressed more than two thousand years ago when Zoroaster reported that Ormazd had created everything good, and all his creatures are pure.

Furthermore, God is infinite, and is all and all-pervasive, therefore there is no room for any other power besides Him. No room for Satan, or any other possible purveyors of evil. God is one, alone, and divides his power with no other entity.

The only possibility that remains is that neither evil nor matter actually exists; they are no more than figments of mortal imagination. For many people, this is a hypothesis difficult to digest. Yet, it is fundamental to Christian Science. Later, we will return to look into this idea further.

The impersonal, transcendental God of Science is no longer masculine in nature, as were his forbears. The God of Christian Science may either be considered sexless, or as embodying the traits of both sexes:

> Love, the divine Principle, is the Father and Mother of the universe, including man. (256:7)

> In divine Science, we have not as much authority for considering God masculine, as we have for considering Him [Her] feminine, for Love imparts the clearest idea of Deity. (517:11)

All other Gods we have considered were both definitely masculine and loving; in the case of the Father God, it was said that God is Love. It is clear that, in Eddy's mind, Love was considered more of a feminine than masculine attribute, and contemporary Victorian depictions of femininity provide ample support for this view. It is also clear from Eddy's consideration of the Adam story as allegory of the falsity of material creation, that the secondary status of woman, as indicated in the follow biblical passage, has no place in Christian Science:

> Thy desire shall be for thy husband, and he shall rule over thee…. (Genesis 3:16)

In Christian Science, women have finally achieved their liberation from the male and pro-masculine God of the patriarchs. This fact is symbolized by the custom of having two readers alternate in Christian Science services, one a man and the other a woman.

We have stated that the Healing God is not Trinitarian. This is correct in the context of comparison with the Mormon and other Gods who have three persons united in one:

> The theory of three persons in one God... suggests polytheism, rather than the one, ever-present, I AM. (256:9)

Nevertheless, the general idea of trinity is not completely lost, but modified to a form of three attributes rather than three persons.

> Life, Truth, and Love constitute the triune person called God....They represent a trinity in unity....the same in essence, though multiform in office: God the Father-Mother; Christ the spiritual idea of son-ship; divine Science or the Holy Comforter....the threefold essential nature of the infinite. (331:26)

Despite this statement, throughout Science and Health, there is repeated insistence on the Oneness of God. Hence, we must interpret this from the standpoint of attributes rather than persons, and avoid any taint of polytheism.

Does the Healing God take a direct personal interest in His individual subjects? There are a few vague statements but precious little evidence that He does. Personal actions on the part of God could take the form of retribution, judgment, or answer to prayer or healing. We will see later that healing comes through man's understanding of God and His purposes, and not through any action of God Himself. Support exists for the concept of control by the healing God:

> Mind's control over the universe....is demonstrable Science. (171:12)

This Healing God, or Mind, also demands obedience, with inevitable consequences if humans do not obey:

> Divine Mind rightly demands man's entire obedience, affection, and strength. (183:21)

> It is quite as impossible for sinners to receive their full punishment this side of the grave as for this world to bestow on the righteous their full reward. (36:21)

This punishment is not saved up by God to be meted out on some apocalyptic Judgment Day, which has no part in Christian Science doctrine.

> No final judgement awaits mortals, for the judgement day of wisdom comes hourly and continually.... (291:28)

The nature of any punishment or reward is nowhere stated, but is left completely to the imagination of the individual. It is definitely not in assignment to Hades or Paradise, for the Healing God has no such establishment. Heaven and Hell for the Christian Scientist are not locations, but conditions.

> Heaven is not a locality, but a divine state of Mind.... (291:13)

> The sinner makes his own hell by doing evil, the saint his own heaven by doing right. (266:20)

As to actions on the part of God in response to prayer, the Healing God does not respond directly to appeals. It is useless to ask God for something through a verbal prayer, because He knows all one's needs before the words are spoken, and He dispenses His blessings as He knows best.

> He who is immutably right will do right without being reminded....the wisdom of man is not sufficient to warrant him in advising God. (3:1)

We are here presented with another aspect of a God who appeals to the philosophical intellectual. The whole attitude toward prayer and its effect on God is a far cry from the primitive who sought to appease God and the spirits with verbal remonstrances and blood sacrifices. This characteristic of the healing God should contribute to His ability to survive in certain modern environments but does not necessarily imply that prayer should be neglected, for it is beneficial in other ways to the supplicant.

> Prayer cannot change the Science of being, but it tends to bring us into harmony with it. (2:15)

> The habitual struggle to be always good is unceasing prayer. (4:12)

> Self-forgetfulness, purity, and affection are constant prayers. (15:26)

And, since God is omniscient and all-knowing, He can respond to prayers—spoken and otherwise expressed—in an appropriate manner.

We have already mentioned that the Healing God has no regard for activities such as rites, ceremonies, sacrifices, fasting or pilgrimages.

> [Jesus] attached no importance to dead ceremonies. (31:13)

We could infer this difference in attitude to formalities—as well as certain other distinctions in the character of the Healing God—from Eddy's description of the spirituality of God and her concentration on the characteristic of Love. Despite the fact that Eddy states that her religion is based on the Bible, from time to time we find this basis modified by her own interpretation, and our inferences are confirmed:

> Mortals believed in God as humanly mighty, rather than as divine, infinite Love. (53:13)

> In that name of Jehovah, the true idea of God almost seems lost. God becomes a "man of war," a tribal god to be worshiped, rather than Love, the divine Principle.... (524:8)

It is interesting to note the derogatory use of the word "worship." Unlike the ancient anthropomorphic Gods, the transcendent, infinite God of Christian Science does not suffer the mortal vice of pride, and hence, does not require worship or servile demonstrations of gratitude, expecting only proper behavior on the part of His creations. Likewise, the "jealous God" of the second commandment has disappeared with the passing of the ages. When God is all, there is nothing apart from Him of which he might be jealous.

We remember that the earlier Gods were vengeful; that the God of the Patriarchs spoke and behaved in such a manner that we could actually consider Him cruel and bloodthirsty. Speaking of Jehovah as a "man of war," Eddy thereby implies that the Healing God is in no way a martial or vengeful God. This is perfectly logical, since one could not expect a God whose name is synonymous with Love to foment wars, support belligerents, or wreak revenge on dissidents. The subject is not even mentioned. Even the lesser quality of wrath is not a characteristic of the Healing God:

> Whoever believeth that wrath is righteous does not understand God. (22:27)

Favoritism or discrimination on the part of God is not even dignified by mention, other than the equality of the sexes which we have already discussed. The Healing God is completely impartial, never once mentioning any preference for a chosen people, a skin color, a sex, or a national origin.

As for asceticism, indulged in by many in the early and middle eras of the Catholic Church, and roundly condemned by Allah, the nearest the Healing God comes to approval of such is a recommendation of abstinence, which was also approved by Allah:

> ....the use of tobacco or intoxicating drinks is not in harmony with Christian Science. (454:2)

Two other attributes that are often discussed in considering the Christian God—forgiveness and mercy—are a little more difficult to pin down. When considering these characteristics in relation to Christian Science, it is important to remember that these two attributes are normally associated with highly personal relationships, and the Healing God is not highly personal. In His transcendent infinitude, He is much more inclined to be aloof. While one certainly could not say that the opposite characteristics—unforgiving or merciless—could ever apply, this does not at the same time require that the positive characteristics must therefore be necessarily typical. We have seen that punishment is stated to follow transgression, but of the nature of that punishment, we have only the vague indication that it may relate to an agonized conscience.

When Science insists that evil does not exist, nor does sin have any reality, what is there to forgive? Sinners can only work their way out of the suffering caused by their sins by a realization and understanding of the Truth, which will automatically bring them into harmony with God, as long as they can avoid reverting to their sins. This is expressed by Eddy herself in the following passage:

> The destruction of sin is the divine method of pardon....being destroyed, sin needs no other form of forgiveness. (339:1)

To the Christian Scientists "forgiving" and "merciful" are not necessary labels to be attached to the Healing God.

Practically no mention is made of God's requirements for charity, tithing, or similar works. It is likely that Eddy relies on the Gospel and her concept of God as Love to automatically cover the subject. We will therefore follow her lead, and refer back to the teachings of Jesus concerning the Father God regarding charity, assuming that the God of Christ, Scientist, approves.

One significant difference between the Healing God and the other Gods we have discussed, as well as the Universal God of the Baha'i Faith whom we will discuss in the next chapter, is that all the others require belief from their devotees. Again, we find a difference which is appealing to the intellectuals: a requirement for understanding rather than belief. Naturally, if one understands, one believes; still, it is more complimentary to a mature mind to ask the person to understand something that will be explained than to ask the person to believe something on the basis of a statement either inadequately explained or only baldly stated.

> Mind (God) must be not merely believed, but it must be understood. (339:27)

> Nothing is more antagonistic to Christian Science than a blind belief without understanding, for such a belief hides Truth and builds on error. (83:9)

Having hopefully now arrived at some understanding of the characteristics and requirements of the Healing God; the God of Christ, Scientist, we now reach the problem of what it is that we are expected to understand. Here, comprehension—or acceptance of the explanation—will not come so easily.

In common with the Father God of Jesus, the God of Mormon, and the Universal God of the Baha'i Faith, the Healing God appeared in a hostile environment. Yet, like the others, He soon found an adequately congenial environment into which to settle, and managed to thrive and develop there.

The definitely spiritual, metaphysical God of Christian Science with His spiritual flock was on the one hand strongly opposed by a society that was rapidly becoming materialistic, and on the other, being misunderstood by those who considered the budding religion to be a form of Mesmerism, animal magnetism, or hypnotism, all of which (essentially different names for the same phenomenon) were forcing their way onto the stage of public interest. Despite this, and because of a combination of persons looking for a new approach to religion and the evident success of Mary Baker Eddy and her students in obtaining cures—in many cases, where contemporary medicine was unsuccessful—the new religion took root and flourished. The zeal, capacity for work, and ability to inspire others innate to Mary Baker Eddy was undoubtedly a prime factor in the success of Christian Science. Other contributing factors were the relatively undeveloped state of the medical art then as compared with today; and the support given a female prophet by women newly inspired by the fight for suffrage and equal rights. Nonetheless, the acceptance of Christian Science, while not as universal as that of some other Christian groups, is enthusiastic, and it is enduring.

There is no doubt that Christian Science is Christian. It is based on the story of Christ as it was related in the Gospels, the idea of God being manifested in the human Jesus. Most Christian religions are based on the teachings of Jesus, with the "miracles" only adjunct to the teaching—to claim the attention of the multitudes. Christ's demonstrations of healing as presented in the Gospels are often relegated to a secondary level of importance by other Christian groups. To Christian Science they are as or more important than the parables and sermons for the true understanding of God.

> ....restoring an essential element of Christianity—namely apostolic, divine healing. (347:18)

This was somehow lost sight of in the early church development, despite the evidence provided by the healing effected by the apostles and the following passage taken from the Bible:

> Truly I say unto you, he who believes in me will also do the works I do, and greater works than these will he do, because I go to the Father. (John 14:12)

This fundamental aspect of Christianity was not lost by the Healing God.

> …he presented proof that Life, Truth, and Love heal the sick and the sinning, and triumph over death through Mind, not matter.….His hearers understood neither his words nor his works. (54:14)

> His purpose in healing was not alone to restore health, but to demonstrate his divine Principle. (51:21)

Hence, we can begin to understand the thinking that the miracles of healing the sick and raising the dead were not actually miracles, but simply the natural functioning of divine law. In this way, Christian Science could be considered closer to Christ than are other, current Christian beliefs.

We cannot expect in a few short pages to be comprehensive in the presentation of so radical an idea. What follows is simply an expository outline of the basic theory of Christian Science, necessary for a better understanding of the Healing God.

We will start with Mary Baker Eddy's words of her discovery:

> That all real being is in God, the divine Mind, and that Life, Truth, and Love are all-powerful and ever-present; that the opposite of Truth—called error, sickness, disease, death—is the false testimony of false material sense…. this false sense evolves, in belief, a subjective state of mortal mind.…thereby shutting out the true sense of Spirit. (108:21)

As we proceed, keep in mind our references to semantics and our caution that Mary Baker Eddy often uses words in a non-pedestrian way—a necessity, as she pointed out, because there is no accepted vocabulary for what she is trying to express. She must use essentially material terms in an effort to explain spiritual matters. It is important to be especially aware of her usage of the words "real" and "substance" when they are used to express spiritual concerns.

Even more elusive is the phrase "mortal mind." As frequently as the expression is used, Eddy often prefixes it with "so-called" to indicate her belief that it is a misnomer for which no term exists that will come closer to expressing her meaning. This is unfortunate, as the concept is basic to her reasoning, since what she calls "mortal mind" is the origin of the "false" beliefs in matter, sin, disease, and death.

> As Mind is immortal, the phrase "mortal mind" implies something untrue and therefore unreal; and as the phrase is used in

teaching Christian Science, it is meant to designate that which
has no real existence. (114:13)

Using Eddy's definitions the "real existence" would mean "spiritual existence." Watch that word "real" here! In this context, meaning real related to spiritual existence. Yet we must have some peg on which to hang the ideas.

Beyond semantics, we must also consider the possible relation of opposites. Opposites can, for instance, be considered as either antagonistic or complementary. As examples, the opposites of right and left are antagonistic. Anything that is to the right of us cannot be in any way to the left. The opposites of key and lock, however, are complementary. Fitting together, and thus useful, neither would be of value without the other. Other opposites are not so obviously either antagonistic or complementary, such as material and spirit; matter and soul. Orthodox religions consider them complementary; that a soul or spirit inhabits the body of man. Eddy denies this, maintaining the viewpoint that these are opposites which are antagonistic.

> God, Spirit, being all, nothing is matter. (113:18)

> Matter and Mind are opposites. One is contrary to the other in
> its very nature and essence; hence both cannot be real. If one
> is real, the other must be unreal. (270:5)

Proceeding further, "cause" and "cure" are similarly antagonistic opposites:

> It is absurd to suppose that matter can both cause and cure disease.... (208:4)

There is no consideration here that one form of matter might cause a disease which another form could cure. Here, frequently as elsewhere in Eddy's teaching, matter is matter, not to be subdivided by characteristics and classifications. It is all unreal.

Following along this line of reasoning, we arrive at the hypothesis that God, infinite and spiritual, cannot create anything finite and material. We have already spoken of this, but it is important to emphasize, because it is so fundamental to Science. Because the opposites are antagonistic, God cannot create matter, and as nothing else did, it simply does not exist.

> ...nothing possesses reality nor existence except the divine
> Mind and His ideas. (331:12)

> Matter is a human concept. (469:3)

Students of philosophy are aware that such ideas did not originate with Eddy. There is an important school of philosophy which holds that matter exists only in the concepts of the mind, and these theories were developed without any relation to religious connotations.

Students of comparative religion will note that this idea is ancient. Many centuries before Christ, there was in the Hindu religion the conviction that Brahmanism was the reality of the spirit, and that spirit was the only reality. Sankara is quoted as saying, "The world is not-being. It is appearance without reality, a delusive show."

If matter does not exist as such, then it obviously follows that there is no validity to anything related to matter, including what we term natural laws and physical science.

> There is no physical science, inasmuch as all truth proceeds from the divine Mind. (127:23)

This applies equally well to disease:

> What is termed disease does not exist. It is neither mind nor matter. (188:3)

This principle can also be applied to "mortal man," who does not exist either. But man himself, the real man, the immortal, spiritual man created by God, does exist. In order for him to regain his rightful position, or to understand that it really does belong to him, he must rid himself of the error of his material thoughts.

What can we know of the real man? Unfortunately, we cannot know him with any certainty, for the mortal senses which are our present consciousness do not react to spiritual man. Therefore:

> We know no more of man as the true divine image....than we know of God. (258:16)

Neither God nor the perfect man can be discerned by the material senses. This does not imply that we are completely ignorant; we do know something of God, and can imagine more. Among other things, we have been informed that man was made in the image of God. And since God is spiritual, without form, this requires that man also must be spiritual.

> ...God....makes man in the image and likeness of himself—of Spirit, not of matter. (94:1)

Man continues to function as an image of God, not identical, for he cannot possibly have all the attributes of God, but as an image reflected in a mirror, presenting a likeness of God without being a copy of God.

Infinite Mind can never be in man, but is reflected by man. (336:13)

Being spiritual, man is in no way material, and any such inference is simply in error:

....the material personality which suffers, sins and dies....is not man, the image and likeness of God, but man's counterfeit.... (285:7)

Mortal man is really a self-contradictory phrase, for man is not mortal...man is immortal. (478:30)

From this certainly follows the logical inference that man is also eternal and perfect:

God could never impart an element of evil, and man possesses nothing which he has not derived from God. (539:10)

....man is in a degree as perfect as the Mind that forms him. (337:10)

Christian Science maintains that the common religious belief that man is composed of a mortal body occupied by an immortal soul is an error, incompatible with their idea of God Himself being Soul. Besides, since what we look at as physical, material man is not the real man, what is the point in endowing him with a soul?

Man is not a material habitation for Soul; he is himself spiritual. Soul, being Spirit, is seen in nothing imperfect nor material. (477:6)

There is no finite soul or spirit. (466:21)

In short, the real man is spiritual, and what we have been mistakenly regarding as man is summed up by:

To the five corporeal senses, man appears. to be matter and mind united; but Christian Science reveals man as the idea of God, and declares the corporeal senses to be mortal and erring illusions. (477:9)

The senses themselves, being part of our material ideas, cannot have any validity:

> Christian Science sustains with immortal proof the impossibility of any material sense, and defines these senses as mortal beliefs, the testimony of which cannot be true either of man or of his Maker. (488:16)

It is interesting to note that this material age would reconfirm the validity of sense perceptions. Whether we go as far as did Eddy and state that the "testimony cannot be true," we do know that one must definitely interpret the testimony of the senses and not accept it at its face value.

We are all familiar with tricks of drawing that can produce optical illusions. Our taste buds can be so easily fooled that labels are required to identify real or imitation products.

We say a thing "feels cold," when our materially inclined physicists know that there is no such thing as cold—it is just less warm than something else. The people in the cinema seem to be moving and talking, but we know this to be an illusion.

So what do we really know for sure?

If our senses of the material world around us can be false, where did they originate?

No hint exists in *Science and Health*. There are explanations for what will aggravate the situation, and a dream theory offered to help the understanding. But for the origin of man's false and self-perpetuating beliefs there is no explanation.

How important actually is an explanation? We do not understand what electricity is or how it originated, but we can use it. Archeology gives us some idea of the origin of tools and of writing; but of the origins of the non-material subject, man's language, nothing at all is known, nor do we have any idea where to look. Yet this fact does not hinder our use of language for communication.

Eddy suggests that man's sense-experiences may be a sort of dream. As the mortal mind can dream all sorts of wildly varied experiences in its sleep, spiritual man may be dreaming what we conceive as material existence. The material body, its functions, its trials and tribulations, could have the same relations to the "real" spiritual man that sleeping dreams have to the material man.

> Mortal existence is a dream of pain and pleasure in matter, a dream of sin, sickness and death.... (188:11)

Acceptance of such a hypothesis or a similar explanation would make it much easier to give credence to Science's assertions that such things as sensations, sin, evil, disease, and death have no reality.

> Sin, sickness and death are comprised in human material belief....They are without a real origin or existence. (286:31)

> Human mind produces what is termed organic disease as certainly as it produces hysteria.... I have demonstrated this beyond all cavil. (177:1)

For someone with a migraine headache, a toothache, a high fever, gangrene or simply the debilitating weakness of a virus attack, credence does not come so easily. If illness is not real, whence these damnable symptoms and pains? The sensations certainly seem real enough.

But it is not the body, the matter, which feels the pain. Matter itself does not suffer. A leg cut off can be stuck full of pins, and does not react. If the mind is disconnected, even temporarily, say by hypnotism or by the effect of an injection of morphine, the sensation of pain or burning ceases to exist.

> ....matter has no sensation of its own, and the human mind is all that can produce pain. (166:1)

The Christian Science affirmation that pain is the result of a belief in pain can certainly be supported by the non-religious, non-drug use of hypnotism, which demonstrates the premise that it is only necessary to remove the belief in pain and the sensation of pain ceases. Not only do certain stage demonstrations show this; many operations are carried out with no anesthetic other than hypnotism.

Descriptions of diseases can cause some people to feel the symptoms of those diseases. Scientific medical research and general conversation can spread these beliefs, aggravating the situation, a contagion of morbid ideas.

> Sin and disease must be thought before they can be manifested. (234:25)

> Treatises on anatomy, physiology and health....are the promoters of sickness and disease. (179:21)

> All disease is the result of education.... disease can carry its ill effects no farther than mortal mind maps out the way. (176:25)

Such is the dilemma of mortal man in the eyes of Christian Science. The premise is that man has worked himself into an infelicitous impasse, relying on beliefs that he had no way of knowing were spurious and illusory. The Healing God, who created man, but who did not create the sin and sickness in which man's mind alone got him involved, has ordained a universe which will allow man to reverse this process.

For the convert to Christian Science, arriving at that point requires some effort and is not so facile.

> ....they will not be able to glean from Christian Science the facts of being without striving for them. (323:2)

If mind got us into these troubles, mind can get us out. It is enough to understand that what we are experiencing is unreal, and it will disappear. Realizing it is a dream, will shake us awake from the dream.

> If a dream ceases, it is self-destroyed, and the terror is over. (346:20)

> A change in human beliefs changes all the physical symptoms...when one's false belief is corrected, Truth sends a report of health over the body. (194:6)

The theory is simple, but the application of the theory requires effort, at least the first time.

> The sick are not healed merely by declaring that there is no sickness, but by knowing that there is none. (447:27)

Concentrated, serious study is required to turn wishful thinking into belief, belief into understanding. It is claimed that even if one has not arrived at a sufficiently advanced stage of understanding to be able to cure himself, he can be cured by the help of one or more persons who are adepts. One must cooperate, of course; any lack of faith is detrimental, if not actually fatal to the cure. Various complicating factors can affect the efficacy of an attempted cure. Beliefs of others, reading of published articles or hearing physician's comments on the disease; attempts to use drugs, hygiene or other material cures will all detract because they divert or belittle the efforts of Science at healing, which are most effective when they are pure and concentrated.

Both cause and cure are occasioned by beliefs. As an illustration from familiar aspects of life of the efficacy of belief in producing symptoms:

> A blundering dispatch, mistakenly announcing the death of a friend, occasions the same grief that the friend's real death would bring.... another dispatch, correcting the mistake, heals your grief. (386:16)

The accumulation over eons of time of various detrimental beliefs acts on both the conscious and subconscious mind of the individual. Therefore it is not only what a person consciously thinks and believes, but also, what others are thinking that can both cause the appearance of symptoms and produce the healing by having the symptoms disappear, as in the case of the mistaken dispatch, medical research, medical publications, conversations of hypochondriacs all contribute. This applies to material cures as well as to occurrence of symptoms of disease, since all is unreal:

> When the sick recover by the use of drugs, it is the law of a general belief, culminating in individual faith, which heals.... (155:3)

If the beneficial effect of healing drugs on the body is due to belief, it is only logical to assume that the same may be said in the reverse cases—the harmful effects of poison. But the danger is that not only the belief of the individual is controlling, but also the cumulative beliefs of others contribute their effect.

> If a dose of poison is swallowed through mistake, and the patient dies even though physician and patient are expecting favorable results, does human belief....cause this death?...[Yes], in such cases a few persons believe the potion to be harmless, but the vast majority of humankind, though they know nothing of this particular case and this special person believe the arsenic....or whatever the drug used, to be poisonous, for it is set down as a poison by mortal mind. (177:25)

Likewise, symptoms of disease unknown to an individual before the symptoms appear, may have been injected into his subconscious by beliefs of others.

It is important, then, for effective cure, that not only the patient, but also those around him have full faith. The beliefs and attitudes of his friends, his relatives, his physician, his Christian Science practitioner, what he reads, all will contribute to the efficacy of healing. Mixing material cures with Science efforts at healing will naturally diminish the faith requisite to a cure by Science, and should be avoided if at all possible.

> If Mind is foremost and superior, let us rely on Mind, which needs no cooperation from lower powers, even if these so-called powers are real. (144:3)

> You weaken or destroy your power when you resort to any except spiritual means. (181:12)

It is interesting to note that the God of the Patriarchs sees things in the same light:

> ....Asa was diseased in his feet, and his disease became severe; yet even in his disease he did not seek the Lord, but sought help from physicians. And Asa slept with his fathers, dying in the forty-first year of his reign. (2 Chronicles 16:12, 13)

Under unusual conditions, exceptions may be allowed:

> If from an injury....a Christian Scientist were seized with a pain so violent that he could not treat himself mentally....a surgeon [could] give him a hypodermic injection, then, when the pain was lulled, he could handle his own case mentally. (464:13)

Fortunately the effects of conflicting belief can turn out positively as well as negatively:

> Atheism....and agnosticism are opposed to Christian Science....but it does not follow that the profane or atheistic individual cannot be healed by Christian Science. (139:28)

With the discussion of effects on and by beliefs, we are ready to consider just how the healing is done. The methods are said to be the same as those used by Jesus, who as we remember from reading the Gospels generally assured Himself of the faith of the supplicant, even though it was often taken for granted that anyone who asked Jesus for a cure must have asked with the belief that He was capable of healing. It is also important to keep in mind that healing is actually a by-product of the effort to become the real spiritual man created by God; eliminating sin at the same time as disease is eliminated. Jesus not only healed; He also preached against sin, often bringing out the relation of the two while healing. When it was deemed by Him that the supplicant approached Him after repenting of his sins, He assured him or her that the sins were forgiven.

> He [Jesus] showed that diseases were cast out....by the divine spirit, casting out the errors of mortal mind. (138:11)

> The efficient remedy is to destroy the patient's false belief by both silently and audibly arguing the true facts in regard to harmonious being—representing man as healthy instead of diseased.... (376:21)

> Truth has a healing effect, even when not fully understood. (152:8)

Eddy herself did not claim to understand things fully, and it is quite probable that most of her followers are not much farther advanced than she was. She has admitted that the present state of understanding is not profound enough to remove the extremely strong belief in death, which should disappear once understanding has been perfected. And even though she has catalogued testimonies of cases of broken bones being repaired by Christian Science, the understanding has not yet arrived at a point where this can be a common occurrence:

> Until the advancing age admits the efficacy and supremacy of Mind, it is better for Christian Scientists to leave....the adjustment of broken bones....to the....surgeon.... (401:27)

Even the passage of the barrier which we know as death will not automatically clear up everything until understanding has progressed a great deal farther:

> Death will occur on the next plane of existence as on this, until the spiritual understanding of Life is reached. (77:9)

A corollary of this lack of understanding is the fact that Christian Science treatment, like many material medical treatments, is not one hundred percent successful. Perhaps the body has already been weakened beyond repair by excessive detrimental beliefs. The presence of pride or superstition will interfere. It is necessary that the patient and the practitioner both conduct a reasonably good moral life. One should avoid mixed material and spiritual treatments, as we have previously mentioned; and the neighboring minds should cooperate. Whenever failure occurs, the reason may be found. It could be a simple lack of faith, even on a subconscious level. Failure of an attempted cure is thus seen not to be a reason to deny Christian Science, or not to try again on a later occasion.

> If you fail to succeed in any case, it is because you have not demonstrated the life of Christ, Truth, more in your own life.... (149:12)

> A moral question may hinder the recovery of the sick. Lurking error, lust, envy, revenge, malice or hate will perpetuate or even create the belief in disease. (419:1)

There is much to Christian Science besides simply being cured by believing in the non-existence of sickness. The aim of the devout Scientist includes the avoidance of all error, including sin; avoidance of vices such as passion, selfishness, envy, hatred, and revenge; and above all an effort to increase understanding to the point that man can take his rightful (spiritual) place as the unsullied image of God.

> We can, and ultimately shall, so rise as to avail ourselves.....of the supremacy of Truth over error, Life over death, and good over evil.... until we arrive at the fullness of God's idea. (406:20)

As for the sufferings and discomforts that are the by—products of sin, Eddy has a simple answer:

> The way to escape the misery of sin is to cease sinning. There is no other way. (327:12)

We have in the foregoing presented the general theory of Christian Science. In the following, taken from the advice of Mary Baker Eddy to the practitioner of Christian Science who is trying to help the patient cure himself, we can see some of the methods of application of the theory:

> The physician who lacks sympathy for his fellow-being....has not that recognition of infinite Love which alone confers the healing power. (366:12)

> Always begin your treatment by allaying the fear of patients. Silently reassure them as to their exemption from disease. If you succeed in wholly removing the fear, your patient is healed. (411:27)

> The sick know nothing of the mental process by which they are depleted, and next to nothing of the metaphysical method by which they can be healed. If they ask about the disease, tell them only what is best for them to know. Assure them that they....have already heard too much on that subject....Teach them that their being is sustained by Spirit, not by matter.... (416:24)

> To the Christian Science healer, sickness is a dream from which the patient needs to be awakened. (417:20)

Thus we have a picture of the Healing God as He exists today. Of all the Gods that we have considered, He is probably the least likely to fit the suggestion of God being made in the image of natural man. At the same time, the revelation of Mary Baker Eddy has fundamentally altered the idea of man himself in order that man can be a reasonable facsimile of the Healing God. This is, in a way, a much more radical change than even the great change in God himself, more radical than the change from the strictly mortal man of the days of the patriarchs, to the man equipped with an immortal soul to whom Jesus and Mohammed preached.

Humanists, and even some religionists who are not convinced of the existence of heaven and hell, consider the idea of an immortal soul to be simply wishful thinking. What must these people think of Eddy's dreaming spiritual man whose dreams sometimes turn to nightmares, but who has the possibility of shaking himself awake and shrugging off the terrors of the dreams?

Our present, advanced state of medical knowledge is still far removed from the possibilities offered by Christian Scientists. We find a medical cure for one disease, like smallpox or consumption, and nature invents another, like AIDS.

The time is still out of sight when our ability to treat disease through scientific means will keep us so healthy that Christian Science will have no appeal. Meanwhile, some people will always be attracted to a metaphysical approach to healing, to a transcendent God who relates better to infinity and eternity than the anthropomorphic Gods, and to the idea of a less complicated spiritual immortal existence. So, it can be anticipated that the Healing God will thrive for some time to come.

# Chapter 10: The Universal God

> The Prophetic Cycle hath verily ended,
> The Eternal Truth is now come. (Baha'u'llah)
>
> The worlds of God are countless in number and infinite in their range. (Baha'u'llah)

We now come to the Universal God. Perhaps there may be some objection to our designating the God of the Baha'i faith as the Universal God, on the grounds that all the Gods previously discussed were supposed to be monotheistic Gods, and hence hold sway over all creation. Even Jehovah, who had His origin as the tribal God of the Hebrews, claimed to have created the whole universe unaided.

Yet, despite the claim that God was one God and alone, the real appeal of all previous Gods was essentially regional. The Old Testament Gods limited their interactions mostly to the Chosen People, only extending their jurisdiction at times to influence nearby people and cultures, such as the Egyptians, Cyrus, and Nebuchadnezzar.

The works of Jehovah never occurred outside of the general area of the Middle East. The Father God did approach the Gentiles, and Allah went even farther afield as a result of Islamic conquests. Admittedly, Allah told Mohammed that he sent prophets to all the nations, but these were essentially ignored in the Koran and the Hadith. The God of Mormon is in essence still an American God. The Healing God may be thought of as a universal Mind, yet the direction of thought of Christian Science seems more focused on the individual's relationship with God, rather than any particular group's.

To the Baha'is, however, the very nature of God is His universality, which is expressed in a variety of ways. At the level of our planet, the prime aim of God is the development of a universal world society in which everyone—irrespective of race, color, or gender—feels like citizen of the world and can interact on an equal basis. The domain of the Universal God also reaches beyond the Earth and its creatures:

> The worlds of God are countless in number and infinite in their range....the creation of God embraceth worlds besides this world, and creatures apart from these creatures....(T, 187)

The universal God's domain also extends beyond the three common dimensions. To get us into the fourth or other further dimensions, the Baha'i texts refer to dreams as evidence of other worlds of the spirit.

More basically still, the universality of God transcends all geographical boundaries and brings universality to the world of the spirit, to religion itself. Before the advent of Baha'u'llah, the great prophets Moses, Christ, Zoroaster, Krishna, and Mohammed, each propounded a separate set of religious beliefs. Followers of any doctrine besides their specific preachings were living in deadly error. Now, the latest Messenger of God tells us that this competition between religions was only apparent, not real. According to Baha'i faith, discrepancies between the teachings of the various representatives of God arose due to the necessity of presenting the will of God so that it would be understood and accepted by the people to whom it was presented. Much of what seemed concrete at the time was actually symbolic. Rules and regulations were presented that suited the societies as they existed. Still, for each of these sets of rules, revelations that seemed to exhibit apparent differences from those delivered by other messengers of God, revealed, on closer inspection, only superficial differences, which had no effect on the basis of religion. Some important similarities existed between all faiths: one's fellow man should always be treated with love and concern, charity and faith were never absent, belief was required; reward and punishment may have varied in detail but remained ever the foundation of justice. (This idea was also propounded independently by the Hindu theologian, Chunder Sen, who believed that all the great religions of the world are one.)

In short, all Gods worshiped by adherents to the various religions, whatever name they are given, are the same God; He is ever the One God regardless of what rites and ceremonies are dedicated to Him, and, with the possible exception of a few minor deities that were obviously incompatible with the system, all religions everywhere are one and the same. Only different costumes to accommodate them to the different customs of the nations. As transportation and communication throughout the world has become increasingly accessible, religion has responded by introducing and enlarging upon this concept of the Universal God.

In the year 1844, a young Persian merchant, born twenty-five years before in Shiraz, announced himself to be a Manifestation of God, and began to preach a new approach to religion. He was accepted by the leaders of a Persian sect that had been looking for the arrival of a Promised One, who they believed was already somewhere on earth. Handsome, charming, and charismatic, Ali

Mohammed, a descendant of the Prophet himself, took the name of "the Bab"; Arabic for The Gate, signifying the entrance to the path toward God.

He soon surrounded himself with enough enthusiastic converts to make the contemporary ecclesiastics concerned about their own positions of power and their favorable relations with the temporal authorities. At that time, Islam was the state religion and control was in the hands of the Shi'ite sect, to which the majority of the Persians belonged. Their alarm grew as they realized that their counter-propaganda was ineffective, and they soon threw the Bab into prison. However, by this time the rapidly spreading religion of the Babis had already produced a few powerfully influential apostles, including a Husayn 'Ali, a young man of good family with no formal education, but who evidently had acquired quite a bit of informal learning. Finally, in an ultimate attempt to discourage the new faith, the authorities executed the Bab in front of a firing squad in 1850, only six years after he had begun his mission.

Three years later, a pair of ill-advised young Babi fanatics made an attempt on the life of the Shah. The Shah escaped with minor wounds, but this was the signal for a violent program of extermination of the Babis. In a short space of time, twenty thousand Babis were submitted to atrocious tortures and killed, and many others, including Husayn 'Ali, were imprisoned. At some point, Husayn 'Ali took the name of Baha'u'llah (Glory of God) and assumed leadership of the cause. In a letter to the Shah from prison, he tells of a vision which was the basis for his declaration of his mission from God, but only ten years later, in 1863, did he lay claim to being himself a manifestation of God.

> O King! I was but a man, like others, asleep on my couch, when lo, the breezes of the All-Glorious were wafted over Me, and taught Me the knowledge of all that hath been....and He bade me lift up my voice between earth and heaven.... (B, 55)

Upon his release from prison, Baha'u'llah was exiled to Baghdad, where he continued to work for the new faith. Thence he was sent ever farther away to exile, first to Constantinople, then to Adrianople, and finally to the gloomy prison of Akka, near Haifa. Ultimately, he was allowed a home in Akka, but not allowed travel.

At least, he was permitted visitors, correspondence and composition. It is said that, during his exile, he wrote about a thousand books and articles. Much of this was dictated at high speed to his secretary, and copies of all his letters were kept, so that the writings of Baha'u'llah—the New Testament of the Baha'i Faith—are as voluminous as all the preceding Holy Scriptures put together.

By the Will and Testament of Baha'u'llah, his eldest son was made his Interpreter, and announced as infallible, inspired by God. The son, taking the name of Abdu'l Baha (Servant of the Glory), was a prisoner in Akka for forty years, and was finally released during the revolution of the Young Turks in 1908. Subsequently, he traveled extensively in Europe and America, spreading the word.

Abdu'l Baha, in moving out of the Middle East and carrying the message to Europe and America, performed the same function for the Baha'i faith that St. Paul did for Christianity, taking it out of its narrow, local sphere and laying the foundations for a worldwide acceptance of his religion. Upon his death in 1921, Abdu'l Baha named his grandson, Shoghi Effendi, the Guardian of the Cause of God. The Guardian continued the work till his death in 1957.

Shoghi Effendi had no offspring capable of carrying on his work, but he had by then anticipated the need for a greater organization and had built up an administrative order capable of taking the helm. Thus, in 1963 they established the Universal House of Justice originally called for by Baha'u'llah as the controlling body of the Baha'i Faith. Local organizations are called "Spiritual Assemblies" and function similarly to a church, except that they don't include clergy.

The Baha'i faith, though not yet well known in the United States, is growing. It is said to have several hundred thousand adherents worldwide, possibly a million or more—no statistics are presently available. The Baha'i writings have been translated into nearly six hundred languages, and, according to a count taken in 1973, Baha'i groups exist in more than 330 countries and territories (F, 258). The Baha'i Community is accredited in the United Nations, and supports a variety of international organizations, in conjunction with its belief in world unity. At the same time, Baha'is are forbidden to take an active part in politics (F, 287).

Although the Baha'i Faith has a social as well as a spiritual aspect, Baha'u'llah enjoins his followers to respect constituted authority, and Baha'is are in no way expected to substitute their own organizations for the normally existing governing bodies.

The Baha'i Mother Temple of the West, whose foundation stone was laid by Abdu'l Baha, is located in Wilmette, near Chicago. Round in shape, it has nine entrances, signifying that one can enter from any direction (from any of the world's nine major religions) in respect for the number nine, a "sign of perfection" for the Baha'is, which also in the Arabic is the numerical value of the word Baha.

> [The Bab] stated that in the ninth year the expected one would be known; in the ninth year, they would attain to all glory and felicity. (B, 221)

Much of Baha'u'llah's writings still remain untranslated in the original Arabic or Persian, and are thus inaccessible to most English-speaking students. Even his "Most Holy Book," the Kitab-I-Aqdas, containing the laws promulgated by Baha'u'llah, had been translated into English only as a synopsis, with a simple listing of the laws. Still, with the translated writings and speeches of Abdu'l Baha, who explained and interpreted Baha'u'llah's mission, and much written originally in English by Shoghi Effendi, we have a clear if not complete picture of God as seen by Baha'u'llah.

It must be admitted that this "clear" picture often requires careful reading. The concepts of Baha'u'llah are frequently swaddled in such florid grandiloquent verbiage that it would require an extremely discerning mind to fathom the structure of his thought. His rhetoric is at times reminiscent of the elegant intricacies of Arabesque decorations. An example follows:

> When the stream of utterance reached this stage, We beheld, and lo! the sweet savors of God were being wafted from the day-spring of Revelation, and the morning breeze was blowing out of the Sheba of the Eternal....it made all things new, and brought unnumbered and inestimable gifts from the unknowable Friend. The robe of human praise can never hope to match Its noble stature, and Its shining figure the mantle of utterance can never fit. Without word It unfoldeth the inner mysteries, and without speech it revealeth the secrets of divine sayings. It teacheth lamentation and moaning to the nightingales warbling on the bough of remoteness, instructeth them in the art of love's ways, and showeth them the secret of heart-surrender.... (KI, 59)

For the lover of poetry there are extensive areas of allegory, seas of similes, and mines of metaphors rich enough to satisfy the most demanding. The writings of Abdu'l Baha are much closer to the demands of contemporary consumption.

Whether the Universal God will survive and flourish in the modern environment only time will tell. Many Baha'i precepts are certainly compatible with the direction of today's world. Abdu'l Baha approved of the League of Nations, and would undoubtedly have considered the United Nations a further step towards the ideals of Baha'i. Equality of the races and the sexes was an idea ahead of its time when propounded by Baha'u'llah, but today, only a century and a half later, it is central to the issues with which contemporary cultures are struggling. Universal education has come, miracles have gone, and more people consider a concrete concept of God to be something beyond the capability of the human mind. He is for many no longer the benevolent long-bearded gentleman in a flowing white robe.

And if we accept Baha'u'llah's dictum, there will be no new Gods appearing for quite some time:

> In this most mighty Revelation all the Dispensations of the past have attained their highest and final consummation. Whoso layeth claim to a Revelation after Him, such a man is assuredly a lying impostor. (G:cxv)

It must be admitted that the Universal God has already well demonstrated his staying powers. He was born in a viciously hostile environment, a God of change and progress in a land that had gelled and solidified, a non-political God in a nation where religion and politics were inextricably intermingled. Prudently, he has moved to parts of the world where he is better adapted to the environment, and more likely to survive.

Before considering in detail the characteristics of the Universal God, we can prepare by presenting a brief sketch. Strictly monotheistic, as are all our other Gods except the Christian Trinity and the tribal primitive Jehovah, the principal concern of the Universal God is the unity of the world, across national boundaries, across pre-existing religions, across racial barriers. He is concerned with reversing the divisive effect of the infelicitous debacle initiated by jealous Jehovah when he decreed the confusion of Babel. He is progressive, demanding education, and insisting that science and religion must be compatible. He still requires belief in both himself and his Messengers, but he has abolished the eternal tortures of the damned, and given all a chance to progress toward God, even after death. He is a thorough-going organizer, with plans for his church administration that can serve as examples for an eventual world government, but only as an example, since he does not want his people in politics, and wants no forcing of his ideas on anyone.

Peace is all important, and anything that will lead in the direction of peace is approved. Furthermore, fighting, even to propagate the faith, is frowned on; holy wars are strictly forbidden. All previous religions of any significance are considered valid, and differences are explained both by an indication of necessary adaptation to the circumstances and by introduction of interpretations based on allegory and symbolism. Not only does he not forbid reading of other religions, he even enjoins his followers to consort with those of all other religions (with the single exception of those who were once Baha'is and have broken away from the faith).

His is a missionary faith, and his favorite people are his missionaries. He has eliminated miracles, signs, and all types of superstition, including jinns and seers. Although he insists on prayer and fasting, he has no interest in ceremonies, rites or sacrifice. Arising in the midst of Islam, he has made some changes that appeal to the devout Muslims: he allows payment of interest, approves of music, elevates women to equality with men and permits consumption of swine.

To the Universal God, some of the individuals who represent him on earth are beings far removed from the known prophets. There seem to be three classes of humans: ordinary people; Prophets or Interpreters, such as Samuel, Jeremiah, Isaiah, Abdu'l Baha, and the lesser prophets; and Manifestations of God, among which are included Moses, Abraham, Adam, Jesus, Mohammed, the Bab, and Baha'u'llah with origins in the Hebrew religion and Buddha, Zoroaster, and Krishna among those belonging to other origins. The prophets and interpreters are inspired by God, but the Manifestations of God are on a much higher plane, being infused with a spirit sent by God for their continual guidance, and maintaining constant contact with God.

Although Moses and Mohammed, for example, personally made no such claims of super-human status, Jesus did, and spoke and lived as if he were the type of Manifestation of God described by Baha'u'llah. From time to time, whenever worldly conditions deteriorated and it seemed expedient to God to renew the faith of his subjects, he selected a man to be infused with the spirit sent down from heaven. This completely changed the character of this man, making of him a Manifestation of God himself, a person who became all knowing, an infallible being simply because he was under continual direct communication with God's will. A man who had the authority directly from God not only to preach, but also to make changes in the characteristics of a religion to bring it up to date and make it more compatible with the times and conditions.

Baha'u'llah explained that this meant that the individual was no longer a plain ordinary human being, nor even an individual in the sense that one considers a human being. The infusion of the spirit, which was in each case the same spirit sent by God, made each of these Manifestations in some way the same as each of the others. The nature of the spirit, or force sent by God for this purpose was beyond the human comprehension and could not be explained, any more than God himself could be comprehended by humans. It did unify the series of Manifestations of God:

> Since there can be no tie of direct intercourse to bind the one true God with His creation...he hath ordained that in every age...a stainless soul be made manifest....unto this subtle, this mysterious and ethereal Being He hath assigned a two-fold nature....the first...representeth Him as One Whose voice is the voice of God himself....the second...exemplified by "I am but a man like you." (G:xxvii)

> They are all but one person, one soul, one spirit, one being, one revelation....Were any of the all-embracing Manifestations to declare "I am God," He verily speaketh the truth. (P, 34)

In other words, while the Manifestations of God have both human and divine attributes, they are essentially mouthpieces of God, who, unable to relate directly to man, uses this system of communication of his will. The twofold nature of these Manifestations is such that if Baha'u'llah says "I am Baha'u'llah" he is speaking the truth; if he also says "I am Jesus," on another level he is still speaking the truth. And whatever he may say, it should be taken as if God himself had said it. Accepting the Manifestation, unavoidably accepts God.

> Unto no one is given the right to question His authority or to say why or wherefore. (T, 108)

> The source of all learning is the knowledge of God....this cannot be attained save through the knowledge of His Divine Manifestation. (T, 156)

Although there is unity and continuity between the various Manifestations of God, not each one says the same thing, because God has decreed that his revelations would be progressive, adapted to times and conditions, ever moving forward toward the ultimate truth; just as in school one may be taught certain things in the lower grades, then in the advanced grades consider the world from a quite different point of view, once understanding has developed.

> Every Prophet Whom the Almighty...hath purposed to send to the peoples of the earth hath been entrusted with a message, and charged to act in a manner that would best meet the requirements of the age in which He appeared. (G:xxxiv)

> The Cause of Baha'u'llah is the same as the Cause of Christ. The teachings of Baha'u'llah have the same basic principles, but are according to the stage of the maturity of the world and the requirements of this illuminated age. (B, 400)

"This illuminated age" implies the era of humankind when the human race has arrived at maturity, and is finally capable of real understanding. The time has come for one last set of changes of doctrine. Now humankind must begin to lay the foundations for the utopian Kingdom of God on earth, the sympathetic unity of all the peoples of the earth.

> This Day is unique and is to be distinguished from those that have preceded it....The Prophetic cycle hath verily ended. The Eternal Truth is now come. He...is now shedding upon the world the unclouded splendor of His Revelation. (B, 28)

Both Baha'u'llah and Abdu'l Baha lament frequently that while they have accepted Moses, Christ, and Mohammed, the favor has not been returned. Baha'is think it strange that, while these other religions all claim to worship one God only, and that this God is undoubtedly the same that the others are worshipping, they consider their own forms of worship so fundamentally important that they have closed their eyes to this new opportunity of a valid ecumenism revealed by God himself. To the Baha'is, if Jews, Christians, and Muslims would accept the validity of Baha'u'llah's prophethood, the world could unite under the great banner of one religion in the worship of one God.

> Why do you not speak these few words that will do away with all this difficulty? Then there will be no more hatred and fanaticism, no more warfare and bloodshed....(B, 278)

The sacred Scriptures have been full of prophecies of the coming of God's Manifestations; why could not the Jews recognize him when Jesus arrived; why could not the Christians recognize him when Mohammed arrived; why could not the Moslems recognize him when Baha'u'llah arrived?

> How many...have...yearningly awaited the advent of the Manifestations of God in the sanctified persons of His chosen Ones....and whensoever the portals of grace did open...they all denied Him and turned away from His face, the face of God himself.( G:xiii)

> [Christ said] I have yet many things to say to you, but you cannot hear them now. When the Spirit of truth comes, he will guide you unto all truth; for he will not speak on his own authority. (John 16:12, 13)

> [Baha'u'llah says] the promises of God, as recorded in the Holy Scriptures, have all been fulfilled. (G:x)

According to Baha'u'llah, the basic problem is that not even the leaders of the various religions understand their own Scriptures. All is symbol and allegory. It is childish to look for a literal interpretation.

Baha'u'llah endeavors to explain the symbolism behind the second coming of Jesus, which the Gospels present in spectacular grandeur:

> ...the sun will be darkened, and the moon will not give its light, and the stars will be falling from heaven, and the powers in the heavens will be shaken. And then they will see the Son of man coming in clouds with great power and glory. (Mark 13:24–26)

in the Book of Certitude:

> By the terms "sun" and "moon"...is not meant solely the sun and the moon of the visible universe....manifold are the meanings they have intended for these terms. (KI, 33)

Among other possible meanings, the sun can refer to the prophets themselves. Toward the end of the dispensation of any particular prophet, the people have fallen back away from his teachings, and thus the sun is darkened; the light of his teachings no longer brilliantly shines as it once did. So that when the teachings, once fresh, of each Prophet are on the wane; when people no longer turn toward the saints and the companions have passed away, it is time for a new Prophet and a new Revelation. And, since for Baha'u'llah, all of the Manifestations of God are spiritually one and the same, even if they function in different bodies, the term "Son of man" applies to any one of them, including himself and Mohammed. Furthermore, when religion is on the wane mundane conditions worsen, there are wars and rumors of wars, economics disintegrates, hatred increases, and thus the powers of heaven are shaken. As for the arrival of the Son of man, he is certainly not expected to sit on a white mass of water vapor and ride down from heaven to earth. He writes:

> By the term "clouds" is meant those things that are contrary to the ways and desires of men...these "clouds" signify, in one sense, the annulment of laws, the abrogation of former Dispensations, the repeal of rituals and customs current amongst men. (KI, 71)

In short:

> Know verily that the purpose underlying all these symbolic terms and abstruse allusions...hath been to test and prove the peoples of the world.... (KI, 49)

Christians should be able to understand this sort of reasoning, as it was the same sort of reasoning that the Christians used in attempting to convince the Jews that they were making a mistake looking for a literal interpretation of the conditions accompanying the coming of the Messiah. If they had only understood the symbolism and allegory behind the prophesying of Isaiah and others, they would have known that Jesus was the Messiah. We fear, however, that the average modern Christian may be as obdurate as was the Jew of nineteen centuries past. Further, the strangeness of such names as Baha'u'llah and Abdu'l Baha will likely act as an additional impediment to ready acceptance. "Joseph Smith" may have been too commonplace; Baha'u'llah too exotic.

Perhaps it just needs time:

> And the Lord will become king over all the earth; on that day the Lord will be one and his name one. (Zecheriah 14:9)

Before leaving the prophets as such, it is interesting to note that Adam has also been listed amongst the Baha'i list of prophets. Baha'u'llah considers the Biblical story of creation in six days to be an allegory, and not literal truth. He also surmises that man existed, possibly in some more primitive form, from the beginning of creation. On being asked why no records were found concerning the prophets before Adam and the kings in those times, he answered that the lack of records was no proof of nonexistence. Abdu'l Baha later explained that the universe and God are coequally eternal. Parts of the universe decay and are reborn, but the universe as a whole has no beginning and will have no end.

The Universal God is transcendent and unknowable, far beyond even a minimal comprehension by man. As plants have no capacity for understanding the movement and sensual feelings such as sight, hearing, and smell of the animal world, so humans have no concept of the spirits of heaven's existence. God is even above them; so there is absolutely no hope for human comprehension of the Infinite. One can only in some small way get a sense of God by observing his creation and trying to understand what the prophets tell us of God's mercy and God's will.

> Every attempt to visualize and know God hath been limited by the exigencies of His own creation.... Immeasurably exalted is He above the strivings of the human mind to grasp His Essence....will everlastingly continue to remain concealed in His inaccessible majesty and glory. (G:cxlviii)

We find also that the primitive passions of the ancient Gods have to a great extent disappeared. Nowhere does the Universal God claim to be a jealous God. Why should he, when there is nothing to be jealous of? The very nature of his universality makes jealousy irrelevant: as the Universal God considers Jesus, Krishna, and Buddha all as his Manifestations, one can hardly expect Him to be jealous of something that originated from himself. Nor is He a vengeful God. Mention of vengeance and wrath are extremely rare in the Scriptures of Baha'i. Unbelievers are not cast into the consuming flames of hell nor does God threaten to visit evil punishments upon those who follow paths other than those decreed by God through earthly means.

Disappointment aplenty, yes, but where punishment is mentioned, it is as a corrective: a positive attitude rather than the negative attitude of vengeance.

> Man has not the right to take vengeance, but the community has the right to punish the criminal, and this punishment is intended to warn and prevent.... (S, 307)

> It is not advisable to show kindness to a person who is a tyrant, a traitor or a thief, because kindness encourages him to become worse and does not awaken him. (B, 412)

This attitude is one of reasoning, not an emotional reaction related to vengeance or reprisal.

Likewise, the Universal God does not speak often of sin. Again here, his exhortations are mostly in the positive direction, always thinking of performing good acts, rarely worrying about the negative of sin and sinners. One of the few references to sin is:

> Breathe not the sins of others so long as thou art thyself a sinner. (B, 159)

Abdu'l Baha goes as far as saying that evil does not exist, just as darkness has no real existence, but is the absence of light. Evil is the absence of the qualities and perfections of man (S, 301). He goes on to explain that certain attributes of man, which may seem evil, such as desire and anger, have their good sides. If there were no desire, nothing would be done. Anger exercised against bloodthirsty tyrants is praiseworthy, but anger improperly used is blameworthy.

In sum, the Universal God is characterized by a positive approach, and has little time to be concerned with the negative.

Nor does Baha'u'llah's God find anything congenial in the supernatural, other than, of course, the original creation. God does not waste time warning against witches and wizards, mentioning jinns or other invisible earth-spirits.

> Any religious belief that is not conformable with scientific proof and investigation is superstition. (F, 126)

As far as "signs" are concerned, Baha'u'llah follows in the footsteps of Mohammed; no supernatural signs are produced, since the creation is itself considered sign enough for anyone.

> The soul is a sign of God....every created thing in the whole universe is but a door leading to His knowledge. (G:lxxxii)

The one miracle attributed to the Universal God we may consider as suspect, since it is not mentioned by Baha'u'llah or Abdu'l Baha in the Baha'i scriptures; still we recount it as it is repeatedly mentioned in the lay history of Baha'i.

When the religious authorities found that simple incarceration of the Bab was not sufficient to discourage the Babi following, they finally decided that elimination of the leader should eliminate the followers. They tied the Bab to a wall with ropes, lined up a large firing squad, and the command was given. In those days, gunpowder was not smokeless, and when the smoke cleared away, there were bullet marks in the stone and the ropes were cut by bullets, but the Bab was nowhere to be seen. A search found him inside calmly finishing his instructions to his secretary which had been interrupted when they led him away to be executed. Evidently he finished what he wanted to say, for this time when they brought him out and bound him, the volley was effective and the body of the Bab lay on the ground, riddled with lead.

Although Baha'u'llah tells us that preceding prophets also brought the word of God, and that what he says about God was dictated directly from God himself, he makes no apology for discrepancies or changes. Rather, Abdu'l Baha explains:

> Laws for the ordinary conditions of life are only valid temporarily. The exigencies of the time of Moses justified cutting off a man's hand for theft....we must remember that these changing laws are not the essentials, they are the accidentals of religion.... (PUP, 360)

Where no prisons exist, punishment must be direct; where hygienic measures are primitive or non-existent, dietary laws are important. Thus, Bah'u'llah claimed that religion and its revelations were necessarily adapted progressively to the times. In each age, each dispensation of a Manifestation of God, conditions had progressed far enough beyond the message of the previous Manifestation that new revelations could be presented and a new set of rules introduced.

Naturally, for a devout people who have been thoroughly indoctrinated in a religion, change is difficult. To Moslems used to female subservience, it was a shock to be told that women are equal to men; to Hasidic Jews it was blasphemy to be told that:

> The choice of clothing and the cut of the beard and its dressing are left to the discretion of men. (T, 23)

To many strictly orthodox sects, the allowance of music for pleasure is sinful, abolition of dietary laws is equivalent to spitting in the face of God. One example of what strict Moslems could not accept was that, in the Baha'i faith:

> Marriage with unbelievers is permitted. (KA, 40)

The changes introduced by Baha'u'llah affected Islam more than other religions. One that affected the practice of Christianity, especially at the time that it was introduced, was the prohibition of asceticism:

> Living in seclusion or practicing asceticism is not acceptable in the presence of God....practices...begotten of the womb of superstition ill beseem men of knowledge. (T, 71)

> Let [the monks and priests] give up the life of seclusion and direct their steps towards the open world....we have granted them leave to enter into wedlock.... (T, 24)

When the latter injunction was first announced a century ago, Catholics were horrified; today, many Catholic bishops and theologians are agitating for a reconsideration. Perhaps the world will eventually catch up with the Universal God. The admonitions against asceticism carry over into allowing a reasonable amount of materialism:

> Having...reached this maturity, man standeth in need of wealth, and such wealth as he acquireth through crafts or professions is commendable and praiseworthy.... (T, 35)

As with so many other religions, we occasionally run across an admonition which seems to contradict this idea:

> If thou seekest to be intoxicated with the cup of the Most Mighty Gift, cut thyself from the world and be quit of self and desire. (B, 362)

Still, such are far in the minority, and one gets the impression that they are no more than a reaction to excessive materialism or to abandonment of thoughts of God, rather than being a recommendation to relinquish completely worldly goods and return to the hermit's life. After all, considering the tremendous volume of scripture Baha'i has produced, perhaps we should allow here and there something that seems to be contradictory when removed from its general context.

Related to abandonment of asceticism is the Universal God's insistence that everyone should carry his share of the load. While it is recognized that some people besides the widows and orphans cannot take care of themselves, it is incumbent on everyone who can produce in any way to do so. Social welfare is praiseworthy, but should by no means be a shelter for indigent sluggards.

Those unable to earn their own living are to be provided for, begging is not allowed, and to carry it further, it is not even allowed to give to a beggar! (KA, 64) But this is not to be construed that God does not approve of charity. Far from it, but only for those who absolutely require it:

> Man should voluntarily and of his own choice sacrifice his property and life for others, and spend willingly for the poor. (B, 288)

> It is enjoined upon every one of you to engage in some form of occupation, such as crafts, trade....We have graciously exalted your engagement in such work to the rank of worship unto God....Waste not your time in idleness and sloth....The most despised men in the sight of God are those who sit idly and beg. (T, 26)

The Universal God does not rely on admonitions alone, but believes in the legal development of social rights. These are not to be one-sided, but should work for the benefit of everyone:

> Laws should be established....the workmen should receive wages which assure them an adequate support and...a sufficient pension....the workmen should...not demand beyond their rights....they should be obedient and submissive, and not ask for impudent wages. (B, 282 and 283)

If one gets the impression on reading some of this that the Universal God is invading mundane life more than other Gods have done, he has the right impression. Baha'u'llah, it must be remembered, is speaking as the mouthpiece of God, so we must accept what he says as what God wills. And Abdu'l Baha is the officially designated interpreter, on whom the cloak of infallibility has fallen, so that his explanations also we must accept.

For the first time in history, a faith has provided for the efficient following of the Prophet after his passing. Baha'u'llah recognized that no one person could answer all the questions. Having seen what happened after the death of Mohammed, when a tremendous body of Hadith, much of which was of questionable reliability, had materialized, he made a provision for the establishment of the Universal House of Justice, for which he promised God's guidance, which was to formulate all needed rules and regulations after Baha'u'llah's passing from this world. At first, the Baha'i community was not large enough to support such an organization, but as a result of the untiring efforts of Abdu'l Baha and Shoghi Effendi, the Baha'i faith grew to the point where, in 1963, the first Universal House of Justice was elected and provision is being made for regional and national Houses of Justice.

> The conduct of these affairs hath been entrusted to the men of the House of Justice that they may enforce them according to the exigencies of the times. (T, 134)

Note particularly that God has freed it from all error. This applies only to the Universal (world-governing) House of Justice, and not to the national or regional Houses. It is also to be remarked that the Universal House of Justice is for Church matters only and has repeatedly been admonished against political involvement.

The Universal God believes in organization, and has made extensive plans for the basic organization of the Baha'i church, which are to be fleshed out by the regulations developed by the Universal House of Justice. It must be noted that, as with the Universal House of Justice, the lower organization is designed for church use only and is not to mix in affairs that the government will ordinarily handle. God is firmly behind a just state authority, and wants his followers to stay far removed from any political involvement—not even to discuss politics in their assemblies.

Yet church organization goes far beyond a simple administrative body. It is projected that eventually, each temple constructed will be the central edifice of a group of Baha'i buildings, which will consist of a hospital, a pharmacy, a pilgrim's house, a school for orphans, and a university (B, 416). Although the Baha'i administrative and governing structure is in no way to usurp state authority, it is hoped that such a fine example can be set up that ultimately, it will be so admired that states will voluntarily adopt it as a prototype.

Despite the proposed separation of church and state, God does not hesitate to make recommendations. Years before the organization even of the League of Nations, God advocated a genuinely effective Supreme Tribunal to conduct world affairs and maintain peace:

> The Great Being...hath written: The time must come when the imperative necessity for the holding of a vast, all-embracing assemblage of men will be universally realized....Should any king take up arms against another, all should arise and prevent him. (G:cxvii)

This suggested tribunal is to have legislative, executive, and judicial powers. The United Nations and the World Court are steps in the right direction, but their authority has not reached the goals.

We see, therefore, that the Universal God is profoundly concerned with the unity of humankind. Basic to the idea of unity is the principle of equality:

> We created you all from the same dust...that no one should exalt himself over the other. (B, 165)

Not only should all races and both sexes be equal, people are enjoined not to be contemptuous of those having other beliefs. To attain real world unity one should:

> Consort with the followers of all religions in a spirit of friendliness and fellowship. (T, 22)

Baha'u'llah makes one exception to this rule. Everyone must strictly avoid contact with the "breakers of the Covenant," those who once followed Baha'u'llah and then turned aside on their own paths.

Unity was God's original intention, and we must bend our efforts to erasing division. One factor that has brought division to men was Jehovah's introduction of a multitude of languages, when during the construction of the tower of Babel, the God of the Patriarchs became concerned that developing man might become competitive with him:

> The Lord said...they all have one language; this is only the beginning of what they will do; nothing...will now be impossible for them. Let us go down, and there confuse their language, that they may not understand one another's speech. (Genesis 11:6, 7)

The Universal God has no such fears. His wish is to see his creatures progress, and He demands a reversal of the confusion. He advocates the development of a universal language and a universal script that will first be an adjunct language for everyone, will allow world-wide communication, and will eventually become the single world language.

> The counselors of the earth must consult together, and appoint one of the existing languages, or a new language, and instruct the children therein in all the schools of the world.... (B, 192)

However, one must not get the idea that unity requires anything approaching monotonous uniformity. Diversity, when it does not impede cooperation, will make the world more agreeable:

> Consider the flowers of the rose garden...different kinds, various colors and diverse forms....yet they drink from one water, swayed by one breeze, grow by the warmth of one sun....This variation...cause each to enhance the beauty and splendor of the others. The difference in manners, customs, habits and thoughts and temperaments is the cause of adornment of the world of humankind. (B, 295)

God is interested in the well-being of His creatures, wants them to be able to enjoy all the bounties that he has provided, and knows that in order to obtain the maximum benefit, knowledge and training are required. Thus, the Universal God is also a great advocate of education, not only in languages and religious instruction, but in other areas, as well.

> Knowledge is as wings to a man's life, a ladder for his ascent....The knowledge of such sciences, however, should be acquired as can profit the peoples of the earth, and not those which begin with words and end with words. (T, 51 and 52)

Furthermore, he recognizes that the previous inferior position of woman in the world, particularly in the Islamic world, is undoubtedly a result of her lack of education, which prevents her from exercising her talents and capabilities to the full. God, through Baha'u'llah, has stated that he expects woman to be fully equal to man once she has been given an equal educational opportunity.

> Strive by all possible means to educate both sexes...girls like boys, there is no difference whatsoever between them. (B, 399)

Education will be better for everyone and lead to the utopian world visualized by Baha'u'llah, but lest we forget, it will be under God's guidance:

> Schools must first train the children in the principles of religion...but this in such measure that it may not injure the children by resulting in ignorant fanaticism and bigotry. (B, 182)

God expects and requires that each man conduct his own independent inquiry into religion. He evidently has no fear that any intelligent person could logically accept any religion other than His if he considers all the alternates with an open mind. Besides, all religions have a connection to Baha'i if one is willing to be flexible, and not be chained to a rigid, detailed dogma.

If one can only accept the principle of progress and progressive revelation, the rest is simple. How many people already agree that "your God must be the same God as mine." Once a person is convinced as a result of his own independent search, he is more likely to remain convinced. Hence, it is better that each person discover the truth for his/herself.

> The first teaching of Baha'u'llah is the investigation of reality. Man must seek the reality for himself. (B, 238)

Meditation is recommended as a way of arriving at a knowledge of God in the solution of his mysteries. People must be given the basic information, and then proceed on their own, for humans were not intended to see through the eyes of others. And yet meditation alone is not enough; the searcher needs a guide. Hence, it is requisite first to study what the prophets have written.

> The source of all learning is the knowledge of God...and this cannot be attained save through the knowledge of His Divine Manifestation. (T, 156)

The Universal God believes in proselytizing, and wants an effective following of missionary teachers. Baha'u'llah himself spent the greater part of his adult life in restricted quarters, and had to spread the word by mail. This he did assiduously, writing to the Czar of Russia, the Queen of England, and many other monarchs, as well as carrying on voluminous correspondence with ordinary folk, answering through his secretary anyone who expressed an interest in the Baha'i faith. His son and great-grandson were more mobile, carrying their missionary efforts to many countries, predominantly in North America and Europe.

Provision was made for a group of men, appointed by the Guardian and called the Hands of the Cause of God, to engage in missionary work in various parts of the world. At the death of the Guardian, Shoghi Effendi, these men were available to carry on this work. The Hands were able to keep the movement going and get it sufficiently well-organized that, six years after the Guardian's death, they were able to set up the first Universal House of Justice. As there are no more Guardians, the institution of the Hands is gradually disappearing. Only a few members of the original group, once numbering twenty-seven, are still alive.

Overall promotion of the faith has therefore devolved upon the Universal House of Justice, and multifarious publications are issued through the Baha'i World Center in Haifa and the Baha'i Publishing Trust in Wilmette, Illinois.

Each individual Baha'i is also expected to disseminate the faith. But, like all other admonitions of Baha'i, the missionary work should be pursued with moderation. One should not be too insistent in promulgating the Baha'i faith.

> If ye find one endowed with an attentive ear, read unto him the verses of God....unloose the tongue with excellent utterances....

otherwise abandon them unto themselves and forsake them in the abyss of hell. (B, 207)

This is analogous to many injunctions of Allah. In the Koran, Allah instructs Mohammed not to waste time with those who do not want to listen. On the other hand, there are many verses of the Koran that advocate conversion by the sword, while the Universal God wants no part of violent acts even where they have the benevolent aim of saving souls.

Not only are God's admonitions in all concerns, particularly that of equality and unity, aimed toward the eventual attainment of what he calls the Most Great Peace, but also, the organizations which are recommended for both Baha'i and the secular world (the Supreme Tribunal previously mentioned) are all directed toward the realization of what in other religions is called "the Kingdom of God on earth." The great difference between the other faiths and Baha'i is that the previous promises of this Kingdom require the arrival of a Messiah or other high ambassador of God who will set this peace into motion. The Universal God intends that the Most Great Peace be brought about by working from the bottom up, rather than from the top down. Baha'u'llah has indicated the direction, it is up to man himself to follow the road.

Meanwhile, not only is violence forbidden, but Baha'u'llah even admonishes against argument and confrontation in the Spiritual Assemblies and in the House of Justice. Differences of opinion must be discussed calmly:

> ...but if, God forbid! disagreement occurs, then the decision must be according to the greater number in harmony. (B, 406)

During the original persecution of the Baha'is in Iran, after many had been killed by the populace and the authorities, one or two groups armed themselves and for a while attempted a fortified defense. A certain general finally promised them free passage if they would lay down their arms, but he treacherously broke his promise and butchered the whole group. No Baha'is have since taken up arms even in self-defense, preferring the martyr's death to violent resistance, and there were twenty thousand martyrs. This attitude was further encouraged by Baha'u'llah:

> Seek a martyr's death in My path....that thou mayest repose with Me beneath the canopy of majesty behind the tabernacle of glory. (B, 161)

Like the Christian martyrs fed to the lions in the Coliseum, the Baha'i martyrs accepted the horrendous physical tortures, secure in the belief that they would last only a few hours, while their souls would thereby achieve an eternal bliss.

Certainly, if the world were made up of people who all had the same faith and the same abhorrence to violence, no dictator would be able to raise an army, and the world would see peace. But this is not a new idea, and it is dependent upon the same "if" we have been hearing since Christ admonished his followers to turn the other cheek.

Like His progenitors, the Universal God insists on belief in Himself, as well as His manifestations, as a prerequisite to salvation of the soul.

> No man can obtain everlasting life, unless he embraceth the truth of this inestimable, this wondrous, this sublime Revelation. (G:xcii)

Baha'u'llah is not, however, as insistent as is Mohammed on belief. While Allah unequivocally divides the people between believers and unbelievers, the Universal God is not quite so dramatically dogmatic. Upon looking into the fate of the soul and immortality, we find that the door is not really slammed shut, since the Universal God provides for progress of the soul after death, an arrangement which is completely different from Allah's. Jesus once commented that the wise men and the learned did not grasp their messages, while the simple folk were the mainstay of the converts. Baha'u'llah remarked on the same phenomenon:

> How vast the number of the learned who have turned aside from the way of God and how numerous the men devoid of learning who have apprehended the truth and hastened unto Him.... (T, 235 and 236)

It ever remains one of the great universal mysteries of religion that the prophets find the majority of their following among the ignorant and innocent, not among the "wise" and scholarly. It must be that faith finds a more facile entrance through the heart than through the mind.

At one point Baha'u'llah endeavors to prove the validity of his preachings by the martyrdom of the believers, going on at some length to argue that these extreme sacrifices should be sufficient proof to any fair-minded person of the authenticity of their faith. Unfortunately, one can point equally to the sacrifices of the Viking warriors for the faith of the pagan gods, the sacrifice of the kamikaze for the Emperor-god, and even, unhappily for our time, the sacrifice of the followers of the Reverend Jones, who first gave him all their worldly goods and then their lives in the holocaust of Guiana. As much as we can admire the strength of the faith of these people, we must admit that their examples have not been a central force in convincing people to adopt a particular religion.

Thereafter, Baha'u'llah concentrated upon consolidating and strengthening the group of Bah'ai followers. For example, there is even a provision for a sort of excommunication of the heretics:

> The Hands of the Cause of God must be ever watchful and so soon as they find anyone beginning to oppose...cast him out from the congregation of the people of Baha'i.... (B, 443)

> Do men think when they say "We believe" they shall be let alone and not be put to proof? (KI, 8 and 9)

Who believes, and who passes the tests and avoids the temptations will find that he is rewarded with immortality. But what is the state that described immortality to the Baha'i? In following along the series of Gods preceding the Universal God, we found that first, reward or punishment was through retribution for the living, then a vague Judgment Day was introduced, then the Paradise of the Father God followed, rather vague in its presentation, then a very concrete picture of Paradise and Hell was presented by Allah. Now we become vague again, as nowhere does Baha'u'llah give us a distinct delineation of the afterlife.

> The nature of the soul after death can never be described....
> (G:lxxxi)

Nor is an attempt made to describe either Paradise or Hell. Though, at one point, Baha'u'llah says:

> They that have disbelieved in God...shall return to their abode in the fire of hell.... (B, 112)

Still, this is obviously a case of Baha'u'llah's ubiquitous use of symbolism, for customarily, the torture assigned to the damned is remoteness from God.

> ...punishments consist in being deprived of special blessings, and falling into the lowest degrees of existence. (S, 261)

For those who have believed and who have followed the admonishments of the Manifestation of God:

> The followers of the one true God shall, the moment they depart out of this life, experience such joy and gladness as would be impossible to describe.... (G:lxxxvi)

Those who have not had the opportunity to learn about the Universal God and His teachings will not be punished unjustly for a deficiency that is no fault of their own:

> ...where the commands of the Prophet are not known.... God treats them with mercy and forgives them. (S, 305)

Baha'u'llah tells us that in the afterlife, it is not at all a question of black or white, either eternal bliss or eternal damnation. The joy of the soul is related to its closeness to God, and that depends in the beginning of its arrival on how it has comported itself in life. However, it is not a simple question of "living happily ever after":

> ...as the spirit continues to exist after death, it necessarily progresses or declines.... (S, 270)

No one is permitted to know how any of this is to be accomplished, but we are given to understand that even the foulest of the unbelievers may find God's mercy and eventually have peace and joy in heaven.

While comparing the Universal God with other Gods, we might in passing mention a particular resemblance to the Healing God of Christian Science. Abdu'l Baha says:

> ...an illness caused by affliction, fear, nervous impressions, will be healed by spiritual rather than by physical treatment....if thou wishest to know the divine remedy which will heal man from all sickness...know that it is the precepts and teachings of God. (B, 376)

Yet he is not as adamant as the Christian Scientist, and does not consider it inappropriate to apply scientific rather than spiritual medicine:

> Illness caused by physical accident should be treated with medical remedies....thou shouldest accept the physical remedies as coming from the mercy and favor of God. (B, 376)

The believers of Baha'i see no conflict between science and religion. Why should there be, since God created the scientific world and ordained the laws of nature. Any apparent conflict must be a misunderstanding of one or the other. This provides just one more bit of evidence that the Baha'i faith is compatible with the modern world, and that the Universal God may well find a suitable environment for His survival.

As in many other religions, Baha'i provides the impression that the whole of creation was designed as a background and supporting cast for man. Given that religions have arisen amongst humans, this is not really an astounding circumstance.

On the subject of the impetus for human creation, the Baha'i faith provides the following reasons:

> The purpose of God in creating man hath been...to enable him to know his Creator and to attain His Presence. (G:xxix)

One infers a certain pride in the Universal God, a pride that demands an appreciative audience. The requirement that people know and appreciate their creators has been underscored in the demand for belief in the Universal God and in His Manifestations. For this man is to be rewarded.

One of the most significant aspects of the Baha'i faith is that it emphasizes the importance of progress and progressive thought.

> Religion is the outward expression of the divine reality. Therefore it must be living, vitalized, moving and progressive...sciences...and philosophies of the past are useless today....ancient laws and archaic ethical systems will not meet the requirements of modern conditions. (B, 224 and 225)

And so God allows for and even encourages the progress of humankind, from tribal man through feudal societies to the present day and beyond. In many ways, the relation between man and God is not unlike that between dogs and their owners. Love is exchanged. Obedience is expected, and freedom is incomplete:

> Liberty causeth man to overstep the bounds of propriety, to infringe on the dignity of his station....true liberty consisteth in man's submission unto My commandments.... (KA, 25)

Other Gods have also required ceremonies, rites, prayers, fasting, belief, pilgrimages, and confessions to support their faith. Rites, ceremonies, and sacrifices are not part of the program of worship decreed by the Universal God through Baha'u'llah. The Baha'i concept of religion does not include creed and ceremony. Prayer, however, is still required; one must maintain communion with God, at least on a personal level.

> ...the laws of prayer and fasting. These...the most fundamental and binding laws of His dispensation. (KI, 38)

> Congregational prayer...is forbidden...with the exception of the Prayer for the Dead. Thus the Daily Obligatory Prayers are to be recited privately, not in congregation. There is no prescribed way for the recital.... (KA, 57)

It should be noted that in forbidding "congregational prayer," this means reciting in unison a predetermined form, as in Islam, or as the Christians recite the Lord's Prayer together. Baha'is do recite both prayers of Baha'u'llah and those of their own design during meetings, but this is done by individuals, not in chorus. It is the strictly mechanical forms that are excluded.

As for fasting, there is an annual period when:

> Abstinence from food and drink, from sunrise to sunset is obligatory. Fasting is binding on men and women on attaining the age of maturity, which is fixed at 15. (KA, 38)

Exceptions are made for the ill, for travelers, pregnant women, those over seventy, and a few others. The discipline of the fast helps to remind the Baha'i of the will of God and of His unity with fellows who are also fasting.

For those who can afford it financially, and are not otherwise prevented:

> Baha'u'llah specifically ordains pilgrimage to the Most Great House in Baghdad and to the House of the Bab in Shirax. (KA, 61)

Here again, as was discussed in the chapter on Allah, the effort and the fellowship of the pilgrimage contributes to the feeling of unity for the religion.

Prayer, fasting, and pilgrimage are added to work and the study of science and arts as acts of worship which are desired by the Universal God. There is further the requirement of belief and the observance of the divine ordinances. Perhaps the most fundamental admonition of Baha'u'llah is:

> The essence of faith is the fewness of words and abundance of deeds. (T, 156)

In demonstrating how the Universal God reflects His environment, we must admit to a seeming paradox. We are studying a God whose fundamental characteristic is peacefulness and who urges the unity of humankind. Yet it is difficult to find these characteristics reflected in the daily perusal of the media. Headlines screaming dissension, televised reports of bombs and terrorism, and cinema violence all seem to indicate a very different God is likely to arise in these times. Still, certain things do indicate a fertile soil for the growth of such a God.

The very existence of the United Nations is heartening. It is through their agency that several wars—which would once have rapidly spread by the action of each combatant's allies, as happened in the past two World Wars—have been contained. There are also numerous non-government-sponsored charities, community funds, Red Cross, cancer drives, and children's camps. Every day someone new knocks on the door with a plea for help for the more unfortunate. Modern governments, with the new social welfare programs, universal education, even the communist dictatorships claim to be working for the benefit of the people. We must admit that we are now far removed far from the old feudal societies, ruled by absolute monarchs who were benevolent only when it suited the whim of an individual ruler.

Regarding the question of the acceptance of the Baha'i Faith, one can only comment that in its first century, it has found more converts in more nations than Christianity did in its first century. Of course, the percentage is still small, and

Baha'i has had the advantage of modern communications, but the main point is that its acceptance is growing.

The survival of the new species, the Universal God, is not yet certain. Still, there is evidence in the recent (historically speaking) development of such organizations as the United Nations, the International Red Cross, the Institute of International Education and a world-wide practice of foreign aid to under-developed nations that a compatible climate may well exist for the survival of a God whose principal doctrine is based on world peace and universal equality. Time will tell—in another five centuries we should know.

John Ferraby, the great student of Baha'i, comments:

> The claim of Baha'u'llah, whether one accepts it or not, must be acknowledged to be rational and suited to the present day.
> (F, 54)

# Epilogue

A person looks into his mirror and sees reflected there the crowning glory of evolution.

This is what he believes. So far, at least.

As much as it may be damaging to Man's ego to consider the possibility that maybe, after all, there will be some creature developed as far beyond man as man is beyond the apes, can we honestly and logically claim that this is the end of the line for Darwinian evolution? A hundred million years ago the torpid dinosaurs were the lords of the creation. These reptiles were far advanced in the evolutionary scale beyond the protozoa and the sea slug. Yet, they could not conceive of the further development of evolution to produce animals like the crafty fox, the agile raccoon, the socially intelligent dolphin, and the curious apes that were around a million years ago.

Nor could these mammals, developed though they were, conceive of the tool-making, fire-using protoman, who was only then preparing to come onstage. No more than could these early humans conceive of the city-living reasoning man of today, surrounded by his personal computers, his volumes of Shakespeare and Keats, reading of trips to the moon and exploration of the outer planets while listening to Beethoven's Eroica symphony on his quadriphonic stereo. The abstruse mathematics of Einstein, the fires of the fusion bomb, the depth of philosophy of Kierkegaard and Kant were alike absolutely inconceivable to our cave-dwelling ancestors.

And yet, our ancestors lived in caves only a hundred thousand years ago, a mere tick of time in comparison with how long the Earth has existed. What will the creatures be like who are lords of the earth a hundred thousand years from now...a million years...a billion years? Yet a billion years is only a fraction of the five thousand million years that our young sun will still have to furnish energy to life's earth forms.

Our science fiction writers have tried to provide some possible clues. They have shown us telepathic people, humans whose technological progress has eliminated all need for effort. Technology has taken us through the universe beyond the stars to find beings even further advanced, such as creatures of organized energy that have been able to dispense with material bodies. They have shown us mature people who have shucked off the infantile contemporary characteristics of war, ambition, and greed—as well as people whose further development of such characteristics have been horribly enhanced via the technology of ever more efficient weapons of destruction.

And yet, it is also possible that the lords of the earth some million or ten million years from now will be something as inconceivable to us as we were to the apes who roamed the savannas a million years ago. They could even develop through some other line of evolution such as the insects or the octopi.

And what of the evolution of God? The primitive animist with his capricious entourage of spirits—sometimes malicious, sometimes benevolent—had no conception of the organized, reasoning, and more predictable deities of our pagan ancestors. Likewise, from the fun-loving gods of the Greeks or the warrior gods of the Scandinavians, it was a long qualitative step to the single creator God of Jesus, of Mohammed, of Baha'u'llah.

What might come next in the evolution of God? Here, the science fiction writers are not so helpful. They may present us with the theocratic governments of the future, or with monasteries that are the repositories of knowledge through the dark ages following a nuclear holocaust, but the presentation of a future God is quite rare.

The viability of any particular species depends on its ability either to find a suitable ecological niche, or to adapt to what it does find. This applies as well to the various species of Gods. If any particular species can find a fertile soil and an equable climate, with the terms "fertile" and "equable" signifying special characteristics suitable to the species under consideration, it will survive and prosper. For example, in the world of plants and animals, some plants need heat and moisture, and thrive best in jungles, while the cactus is quite content with its arid desert; and we find different animals in the plains, in the forest, in rivers, in the sea, and in the arctic tundra. The evolutionary phrase "survival of the fittest" must not be taken too literally. It is not only the absolute fittest which survive; there is room in the world for myriad species to find each its own ecological niche, and "survival of the fittest" applies only when fierce competition for a particular niche arises.

Likewise, there are multitudes of niches in the human ecology in which an adaptable god-species can find an equable climate. Literally dozens of god-species exist today, and hundreds or even thousands of varieties of each species have found themselves a comfortable home. The pagan Gods of Rome, Greece, Arabia, and Scandinavia have long since died out; the Gods of Egypt, of the Incas, and the Aztecs have become extinct; the Japanese Emperor-God is probably gone; and the God of Zoroaster is a threatened species. Who today can feel reverence at the mention of Zeus, Osiris, Wodin, Astarte or Bel? Each of the Gods which we have discussed is today alive and thriving, each in His own compartment, each adapted to a certain environment.

We are on our own. The Gods of Jesus, of Mohammed, of Joseph Smith, of Mary Baker Eddy took only ten thousand years to develop from Isis, from Zeus, from Wotan. Is the Universal God of Baha'i a further stage in the evolution of God, or is He simply another variation on the theme of the monotheistic Creator? Future concepts of God may well be as different from the Father God of Jesus as was the Father God from Zeus.

Or could it be possible that evolution is producing a converging pair of lines that the concepts of God will approach the development and evolution of the descendants of Man, until they merge and become one god-like form? This is a possibility. There are some philosophers who believe that time as we see it is a mirage or illusion, that the past is coexistent with the future, just as the stations along the train track are always there, even though the traveler may only see one at a time. As the passage of time may be merely an illusion, why should not God have created Himself as well as all those parts of Him which we look on as steps in the evolution process? Or are we all just a dream that God is having?

I leave these questions in the reader's lap. Can you conceive in your mind the direction of evolution either of human beings or their concept of God? Think about it. If you dare.

# REFERENCES

**Scripture References**
Scripture references and other sacred writings in this work are from the following sources unless otherwise noted. Abbreviations and explanatory information used in text citations are given in parentheses following the reference, if needed.

**Chapters 4–6 and throughout**
Old and New Testaments, *Revised Standard Version of the Holy Bible*, 1946, Division of Christian Education, National Council of the Churches of Christ in the U.S.A. (book, chapter, and verse)
Apocrypha, *King James Version* (book, chapter, and verse)

**Chapter 7**
*The Koran*, translated by N. J. Dawood, 4th ed., rev. Harmondsworth, England: Penguin Books, 1979 (two numbers indicate chapter [Sura] and verse)
*The Hadith* (arabic numbers are pages, roman numerals are sections)
*The Musnad of Al-Tayalisi: A Study of Islamic Hadith as Oral Literature*, R. J. Speight. Ann Arbor, Michigan: University Microfilms, 1971 (T)
*The Traditions of Islam*, Alfred Guillaume. Oxford: Clarendon Press, 1924 (G, from the Hadith of Al-Bukhari) (G-M, from the Mishkat of Waliu-l-Din Abu 'Abd Allah)

**Chapter 8**
*Book of Mormon* (book, chapter, and verse)
*The Pearl of Great Price* (references to "Moses," "Joseph Smith," and "Abraham")
*Doctrine and Covenants* (D.C., including section and verse)

**Chapter 9**
*Science and Health with Key to the Scriptures*, Mary Baker Eddy, First Church of Christ, Scientist, Boston (page and beginning line)

**Chapter 10**
*Baha'i World Faith: Selected Writings of Baha'u'llah and Abdu'l Baha*. Wilmette, Illinois: Baha'i Publishing Trust, 1956 (B)
*All Things Made New*, J. Ferraby. London: Baha'i Publishing Trust, 1975 (F)
*Gleanings from the Writings of Baha'u'llah*, translated by Shoghi Effendi. New York: Baha'i Publishing Committee, 1953 (G)
*Synopsis and Codification of the Laws and Ordinances of the Kitab-i-Aqdas* (The Most Holy Book), Baha'u'llah. Haifa: Baha'i World Centre, 1973 (KA)
*The Kitab-i-Iqan* (The Book of Certitude), Baha'u'llah, translated by Shoghi Effendi. Wilmette, Illinois: Baha'i Publishing Trust, 1974 (KI)
*The Promise of All Ages*, G. Townshend. Dorchester, England: George Ronald, 1948 (P)
*The Promulgation of Universal Peace*, Abdu'l Baha. USA, 1922 (PUP)
*Some Answered Questions*, Abdu'l Baha. Wilmette, Illinois: Baha'i Publishing Trust, 1957 (S)
*Tablets of Baha'u'llah*, translated by Habib Taherzadeh. Haifa: Baha'i World Centre, 1978 (T)

**Other References**
Boyer, V. *Zoroastrianism*. Leiden: Brill, 1975.
Bulfinch, Thomas. *Mythology*. New York: Crown, 1979.
Cabell, James Branch. *Between Friends: Letters of James Branch Cabell and Others*. Edited by P. Colum. New York, Harcourt, 1962.
Coué, Émile. *Self Mastery through Conscious Autosuggestion*. [New Mexico]: Sun Publishing, 1981.
Cowper, William. *Letters and Prose Writings of William Cowper: Prose, 1756–1798*. Oxford: Oxford University Press, 1986.
Dante, *The Divine Comedy: The Inferno, Purgatorio, and Paradiso*. Translated by John Ciardi. New York: W. W. Norton, 1977.
Descartes, René. *Descartes, His Moral Philosophy and Psychology*. Translated by John J. Blom. New York: New York University Press, 1978.
Farah, Caesar E. *Islam: Beliefs and Observances*. 4th ed. New York: Barron's, 1987.
Feuerbach, Ludwig. *The Essence of Christianity*. Translated by George Eliot. Buffalo: Prometheus, 1989.
Fromm, Erich. *Man for Himself: An Inquiry into the Psychology of Ethics*. 1947. Reprint, New York: Henry Holt, 1990.
Marx, Karl. *Capital, the Communist Manifesto and Other Writings*. Edited by Mary Eastman. New York: The Modern Library, 1932.
Nietzsche, Friedrich W. *Complete Works*. Edited and translated by Oscar Levy. New York: Russell & Russell, 1964.

Pascal, Blaise. *The Provincial Letters*. Translated by A. J. Krailsheimer. Harmondsworth, England: Penguin, 1967.
Rogers, Will. *Ether and Me; or, "Just Relax."* New York: G. P. Putnam, 1935.
Tylor, Edward B. *Anthropology*. New York: Macmillan, 1913.
Williams, John Alden, ed. *Islam*. New York: George Braziller, 1961.